The preparation of editions for performance and study is one of the most important activities and contributions of the music scholar to cultural life. Through accessible editions, previously unknown music enters the repertory, while well-known works receive fresh interpretations. This is the first book to provide an introduction to the methods of textual criticism and their application to music editing, as well as providing a history of the field, and a discussion of the issues and problems encountered.

In this volume, James Grier examines the central issues of music editing and develops a theoretical framework for a critical methodology, drawing examples from the early music repertory through contemporary works, including various genres from opera to the symphony. The author also examines the future of music editing and its application on CD-ROM and related electronic media. The book follows the various activities inherent in music editing, including the tasks of the editor, the nature of musical sources, and transcription. Grier also discusses the difficult decisions faced by the editor such as sources not associated with the composer and necessary editorial judgement.

The critical editing of music

The critical editing of music

History, method, and practice

JAMES GRIER
Associate Professor, Department of Music
Yale University

Published by the Press Syndicate of the University of Cambridge
The Pitt Building, Trumpington Street, Cambridge CB2 1RP
40 West 20th Street, New York, NY 10011–421, USA
10 Stamford Road, Oakleigh, Melbourne 3166, Australia

First published 1996

Printed in Great Britain at the University Press, Cambridge

We gratefully acknowledge the assistance received in publishing this book from the Frederick W. Hilles Publications Fund of Yale University.

A catalogue record for this book is available from the British Library

Library of Congress cataloguing in publication data

Grier, James, 1952–
The critical editing of music: history, method, and practice / by James Grier.
p. cm.
Includes bibliographical references (p.) and index.
ISBN 0 521 55190 0 (hardback) – ISBN 0 521 55863 8 (paperback)
1. Music – Editing. I. Title.
ML63. G745 1996
780′. 149–dc20 95–44092 CIP MN

ISBN 0 521 55190 0 hardback
ISBN 0 521 55863 8 paperback

SE

To my mother, Judith Grier
and to the memory of my father, William D. Grier (1918–1995)

Contents

Preface

Editing is a common and frequent professional preoccupation among musicologists, but until recently there has been very little critical discourse about the nature of music editing, at least in print. This book attempts to redress the balance, to make editing the focus of critical debate, and to challenge editors to recognize the degree to which critical interpretation and editing are inseparable, as the expression textual criticism shows. Over the past century and a half, music editors often strove to present a neutral edition, one that seemed to preserve objectivity and permitted either a limited scope for editorial intervention, or none at all. Again, a term, this time *Urtext*, reveals the mode of editorial thinking. An *Urtext* purports to present the "original" text of the composer, unmediated by the editor. But even the staunchest proponents of the concept, Günter Henle and Georg Feder, recognize the necessity for the editor's critical involvement, as I show below. That admission underscores the central tenet of this book: editing is an act of criticism.

The genesis of the book lies in the influence of two scholars on my perception of sources and editing. Leonard E. Boyle, through his approach to palaeography and codicology, instilled in me a profound respect for the historical significance of the written artifact. Father Boyle read and commented on an early version of Chapter 2. To Jerome J. McGann I also owe a great debt for the tremendous inspiration given me by his book *A Critique of Modern Textual Criticism*. There, Professor McGann shows that much of the meaning of the work of art lies in its socialization, a process that affects the creation of the work as well as its reception. Therefore, the forces that this process exerts on the work of art can materially influence the form of the text, and so can carry great significance for editorial procedure. I find this theory particularly attractive in the field of music, where the processes of socialization usually take place in a very public forum through the medium of performance.

Many other friends and colleagues contributed significantly to the creation of the book. Andrew Hughes and David Fallows both read and commented on an early version of the book, as did Cliff Eisen, with whom I have also shared many stimulating discussions. All my colleagues at Yale have provided me with numerous opportunities to air my views, and I thank each of them for their patience and interest. I note a special debt of gratitude to two graduate students in the musicology programme who argued many of these points with me on a number of occasions, John Gingerich and Matthew Head. And Leo Treitler offered much encouragement and provocative comment.

An earlier version of Chapter 3 appeared in *Journal of Musicology*, 13 (1995), under the title "Musical Sources and Stemmatic Filiation: A Tool for Editing Music." I am grateful to Marian Green, the journal's Editor, and the University of California Press for permission to reprint the article here. The musical examples were prepared with the music-processing software Notewriter, whose author, Keith Hamel, I thank for making the software available to me.

I also gratefully acknowledge the kind and gracious hospitality of my dear friends Claire Harrison and Peter Jarrett, whose home in the *banlieue* of Paris provided a safe haven for many research and writing trips. And finally no prefatory acknowledgement will ever adequately recognize the contribution of my most cherished colleague and harshest critic, my wife, Sally Bick. She was intimately involved with every stage in the process, debated every issue, and continually challenged me to refine the formulation, substance and expression of the book. Any success it achieves will be as much hers as mine.

New Haven
1995

1

Introduction: the task of the editor

No passage in Western art music has created more editorial controversy than the retransition in the first movement of Beethoven's *Hammerklavier* Sonata, Op. 106 (bars 224–26).[1] The facts are well known: two sketches contain the reading A♮; the first edition gives A♯; no autograph survives.[2] Some editors would accept the reading of the print on the grounds that it must represent Beethoven's final thoughts on the matter; others would claim, with equal justification, that a variety of influences other than Beethoven's own compositional thinking may have intervened to generate the reading of the print, and therefore the sketches preserve the correct reading. In fact, both explanations are equally plausible. Either Beethoven changed his mind between the sketches and the first edition, or the natural (that would cancel the sharp in the signature) was omitted erroneously from the print.

And the autograph, were it to reappear, would probably not decide the issue. If it agreed with the sketch, Beethoven could still have changed the text during the publishing process; if it accorded with the print, he might have erred while writing the autograph, an event not

[1] For discussion and bibliography, see P. Badura-Skoda, "Noch einmal zur Frage Ais oder A." See also Mies, *Textkritische Untersuchungen bei Beethoven*, pp. 65–66; E. Badura-Skoda, "Textual Problems," pp. 303–4; and Rosen, *The Classical Style*, pp. 420–21.

[2] The better-known sketch appeared in the "Boldrini" sketchbook, now lost; see H. Schmidt, "Verzeichnis der Skizzen Beethovens," no. 71, p. 47; Johnson, Tyson and Winter, *The Beethoven Sketchbooks*, pp. 347–50; Adler, *Verzeichniss der musikalischen Autographe*, no. 75, p. 20; and Marston, "Approaching the Sketches for Beethoven's 'Hammerklavier' Sonata." The sketch is published in Nottebohm, *Zweite Beethoveniana*, pp. 126–27 (reprinted from *Musikalisches Wochenblatt*, 6 [1875], 297–98, 305–7). The second sketch was once part of the Klinckerfuss collection in Stuttgart, but its whereabouts are today unknown. It was inspected by Rudolf Serkin, whose findings P. Badura-Skoda reports ("Noch einmal zur Frage Ais oder A," pp. 60–61). On the early editions, see Kinsky and Halm, *Das Werk Beethovens*, pp. 292–96; and Newman, "On the Problem of Determining Beethoven's Most Authoritative Lifetime Editions," pp. 132–35. On the autograph, see Kinsky and Halm, *Das Werk Beethovens*, p. 292.

without parallel in other sources of Beethoven's music.[3] Only if the autograph were to exhibit Beethoven's modification graphically would it determine the reading, as, for example, if Beethoven first wrote a natural and then cancelled or erased it, showing that he began with the idea of specifying A♮, and then consciously changed the text.[4]

Editorial theorists would normally appeal, in such a case, to the composer's intentions, but the state of the sources does not permit us to *know* Beethoven's intentions, to hold any certainty about the *truth* as to which reading is correct. Such theorists attempt to return to a historical moment, the moment when Beethoven decided on the reading of the retransition, that is simply irrecoverable. The sources do allow us to know, however, what Beethoven wrote for most of the work. Otherwise we would not be able to acknowledge the existence of a *Hammerklavier* Sonata at all, or to distinguish it from any other sonata, by Beethoven or any other composer. But when the sources transmit genuine ambiguity, a crux in the parlance of Classical Philology, we must recognize the futility of appealing to Beethoven's intentions.

Now critics may feel safe enough in this scholarly uncertainty, and blissfully continue to debate the merits of the two competing readings from that privileged position without committing themselves one way or the other. But the editor who would print this sonata and, especially, the pianist who would play it, enjoy no such luxury. They must decide between A and A♯ for better or for worse. (Editors are always free, of course, to express their uncertainty in some way, for example, through a footnote, but performers cannot have it both ways.) This example shows that the decision, no matter what it is or how it is achieved, is the decision of the editor or the performer alone. We cannot know what Beethoven intended, and the best we can do is to make a choice.

Editing, therefore, consists of series of choices, educated, critically informed choices; in short, the act of interpretation. Editing, moreover, consists of the interaction between the authority of the composer and the authority of the editor. Composers exert their authority

[3] For a selection of Beethoven's own comments on the problem, see Unverricht, *Die Eigenschriften und die Originalausgaben*, p. 22.

[4] Mies, *Textkritische Untersuchungen bei Beethoven*, p. 190, and E. Badura-Skoda, "Textual Problems," p. 311, cite a similar example from the first movement of the *Waldstein* Sonata, Op. 53 (bar 105), where autograph and first edition disagree, but the reading of the first edition originally accorded with the autograph and was subsequently changed at the stage of engraving, presumably on the instructions of the composer.

over sources created by themselves or under their direct supervision, although, as I discuss below, that authority is affected and limited by the social, political and economic institutions through which those sources are produced and disseminated. The authority of composers extends, at least indirectly, to sources whose production they do not directly supervise, for the very act of reproduction exhibits at least a token acknowledgement of that authority.

When editors come to evaluate both types of sources, they invoke their own authority in forming judgements about what the sources transmit. And in some cases, they must call into question the accuracy, the truth of a particular reading that is recorded in a source or sources. Here lies the point of interaction between the authority of the composer, as transmitted in the sources, and the authority of the editor in the course of evaluating and interpreting those sources. Editing, therefore, comprises a balance between these two authorities. Moreover, the exact balance present in any particular edition is the direct product of the editor's critical engagement with the piece edited and its sources.

This position has long been acknowledged in philology, whose practitioners know it as textual criticism. The achievements of textual criticism over its long history show that the critical judgement of the editor is engaged at every stage of the editorial process, beginning with the choice of project. (Textual critics have always focused their most intensive efforts on the texts that hold the greatest importance for them and their culture: Homer for the Greeks, the Bible in medieval and modern Europe, Shakespeare for students of English literature.) But many music editors exhibit a reluctance to address the issue of their own authority, and some actively suppress it in their editions, seeming to feel that its presence is so obvious that it hardly requires stating, never mind discussing.

That behaviour, in itself, reveals much about music editing and the nature of the discourse surrounding it. Joseph Kerman rebukes the discipline for giving too much emphasis to the uncritical reproduction of documents, in place of their critical evaluation.[5] In response, Margaret Bent presents what could be considered a credo for this book. "*Making a good edition is an act of criticism* that engages centrally with the musical material at all levels, large and small."[6] But later in the same address she acknowledges that all is not what it should, perhaps, be. "Much

[5] Kerman, *Musicology*, pp. 31–59, especially 42–44, 48–50.

[6] Bent, "Fact and Value," p. 5 (Bent's emphasis).

editing, for example, *is* less critical than it ought to be. Many so-called critical editions *are* indeed neither very critical nor very interesting."[7]

Philip Brett, in an article whose spirit inspires much of this book, moves beyond these comments to address the central problem in modern scholarly music editing. "But editing is principally a critical act; moreover it is one (like musical analysis) that begins from critically based assumptions and perceptions that usually go unacknowledged. If these assumptions were to be openly stated, if we began to recognize and allow for legitimate differences in editorial orientation, and if we ceased to use the word 'definitive' in relation to *any* edited text, then much of the polemics surrounding editing might subside."[8]

Since the first inscription of Western art music in Carolingian Europe through Petrucci and Artaria to the most recent scholarly editions, music editors, scribes and publishers have acted as mediators between composer and audience. They standardize notation, adapt works for current performing or institutional needs, correct errors that are obvious to them, introduce corruptions of their own, and generally influence the musical text in every conceivable way. Their motivations include, but are not limited to, preservation, the requirements of the moment and caprice. In many cases their actions are governed by astute critical thought based on a profound knowledge, and even love, of the repertory.

But the solution to the problem that Brett identifies comprises the disclosure of that mediation and of the critical acts that constitute it. For music editors are often reluctant to assume authority over the texts they print, wishing to give the appearance that they present only the text of the composer. And so they rely, or appear to rely, on the sources themselves instead of acknowledging their own critical initiative. Nowhere is this tendency more transparent than in the *Urtext* industry, whose products purport to reproduce the "original" text. I discuss, below, the historical and intellectual context of the concept, but it suffices to note here that even its most devout exponents acknowledge that editorial intervention is unavoidable, if not outright obligatory, no matter how undesirable.[9]

It is my aim in this book to examine the nature of editorial mediation, and to show how the editor's critical engagement plays an active

[7] *Ibid.*, p. 7 (Bent's emphasis).
[8] Brett, "Text, Context, and the Early Music Editor," p. 111 (Brett's emphasis).
[9] Henle, "Über die Herausgabe von Urtexten"; Feder and Unverricht, "Urtext und Urtextausgaben"; and Bente, "Ermittlung und Vermittlung."

role in every aspect of editing. I hope to penetrate some of the unstated assumptions mentioned by Brett, and make them the subject of debate, bringing into the open some of the critical perspectives and issues that affect every editorial decision. In the course of making any edition, editors confront many problems, like the one from Beethoven cited above, that admit no definitive answer. At such points, they must assume authority over the text, for the state of the sources leaves it uncertain as to whether the composer's authority generated the reading of the source. In order to reach a decision, they engage in a critical transaction that involves the careful consideration of the evidence bearing on the problem. Understanding of the musical idioms that make up a piece, knowledge of the historical conditions under which it was composed or the social and economic factors that influenced its performance, coupled with an aesthetic sensitivity for the composer's or repertory's style, can all contribute to a heightened critical awareness.

A second aim of the book is the presentation of a generalized theoretical framework for editing, within which each editor can develop a particular methodology for the project at hand. Most of the limited theoretical discourse on editing music that exists is concerned with the practical application of editorial method to specific repertories. While each repertory, indeed, each piece, presents special challenges for the editor (as I discuss below), there is a common group of problems that underlies the process of editing irrespective of the repertory in question.

(1) What are the nature and the historical situation of the sources of a work?
(2) How do they relate to one another?
(3) From the evidence of the sources, what conclusions can be reached about the nature and the historical situation of the work?
(4) How do this evidence and these conclusions shape the editorial decisions made during the establishment of the edited text?
(5) What is the most effective way of presenting the edited text?

I organize the book around these stages in the editorial task, showing how critical thought affects each phase of the undertaking.

The recognition that editing is a critical act leads directly to the corollary that different editors will produce different editions of the same work, even under the most rigorous, scholarly circumstances. Such has always been the case, or the Bach-Gesellschaft edition would not need to be replaced by the Neue Bach-Ausgabe (NBA). The editors of the NBA, operating under different social, economic and cultural conditions, and with access to new sources and new information about familiar ones, felt that the existing edition was no longer adequate. Knowledge continually broadens and deepens, while aesthetic sensibilities remain in a perpetual state of flux. And new critical perspectives inevitably address the concerns of their own historical context. Not only is this the normal situation, but editors would do their audience the greatest service by stating and discussing the critical point of view from which their edition emanates. This is a goal I stress in this book.

Long before the post-structuralists, editing, whether of literature or music, assumed many of the attributes of deconstruction.[10] As the rich tradition of editing in Classical Philology shows (about which I say more below), editors have always shaped the texts of their editions to conform to their personal interpretative conception of the work. This attitude echoes the concerns of recent writings in musicology, which acknowledge the plurality of interpretation, and the necessity to articulate the critical observer's standpoint.[11] Rose Rosengard Subotnik in particular questions the tendency towards objectification and determinism in discourse about music, and suggests that all scholarship originates in subjectively formed value judgements. Although individual editions cannot avoid objectifying a particular state of a work by determining its written text, the discipline of editing, like all critical undertakings, undergoes continual change in response to a changing critical environment. In these two respects, editing is analogous to performance. For each performance creates and objectifies a unique state of a piece, but no two performances of the same piece are exactly the same in all details. Similarly, no two editors would render its score in exactly the same way.

Performers and editors constantly make decisions in response to the same stimuli (notation) on the basis of the same criteria (knowledge of the piece and aesthetic taste). Only the results differ: performers produce sound while editors generate the written or printed page. Before Thomas Edison, performances could only be preserved in memory. But with the invention and ongoing development of recording technology, recorded performances have come to acquire the same

[10] Patterson, "The Logic of Textual Criticism," addresses this issue in literary editing; see especially pp. 69–91.

[11] See, for example, Subotnik, *Developing Variations*; Bergeron and Bohlman, eds., *Disciplining Music*; and Solie, ed., *Musicology and Difference*.

immutable qualities as print. These qualities have not been greeted with universal approval.[12] Nevertheless, they highlight the inherent similarity between the two activities: the interpretation and communication of a piece of music via the fixing of a particular state, in sound or in written form.

This book, then, does not present a specific and prescriptive methodology for editing. All editors will inevitably develop their own methods with each new edition. Instead, the focus is on principles leading to a critical theory of editing, and a discussion of how criticism interacts with practice and method. Accordingly, the musical examples cited below are intended to illustrate the principles behind the editorial process, to raise the critical questions that challenge the editor at every turn. Thereby, I do not prescribe or imply a particular solution, which will vary with each editor. Rather the examples demonstrate that, in each case, a variety of courses is open to editors, and show how critical thought might affect their choice. By conducting the debate in this way, I address the concerns not only of editors, but also of those who use editions, namely scholars and performers. This book brings to the forefront the critical positions that underlie the editions they must use daily in the course of their professional activities, and so it better equips them to approach the printed score with a more critical attitude.

The discussion and musical examples are limited to the literature of Western art music. For the most part, this is music that is closely linked with a written tradition. Obviously, musics of other cultures, especially those in which an oral tradition predominates, pose quite different and equally important problems for the editor. Moreover, editors in ethnomusicology have developed conventions of their own, especially in regard to the use of notation, that establish their work as an independent field.[13] Rather than expanding the current discussion to include this separate but related area of endeavour, I wish to address the process of editing that begins with one written document (the source) and ends with another (the edition).

To return to our example from Beethoven, then, where the sources are irreconcilable, there is no need for despair. Even Heinrich Schenker, who initially declined to edit the work because the auto-

[12] See Hitchcock, ed., *The Phonograph and Our Musical Life*; and Peyser, "Commentary: 'The Phonograph and Our Musical Life'."

[13] For theoretical discussions of transcription in ethnomusicology, see England, *et al.*, "Symposium on Transcription and Analysis"; and Stockmann, "Die Transkription in der Musikethnologie."

graph was lost, eventually relented.[14] He acted as all editors and performers would, and chose the reading that he found most convincing. But that reading is his and his alone. It may coincide with Beethoven's intentions, but no one will ever know for sure, and so that issue is moot. More important to the critical users of an edition are two other matters. First, they seek unequivocal indication that a particular reading arises from editorial intervention. Not all editors are as frank with their audience as they might be. How frequent is the remark "Obvious errors are silently corrected?" Obvious to whom? And corrected in what way? Second, and even more important, the user would like to know why the editor preferred one reading over another. With that information at hand, the editor's choice becomes a point of departure for users of an edition to make up their own minds about the passage.

Within that context, I propose four constituent principles regarding the nature of editing music, each principle emerging as a consequence from its predecessor.

(1) Editing is critical in nature.
(2) Criticism, including editing, is based in historical inquiry.
(3) Editing involves the critical evaluation of the semiotic import of the musical text; this evaluation is also a historical inquiry.
(4) The final arbiter in the critical evaluation of the musical text is the editor's conception of musical style; this conception, too, is rooted in a historical understanding of the work.

Musicology and the practice of editing

Musicology can claim an illustrious history of editorial practice. Since the formation of the Bach-Gesellschaft in 1850, for the production of a complete edition of the music of J. S. Bach, musicologists have produced an enormous quantity of distinguished editions, from the Collected Editions of most important composers to the monumental series and national collections. Much of this enterprise was driven by the sheer necessity of making the music accessible. But a strong element in the undertaking was the creation of a canon, a central core of repertory, whose texts carried the same philological weight as their rivals in literature and political history. These editions constitute, in short, a statement, by the purveyors of the young academic discipline

[14] *Die letzten fünf Sonaten von Beethoven*, despite its title, contains only Opp. 101 and 109–11. His complete edition, *Sämtliche Klaviersonaten*, includes Op. 106, vol. IV, 511–56.

of music, of the seriousness and worthiness of their discipline within the academy.[15] Even their presentation, in imposing folio volumes, reflects the gravity of their intent.

As valuable and important as these publications were, and are, to musicology, some have been found wanting in the light of modern scholarship, and are being superseded by newer editions, themselves not entirely infallible. Even in so scholarly an enterprise as the Collected Edition of Mozart (Neue Mozart-Ausgabe or NMA), some works were edited, in the absence of the autograph, from nineteenth-century sources when authoritative, contemporary (but not autograph) sources were available.[16] These latter were rejected presumably because the editors of the NMA believed that they were more likely to preserve copying errors than nineteenth-century sources produced under ostensibly scholarly auspices. Subsequent scholarship has shown the reverse to be true in some cases.[17]

This succession of events demonstrates that editing music, far from being an exact science, presents, in fact, a moving target. As our knowledge of repertories and their sources deepens, and our critical appraisal of that knowledge continues, new editions are needed to keep pace with, and reflect, the latest developments. No clearer affirmation of that situation can be adduced than the proliferation of new Collected Editions initiated since World War II, such as the NBA and NMA already cited. At the base of these projects lies a sharpening critical perspective. The original Collected Edition of Mozart (Alte Mozart-Ausgabe or AMA) provided an enormous service to musical scholarship by bringing together, for the first time, the works of Mozart in a uniform edition; the NMA presents substantial refinements in virtually every respect, refinements which result from several generations of intensive research that was stimulated and enabled in large part by the AMA; and the NMA, too, already needs revision in places, and will continue to be challenged in the future as research into Mozart's music continues. These editions represent nodal points on the continually changing path of Mozart scholarship, and each subsequent step would have been impossible without the existence of its predecessor.

[15] See Vötterle, "Die Stunde der Gesamtausgabe," p. 288; Finscher, "Musikalische Denkmäler und Gesamtausgaben"; Finscher, "Gesamtausgabe–Urtext–Musikalische Praxis"; Dahlhaus, "Zur Ideengeschichte musikalischer Editionsprinzipien"; and Brett, "Text, Context, and the Early Music Editor," pp. 85–88.

[16] Eisen, "The Old and New Mozart Editions."

[17] Eisen, "The Old and New Mozart Editions," pp. 518b–19a, identifies such a problem with the Piano Concerto in C, K. 415.

Musicological discourse about editing

Only a limited discourse on the theory and methodology of editing accompanied this distinguished history of editorial practice. Most scholars who were interested in editing were doing just that instead of worrying about methodological niceties. They solved problems *ad hoc,* produced the best editions they could, and left questions of method to the philologists. Until very recently, when musicologists have commented on editorial technique, they focused most of their attention on mechanical issues of presentation, and critical issues received a low priority: scholars either skirt them without a clear statement of how criticism affects editing, or they avoid them altogether.

Guido Adler's discussion of editing provides a typical example.[18] Although he makes some stimulating comments about the role of style in evaluating variants, and the need for the critical appraisal of sources, he devotes most of his attention to technical matters such as the modernization of notation, and modes of indicating editorial intervention. Adler assumes that music editors employ philological methods borrowed from literary editing, and so focuses on problems with the scholarly presentation of music. Source study receives much more prominence in a pamphlet by Max Friedländer, who shows that a critical assessment of style provides the only guide for deciding between variant readings in the sources.[19] Despite this promising start, no new contributions to the discourse appeared until after World War II, by which time the intellectual approach to editing had changed drastically.

Musicologists were reacting to two trends in editing. The first was the production of "performing" or interpretative editions, most commonly of keyboard music, but also of music for solo instruments with keyboard accompaniment, and usually prepared by famous performers. Musicologists complained that the numerous performance instructions added by the editors, such as tempo markings, dynamics, phrasing, fingering and pedalling, obscured the original notation, and that, because very little or no effort at all was expended in differentiating editorial marks from those in the source, the editions' users had no means of distinguishing between them. Already in the last decade of the nineteenth century, the Königliche Akademie der Künste in

[18] Adler, *Methode der Musikgeschichte,* pp. 69–84.
[19] Friedländer, *Ueber musikalische Herausgeberarbeit.*

Berlin was issuing editions that claimed to be free of such editorial intervention; their name for this type of edition was *Urtext*.[20]

Although this term is now largely discredited by scholars, it is important to note that the original conception was honourable enough: to provide texts that allowed the composer's notation to speak for itself; to permit performers, especially students, to form their own interpretation of the piece based on that original notation. The problems began with the commercialization of the concept in the immediate post-World War II period, primarily through the editions published by G. Henle Verlag, Munich, although it was by no means the only publisher to capitalize on the term to sell editions. The commercial importance of the term is revealed by Hubert Unverricht's discussion of its unseemly use in music publishing and the possible remedies afforded by the revision to German (BRD) copyright law of 1959.[21]

The objections of the scholarly world to *Urtext* editions centre on the fact that they do not present what they purport. Again, one need not go any further than the two principal statements of the term's leading protagonists. Günter Henle himself notes that sometimes the autograph and the first edition differ, in which case the editor must decide what to print.[22] Aside from failing to suggest how that decision might be reached, Henle also neglects to point out that such a text is no longer the *Urtext*, the composer's own written text, but the editor's interpretation of it. Georg Feder, in his contribution to the article he co-authored with Unverricht, makes the important point that *Urtext* editions must be critical editions, although he distinguishes them by their mode of presentation from the kind of critical editions associated with the Collected Editions and monumental series.[23] He does not, however, pursue the question of how criticism might inform the edition, other than to stress, like Friedländer, the necessity of source studies. This very discussion of critical method reveals that *Urtext* editions are not what they seem, not the composer's written text, but the editor's reconstruction of it. Feder affirms this alarming fact when he

[20] Friedländer, *Ueber musikalische Herausgeberarbeit*, pp. 11–12; Feder and Unverricht, "Urtext und Urtextausgaben," pp. 441–43; and Finscher, "Gesamtausgabe Urtext Musikalische Praxis," p. 194.

[21] Feder and Unverricht, "Urtext und Urtextausgaben," pp. 451–54. See also Berke, "Urtext zwischen Wissenschaftsanspruch und Praxisnähe," pp. 534–35.

[22] Henle, "Über die Herausgabe von Urtexten," p. 379.

[23] Feder and Unverricht, "Urtext und Urtextausgaben," pp. 432–40. See also Bente, "Ermittlung und Vermittlung"; and Berke, "Urtext zwischen Wissenschaftsanspruch und Praxisnähe," p. 533.

notes, in his discussion of five common misunderstandings of the *Urtext* concept, that an *Urtext* edition that has been superseded by subsequent scholarship is no longer an *Urtext*.[24] Clearly more than one *Urtext* simply cannot exist, and an edition that is the product of critical scholarship may be admirable and useful, but an *Urtext* it is not.[25]

The second direction in post-World War II editing that provoked critical reaction centred on the new Collected Editions of the great composers. The initiatives pursued in the 1950s refocused attention on the preparation of scholarly critical editions that could also be used by performers.[26] That approach stands in marked contrast to the attitude of the first series of these editions, starting in the nineteenth century, which consisted largely of philological monuments, as noted above, and, as such, gave less attention to performance matters. Musicologists responded to the challenges of these new projects by opening discussions on the relationship between music of the past (including the recent past) and the performer.[27] Editors were urged to jettison some of the philological purity of their texts (old clefs, for example), in order to make editions more accessible to performers. At the same time, the need for critical intervention on the part of the editor was recognized, without, however, a detailed discussion of what that entailed.

These developments led, almost incidentally, to a consideration of the historical relationship between composer and performer. If that relationship affects editorial practice in the present, should editors not give weight to its nature in the past? The most penetrating assessment of this issue came from Klaus Harro Hilzinger, who was influenced by the method of "genetic" editing cultivated in German philology.[28]

[24] Feder and Unverricht, "Urtext und Urtextausgaben," pp. 444–46.

[25] For criticism of editorial practice in *Urtext* editions, see E. and P. Badura-Skoda, *Mozart-Interpretation*, pp. 139–51; Emery, *Editions and Musicians*, pp. 9–14, 39; Dahlhaus, "Urtextausgaben"; Dahlhaus, "Zur Ideengeschichte musikalischer Editionsprinzipien," pp. 23–24; Hilzinger, "Über kritische Edition," pp. 204–7; Rehm, "Notenschrift und Aufführung," pp. 103–7; Finscher, "Gesamtausgabe–Urtext–Musikalische Praxis," pp. 194–95; Querbach, "Der konstruierte Ursprung"; and Brett, "Text, Context, and the Early Music Editor," pp. 89–91.

[26] Vötterle, "Die Stunde der Gesamtausgabe," pp. 288–91; Finscher, "Musikalische Denkmäler und Gesamtausgaben," pp. 10–13; Dahlhaus, "Zur Ideengeschichte musikalischer Editionsprinzipien," pp. 21–23; Rehm, "Notenschrift und Aufführung," pp. 107–11; and Berke, "Urtext zwischen Wissenschaftsanspruch und Praxisnähe," p. 531.

[27] E.g., Fellerer, "Werk–Edition–Interpretation;" Finscher, "Gesamtausgabe–Urtext–Musikalische Praxis"; pp. 196–97; Gülke, "Philologie und musikalische Praxis"; Wallnig, "'Produkt im Kopf'"; and Gruber, "'Doppel'-Editionen."

[28] Hilzinger, "Über kritische Edition." On genetic editing, see the essays collected in Martens and Zeller, eds., *Texte und Varianten*; and Kraft, *Die Geschichtlichkeit literarischer Texte*.

This approach emphasizes the processes through which a work comes into being, instead of the reification of a particular state of the work. Hilzinger identified the promise this conception holds for scholarly editing in music by recognizing that convention holds the central place in communication between composer and performer via the score. The reconstitution of conventions that governed music of the past requires a consideration of the work's historical context. The interpretative editions, for example, that motivated, in reaction, *Urtext* editions become primary sources for the reception of the work, a kind of oral history.[29] Carl Dahlhaus, in his reply to Hilzinger, reasserts the need to assign authority to the composer, even in the context of a historical investigation of the work and its reception.[30]

To this point, the account of critical discourse about the editing of music has considered contributions by German-speaking authors only, whose concern for editing is rooted in the philological issues surrounding the preparation of the monumental scholarly editions of the last century and a half. Alongside that tradition emerged another in the immediate post-war period, in English-speaking nations, associated with the performance of early music. Its pragmatic approach took as a point of departure the problem of creating clear, usable editions of old music originally written in notation no longer familiar to practising musicians. These editors gave clear precedence to presentation over critical issues.[31] The one publication from this period that does address criticism in editing is Walter Emery's pamphlet *Editions and Musicians*, which Philip Brett in 1988 called "still the best introduction to editing for the general musician."[32]

Yet Emery does not apply his criteria for editorial judgement consistently. He condemns "aesthetic and stylistic criticism," and characterizes editing as "a quasi-science, and the more scientific it is, the better," based on "palaeography and bibliography, and historical facts in general."[33] Quite a few of the observations he makes, however, arise from subjective, critical observations regarding musical style, rather than objective bibliographical, palaeographical or historical facts. He presents an elaborate argument, for example, about the disposition of the voices in the A♭ major fugue in book 2 of the *Well-Tempered*

[29] Hilzinger, "Über kritische Edition," p. 205; see also Finscher, "Gesamtausgabe–Urtext–Musikalische Praxis," pp. 193–94

[30] Dahlhaus, "Philologie und Rezeptionsgeschichte."

[31] Dart, *The Interpretation of Music*, pp. 11–28; and Dart, Emery and Morris, *Editing Early Music*.

[32] Brett, "Text, Context, and the Early Music Editor," p. 90.

[33] Emery, *Editions and Musicians*, pp. 5, 6, 13.

Clavier.[34] His reasoning is convincing, showing that Bach would most likely not have allowed the soprano to rest for fourteen out of fifty bars (that is, bars 8–22), as one of the autograph sources reads. But his conclusion depends on musical, not bibliographical, issues, sharpened through critical and even aesthetic sense, and shows that these qualities, in addition to complete bibliographic control of the sources, are essential to scholarly editing.

The question of textual criticism receives little better treatment in the more recent discussions of editing by Howard Mayer Brown and John Caldwell, both of whom dispense with critical issues in brief introductory passages before turning to the more mechanical aspects of editing.[35] Each, nevertheless, is an important contribution to the field. Brown presents a thoughtful discussion of the practical problems of editing, and his own editions demonstrate the results of creative critical thought. Caldwell's book, moreover, contains much very sound guidance, arising from the author's extensive experience in editing, and supervising the editing, of early music.

Articles by Arthur Mendel and Philip Brett confront critical matters more directly.[36] Both note that performers of early music continue to assume greater responsibility for details in the execution of these works, with increasing sophistication. Consequently, the editor who proposes definitive solutions for all such problems obstructs, rather than assists, the aim of performance. Brett, in the passage quoted above as well as elsewhere in the essay, defines the open acknowledgement of the editor's critical position as the paramount issue in creating a truly critical edition, one that he recognizes musicologists often sidestep.[37]

The most important contribution to date, and the only one that considers the full range of critical issues in editing, is Georg Feder's monograph, *Musikphilologie.*[38] Although I do not wish to give a detailed review here, two central aspects of Feder's treatment elicit further comment in the following discussion. First, even though Feder himself realizes that the entire editorial process requires critical thought, he nevertheless persists in dividing that process into "lower"

[34] *Ibid.*, pp. 10–12. [35] H. M. Brown, "Editing"; and Caldwell, *Editing Early Music.*

[36] Mendel, "The Purposes and Desirable Characteristics"; and Brett, "Text, Context, and the Early Music Editor."

[37] Brett, "Text, Context, and the Early Music Editor," pp. 89–91, 97–99, 111.

[38] Feder, *Musikphilologie.* This book has received very little attention in the scholarly press; the only published review in the periodicals indexed by the *Music Index* and the *Arts and Humanities Citation Index* is by Querbach (see Bibliography).

(bibliographic and mechanical) and "higher" (interpretative and critical) stages. Second, Feder implies throughout that the goal of editing is the determination of final compositional intentions. Both issues take on importance in the context of the critical theory of editing I develop in this book.

Philology and editing

Since the beginning of scholarly editing in music, musicologists have borrowed the methods and approaches of philology. Even Kerman, in attacking what he sees as the deficiency of musicological method, borrows an approach from English philology. In this field, many scholars believe in the division of labour between Low and High Criticism that forms the basic structure of Feder's book on editing, as noted above.[39] Brett's position, so eloquently stated in the passage quoted at the beginning of the chapter, also owes much to philology, and he devotes a good deal of space to summarizing the principal approaches and how they relate to editing music.[40] My ideas, too, are shaped by thinking in philology, by the two streams that inform Brett's discussion, as the ensuing argument will reveal.

Nevertheless, editing music is, fundamentally and in essence, different from editing literature. The fundamental distinction stems from the relationship between the work and its written text in music, while the essential difference lies in the character of the written text of a musical work. My intention here is to present a theory of editing that acknowledges these unique aspects of the musical work and places them as central issues in the methodology and practice of music editing.

Before proceeding to that discussion, I shall outline the approaches from philology that have influenced my thinking about editing. The first is the very venerable and learned tradition of textual criticism in Classical Philology.[41] To many, this is identified principally with the technique of stemmatic filiation derived from the principle of common error, which, in turn, is usually associated with the German scholar Karl Lachmann. Below, in Chapter 3, I devote a good deal of space to a description and critical evaluation of this tool and its usefulness in music editing. But Classical Philology has a good deal more

[39] A classic statement of the goals of High Criticism is Frye, *Anatomy of Criticism*.
[40] Brett, "Text, Context, and the Early Music Editor," pp. 99–114.
[41] See Brett, "Text, Context, and the Early Music Editor," pp. 99–103.

to offer students of editing than stemmatics. I look, rather, to the tradition within which editing is an integral part of a thoroughgoing critical appraisal of the work as a whole. Lachmann was a part of that tradition, although that fact is almost forgotten in the frenzy, pro and contra, about stemmatic filiation.

Indeed the idea of a critical reading of a work reaches back to antiquity, to the scholars at Alexandria who strove to establish a text of Homer.[42] In this tradition, every editorial decision is taken in the context of the editor's understanding of the work as a whole; and that understanding can only be achieved through critical evaluation. The establishment of the text, then, far from being mechanical, forms part of the ongoing critical dialogue between work and scholar. The meaning of the work and the reading of the text are fully complementary and interdependent phenomena. This is precisely the situation that I described at the outset, when I located all editorial decisions squarely within the realm of critical inquiry.

The second idea from philology that has influenced my approach to editing is Jerome J. McGann's theory of the work of art as a social phenomenon.[43] McGann begins by attacking the notion of "final authorial intentions." This construct requires the editor to consider only the artistic wishes, or intentions, of the author in establishing the text.[44] McGann shows, however, that the act of communicating the work to an audience is a fully integrated part of the creative process. By entering into this dialogue, artists abandon their autonomy, and inevitably shape the work somehow to accommodate and facilitate that act of communication. The context, then, social, cultural, political and economic, impinges on the final form and meaning of the work, which can only be understood as a social artifact, rather than an autonomous entity subject only to the will of its creator.

Much the same relationship exists between a piece of music and its context. The work enters into a dialogue with its context, which it

[42] On the Classical tradition of textual criticism, see Pfeiffer, *History of Classical Scholarship: From the Beginnings to the End of the Hellenistic Age*; *idem*, *History of Classical Scholarship: From 1300 to 1850*; Kenney, *The Classical Text*; and Reynolds and Wilson, *Scribes and Scholars*. On Lachmann's contribution, see Timpanaro, *La genesi*.

[43] McGann, *The Romantic Ideology*; *A Critique*; the essays collected in *The Beauty of Inflections*; *Social Values and Poetic Acts*; *Towards a Literature of Knowledge*; and *The Textual Condition*. See also Thorpe, *Principles of Textual Criticism*; and McKenzie, *Bibliography and the Sociology of Texts*.

[44] Bowers, "Some Principles for Scholarly Editions"; and Tanselle, "The Editorial Problem of Final Authorial Intention." Most of McGann, *A Critique*, constitutes a refutation of this view, but see, especially, pp. 29–80. On this issue in music, see Dadelsen, "Die 'Fassung letzter Hand'." Jeffrey Kallberg, "Are Variants a Problem?" adapts McGann's approach to the issue in the music of Chopin.

then helps to shape. Palestrina wrote music for the celebration of the Catholic liturgy, which required a certain amount of accommodation on the composer's part; the style he created for this type of music then went on to dominate the composition of Catholic liturgical music for the next two centuries or more: context affects the music, and the music affects the context. This idea is certainly not new to musicologists. It forms a central concern of research in ethnomusicology, whose practitioners study culture and behaviour as a unified whole within which they place the functional and aesthetic import of music.[45]

Historical musicologists, too, have made material contributions to the discussion. In one of this century's monuments of musicological literature, Paul Henry Lang devoted 1,000 pages to the place of music in its cultural context, and Hugo Leichtentritt prefaced his survey of music history with an eloquent plea to view historical study as a necessary complement to the study of musicology.[46] More recent scholars, such as Gary Tomlinson and John Shepherd, refine the debate by seeing music as an active participant in the social and cultural matrix.[47] And, in a study of nineteenth-century instrumental music, Lawrence Kramer shows that meaning in music is referential and dependent upon context.[48] Nevertheless, McGann's theory shows how the social aspects of the creative process materially affect editing, and therefore it holds a central place in my conceptualization of editing music.

By rejecting the concept of final authorial intention, and replacing it with his theory of the social nature of the work of art, McGann transforms the process of editing from a psychological endeavour (in which the editor attempts to determine the author's intentions) into a historical undertaking. Under this principle, each source attests to a particular historical state of the work; the editor assesses the value of that evidence against the background of the larger historical context in which the piece was created; and the final edited text reflects the editor's conception of the piece as it existed in its historical and social environment. Thus each source and each reading is considered as an individual piece of evidence for the history of the work.

Two examples illustrate how the creative process in music reflects the socialization that McGann describes in literature. Boris Schwarz

[45] Representative statements of these goals are Merriam, *The Anthropology of Music*, and Blacking, *How Musical is Man?*

[46] Lang, *Music in Western Civilization*; Leichtentritt, *Music, History, and Ideas*, pp. xi–xxv.

[47] Tomlinson, "The Web of Culture"; and Shepherd, *Music as Social Text*. See also the essays collected in Leppert and McClary, eds., *Music and Society*.

[48] Kramer, *Music as Cultural Practice*.

documents how Brahms, during the composition of his Violin Concerto, Op. 77, sought and received advice from Joseph Joachim.[49] Brahms, of course, was ultimately responsible for the compositional decisions that shaped the piece. When, however, we accept into the text of the Concerto readings that originated with Joachim, we accept that Brahms engaged in a social dialogue that affected those compositional decisions. The dialogue itself and its effects on the compositional process are matters of historical investigation based on the surviving documents; they are not subject to a psychological interpretation that attempts to determine levels of intention.

A similar process of socialization was carried out in a more public forum by Schumann when, as Jon W. Finson shows, he revised his orchestral piece, Op. 52, in the interest of increasing its commercial viability.[50] This example is particularly interesting because the nature of the surviving documents sets the issue of compositional intention in high relief. Schumann's motivation in revising Op. 52 was apparently to promote its performance and publication. Does his commercial intention for the work differ from his artistic intention in creating it in the first place? If we can separate these two facets of intentionality, then perhaps we should view the original, 1841, version of Op. 52 as that which Schumann created from a primary artistic impulse, and the 1845 revision as a commercial adaptation of the original work.

But that analysis may well not square with Schumann's own appraisal of the situation, and the state of the autograph, in which he made the revisions, does not support this interpretation. From the time of the piece's première, on 6 December 1841, he expressed concern for its reception, and, after several unsuccessful attempts to place the work with a publisher, he yielded to the inevitability of revision.[51] Can we reasonably separate artistic and commercial intentions? Did Schumann's revisions of 1845 compromise the artistic and aesthetic qualities of the work? We can never know, for certain, what his true, innermost feelings about the piece were. Nevertheless, the historical circumstances show that, whatever his opinion of the earlier version, and whatever his motivations for the revisions, the only version he left for posterity was the later one.

A convincing piece of evidence for this argument is the state of the Finale in the autograph. He discarded most of the 1841 version of this

[49] Schwarz, "Joseph Joachim."
[50] Finson, "Schumann, Popularity, and the *Ouverture, Scherzo, und Finale*, Opus 52."
[51] *Ibid.*, pp. 3–7.

movement, and replaced it with a new version written on different paper and dated 20 October 1845.[52] Here, his actions leave no room for speculation. Wherever the 1841 version can be reconstructed, its readings make for interesting comparison with the revisions to illustrate Schumann's compositional method, as Finson shows in his article. Most editors, however, would print the 1845 version, if for no other reason than the incomplete state of the earlier version. Yet this conclusion is anything but definitive. It depends on a critical appraisal of the source and the historical circumstances of its creation and revision. Moreover, it represents not so much an attempt to understand Schumann's intentions, as to interpret the historical evidence of the sources. And that historical interpretation requires us to find our own meaning in the testimony left behind by Schumann.

That meaning arises from the social nature of artistic communication, a factor that artists, like Brahms and Schumann, take into consideration when they create their works. Nevertheless, the work of art begins from the original conception of the artist, and through all the metamorphoses it undergoes during the process of its socialization, it is the artist who is responsible for its shape.[53] When textual criticism is undertaken within a historical frame of reference, it discerns the possible influences on the artist and how those influences are reflected in the sources. And so, under McGann's influence, the second tenet of my approach to editing holds that editing is, in essence, a historical enterprise.[54]

History and editorial method

Every piece of music is created under a unique combination of cultural, social, historical and economic circumstances. An acknowledgement of those circumstances, and thus of the uniqueness of each creative product, affects the conception of all editorial projects: each piece is a special case, each source is a special case, each edition is a special case. This attitude leads naturally to the corollary that different

[52] *Ibid.*, p. 9.

[53] Tanselle, "Problems and Accomplishments in the Editing of the Novel," presents a sensitive account of some of the influences on novelists and the possible editorial solutions that might accommodate them.

[54] For criticism of McGann's approach, see Tanselle, "Historicism and Critical Editing," pp. 19–27; Shillingsburg, "An Inquiry into the Social Status"; Howard-Hill, "Theory and Praxis" (see McGann's reply, "A Response to T. H. Howard-Hill"); and Howard-Hill, "Variety in Editing and Reading" (replying to McGann, "Literary Pragmatics and the Editorial Horizon," and Shillingsburg, "The Autonomous Author").

repertories of music require different editorial methods, or even that each edition calls for a unique approach. This idea, too, is not new to musicology, nor to musicological discourse on editing. The editorial boards of several of the new Collected Editions from the post-World War II period have issued specific guidelines for editorial procedures in their series.[55]

The organization of most recent literature on editing also reflects this attitude. Brown and Caldwell both devote separate sections of their discussions to editorial problems in the music of discrete chronological periods, and Thrasybulos G. Georgiades has edited a series of essays on the editorial problems of several distinct repertories.[56] Because of the diversity of approach required for different editorial projects, it would be sheer folly to attempt to stipulate a particular methodology by which any and all musics can be edited. The historical nature of editing prohibits such an attempt, and no book could suggest solutions or even guidelines for the multitude of problems that any edition generates, nor should it: all editors will resolve them in their own way. Moreover, all editors exist in their own historical context, which directly affects the attitude they take in approaching any editorial project.

Above I formulate a group of questions that constitutes a framework for an editorial methodology. These questions form a point of departure for each editorial project, and for each editorial project the answers will assuredly differ. But the formulation of this set of questions constitutes a critical theory for the editing of Western art music. For the creation of a truly critical edition demands not only that they be asked, but that some kind of critical discourse be offered by way of response. The authorial intention of this book, then, is to formulate the theoretical framework outlined above, within which editors can found their work on a solid basis of critical and historical inquiry.

Work and Text

That inquiry begins with a consideration of the relationship between the text of a work of music, and the work itself. G. Thomas Tanselle, in describing this relationship in literature, differentiates between the

[55] Some are collected in Dadelsen, ed., *Editionsrichtlinien*; see also Bennwitz, *et al.*, eds., *Musikalisches Erbe und Gegenwart*.

[56] Brown, "Editing," pp. 843a–47b; Caldwell, *Editing Early Music*, pp. 13–94; and Georgiades, ed., *Musikalische Edition*.

text of a work and the text of a document, that is, the physical artifact that carries a text.[57] His locution demonstrates the central place of textuality in literature, something McGann calls the textual condition.[58] Sound, metre, rhyme all contribute to the effect of the poem, with the result that the meaning and the physical, verbal, textual form of a poem are inextricably interwoven. Furthermore, editing in literature consists of the mediation between the texts of preserved documents and the editor's conception (formed from a historical inquiry into those documents and their context) of the text of the work.

The work of music, however, participates in a very different relationship with its physical manifestations, whether in sound or in writing, a relationship that fundamentally affects the textual condition of the work in music. That difference begins from the recognition that the written text of a work, its score, is not self-sufficient, that text and work, therefore, are not synonymous. Where, then, does the work of music exist? Roman Ingarden locates it in the collaborative intentionality of composer and performer through the mediation of the score.[59] Critics of Ingarden have attempted to limit the application of his concept geographically and chronologically. In particular, Lydia Goehr presents a sophisticated account of the historical development of the work-concept beginning around 1800, when musicians began comparing their creations to those in the visual arts.[60]

A graver difficulty in Ingarden's formulation for the purposes of this book, grounded as it is in McGann's historicist theory, is that it identifies the work as a psychological entity, existing in the minds of composer and performer. Such reasoning immediately calls to mind the notion that the work exists in its only true form in the mind of the composer, with the corollary that any score (never mind a performance) could only be a pale imitation of it.[61] Ingarden and Jean-Jacques Nattiez combat this association by insisting that the performer is a full and active participant in the creation of the work. Nevertheless, Ingarden's theory situates the work in a place that can

[57] Tanselle, "Literary Editing"; and *A Rationale*.

[58] See McGann, *The Textual Condition*, especially pp. 3–16.

[59] Ingarden, *The Work of Music*, especially pp. 34–40, 116–22, 137–58. See also Dahlhaus, *Musikästhetik*, pp. 19–27; Dahlhaus, "Ästhetik und Musikästhetik," pp. 90–99; Feder, *Musikphilologie*, pp. 13–21; and Nattiez, *Music and Discourse*, pp. 69–90.

[60] Goehr, *The Imaginary Museum*, especially pp. 148–286. See also Lissa, "Some Remarks on Ingardenian Theory of a Musical Work."

[61] For a commentary on how this attitude, whose originator seems to have been Richard Wagner, came to dominate musical life in the twentieth century, see Salzman, "On Reading Cosima Wagner's *Diaries*," pp. 344–52.

never be subject to critical scrutiny, in the intention of composer and performer.

It is more fruitful, I believe, to seek those aspects of the musical work that are not transmitted through its score in the sphere of performance practice. The works of Chopin exemplify the relationship between the piece, as it is recorded in writing, and performance, as Jeffrey Kallberg and Leo Treitler show.[62] Autographs and contemporary prints of certain piano music preserve an assortment of variants that denote some indeterminacy in the mind of the composer himself regarding the text. The exact details, therefore, can only be realized in performance, and individual performances could differ somewhat, either by observing some of the variants in the written tradition or by introducing new ones in the same vein. To illustrate the practice, Treitler documents some of the variation he encountered in early recorded performances of some of Chopin's piano music.[63] The score, therefore, the composer's direct product, does not precisely define the piece, nor does any performance or combination of performances.

The variations that we observe in the written and performing traditions of the piece suggest, but do not fix, the limits of indeterminacy. Some of that indeterminacy arises from the limitations of notation, but most of it from the prevailing conventions of performance and written transmission. Moreover, for any music that continues to be performed those limits will never be fixed, as new performers will (and should, I believe) continue to redefine them. The piece, therefore, resides equally in the score and in the performing conventions that govern its interpretation at any particular historical moment. These conventions are fixed in practice, and practice changes over time, changing convention with it. The identity of the work, then, varies with the conventions under which the score is understood.

This conclusion leads to an investigation of the textual condition of the score. For most of the Western art tradition, the act of creating a musical work consists of two stages, composing (which is usually synonymous with the inscription of the score) and performance. These two intermediary steps place the musical work on the same plane as dance and drama, in which the execution of a work, which could exist in written form (the script in drama and choreographic notation in dance), occurs in performance. At the same time, it marks

[62] Kallberg, "Are Variants a Problem?" and Treitler, "History and the Ontology of the Musical Work." [63] Treitler, "History and the Ontology of the Musical Work," pp. 487–91.

a distinction between the work, which depends equally on the score and performance for its existence, and a text, either written (a score) or sounding (a performance) that defines a particular state of the work. This is the distinction I maintain throughout this study: the work exists in a potentially infinite number of states, whether in writing (the score) or in sound (performance); the text is one of those states.

In McGann's theory, the written text holds a central place in our understanding of the work. Although the text is not identical with the work, it is the principal concern of editing, which begins and ends with this physical entity. The critical position adopted by the editor observes the distinctions between work and text and between written and sounding texts, and many of the critical decisions made by editors depend on their understanding of the work (as opposed to its text). Nevertheless, editing depends principally on the texts of the work's sources, and ultimately generates a text as its product.

Musical notation also carries a distinctive type of meaning, for the text of a musical work addresses not the listener, who occupies the same position as the reader in literature, but a quite different person, the performer. This individual, even when he or she is the composer, acts as a second intermediary between the work and its audience, through the medium of performance. And the text of a musical work functions, in the first instance, as the means of communication between composer and performer. This relationship clarifies the nature of a musical text: a musical score contains of a set of instructions to the performer for the execution of the work transmitted in the score.[64] Perhaps John Cage's *4′33″* most graphically illustrates the relationship.[65] The printed score instructs the performer or performers to remain silent; any sound that forms a part of the piece comes from the audience or the acoustical ambience, and both sources are, of course, completely indeterminate.

The instructions found in a score vary as to specificity, but throughout the Western art tradition at least some details are left to the discretion of the performer. (Some would say that those compositions created and executed entirely on electromagnetic media constitute exceptions to this situation.[66] Even here, though, vagaries in the hard-

[64] Ingarden, *The Work of Music*, pp. 34–40; Dahlhaus, "Ästhetik und Musikästhetik," pp. 94–96; and Goehr, *The Imaginary Museum*, pp. 21–43. For a less flexible interpretation of the relationship between work, score and performance, see Goodman, *Languages of Art*, pp. 177–92.

[65] Cage, *4'33"*. [66] E.g., Feder, *Musikphilologie*, p. 98.

Example 1–1

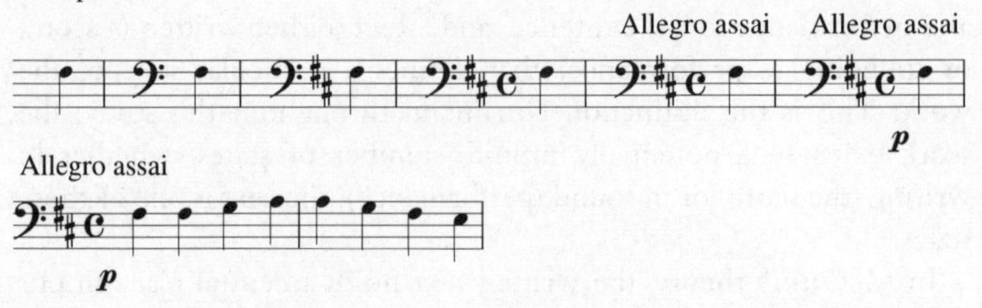

ware used for reproduction and the room acoustics of the place of performance can materially affect the aural impact of the piece in ways that are beyond the composer's control.) Trained musicians can aurally imagine the sounds indicated by the score, but this action is not equivalent to reading: rather it is the aural replication of a performance, and the silent score reader must make the same decisions, interpret the symbols of the musical notation, just as a performer does, in order to re-create the work.[67]

The nature of those interpretative processes emerges from a consideration of the manner in which notation communicates. The individual symbol of musical notation carries no independent meaning whatsoever. The following symbol has a name, but no meaning.

Its meaning arises solely from the context in which it occurs (see Example 1–1). Gradually its meaning is created by the addition of more elements of its context, giving it pitch, duration and volume, before it takes its place, in the second line of the Example, in a musical phrase, where it gains more meaning through its position in the melodic and metrical scheme of the phrase in relation to other notes in the phrase. Any musician would recognize that the symbol's meaning could have been made even more specific through the multiplication of modifying notational symbols in the context, like marks of articulation. That Beethoven chose not to do so in this passage does not change or diminish the meaning of the individual symbols in it; rather the degree of detail in the notation defines the context within which those individual symbols derive their meaning.

[67] On the difference between text in music and literature, and the nature of communication in the musical text, see Tanselle, *A Rationale*, pp. 22–24.

The semiotic nature of musical notation

Therefore the meaning that the text of a musical work carries is inscribed in the semiotic import of its notational symbols; and I use semiotics in its most strictly literal sense, as derived from τό σημεῖον, "a mark" or "sign."[68] I also distinguish it from semiology in the sense that Jean-Jacques Nattiez uses the term to denote the study of meaning in musical gesture.[69] As Leo Treitler points out, the fullest interpretation of musical notation requires not only a consideration of morphology, in which the identity of the notational symbol is determined, and meaning, but also the way in which meaning is conveyed, that is, the semiotics of the notation.

For example, in much music of the period *c.* 1550–1800, composers indicated tempo by the predominant note values used in the course of a piece: longer note values convey slower tempos.[70] Arcangelo Corelli observes these distinctions in his Trio Sonata Op. 3 no. 2, for example, where the second and fourth movements, both marked Allegro, use eighth notes predominantly, while the third movement, marked Adagio, moves in half notes for the most part. (The Italian character designations, therefore, reinforce the implications of the notation.) In both fast and slow contexts, the same symbol indicates the same relative duration (i.e., a quarter note is half the duration of a half note, or double the duration of an eighth note), and this relationship arises from the morphology of the symbols. The two contexts, however, require that the same symbol denote different absolute durations, a deduction that cannot follow from the morphology of the symbol alone.

This meaning derives from two complementary factors, both central elements in Ferdinand de Saussure's conception of semiotics, that together form the semiotic framework within which musical notation communicates. The first is convention.[71] That is, the assignment of a particular meaning to a specific symbol is arbitrary. This is true at the level of morphology. There is nothing intrinsic about the

[68] Semiotic issues in notation are addressed in Seeger, "Prescriptive and Descriptive Music-Writing"; and Dadelsen, "Über das Wechselspiel von Musik und Notation." See also Kurkela, *Note and Tone*; Goehr, *The Imaginary Museum*, pp. 21–43; and Treitler, "Observations on the Transmission," pp. 48–60; "The Early History of Music Writing in the West"; "Reading and Singing"; "Paleography and Semiotics"; and "The 'Unwritten' and 'Written Transmission'."

[69] Nattiez, *Music and Discourse*; see also Dunsby, "Music and Semiotics."

[70] Vicentino, *L'antica musica*, fol. 42r–v.

[71] Saussure, *Cours de linguistique générale*, pp. 100–2, 180–84.

addition of a stem that requires a half note to last half as long as a whole note, but convention dictates it. Convention operates equally in the use of note values to indicate tempo, as described above. And the arbitrary nature of the convention is revealed when it is contradicted, as in the piano works of Beethoven, who habitually writes slow movements in short values and fast ones in long notes (e.g., the *Pathétique* Sonata, Op. 13, first movement, where the Grave passages move in sixteenth notes and the Allegro di molto e con brio in eighth notes). Corelli and Beethoven are working in opposite but equally arbitrary conventions.

The second factor is the system within which individual signs operate.[72] This aspect of semiotics concerns the relationships between signs, the ways in which their individual meanings depend on the significance of one another. Again, morphology constitutes one system: here the relative durations of symbols are arbitrarily determined. But more than one morphological system exists in the history of notation, and different systems operate within different conventions. In notation of the common practice period, duple subdivision is always assumed and triple must be indicated with a dot.

In fifteenth- and sixteenth-century notation, however, triple subdivision is indicated by the mensuration with the result that the dot is not obligatory.

These two systems, morphologically similar, employ two different conventions for indicating triple subdivision, and again both conventions are arbitrary.

In a parallel way, the method of indicating tempo by note values constitutes another semiotic system. The meaning of individual symbols arises from their relationship to other symbols within the system. Therefore, a movement that predominantly uses quarter notes is to be

[72] The whole of Saussure, *Cours de linguistique générale*, is concerned with language structure; see pp. 23–35.

performed more slowly than one that moves in sixteenth notes. Corelli's addition of the Italian character indications provided a supplement to the convention that eventually became a system in its own right, which in turn gave way to the greater precision of metronome markings.

Each musical sign, therefore, carries a significance dependent on context and convention. Composers who set these signs down are aware of these factors, and fix the text of their work within that framework. Once the historical moment of inscription has passed, however, the particular context and set of conventions in place at that time are subject to change, and new observers will bring their own set of conventions to the interpretation of the signs.

The interpretation of these signs, therefore, whether in performance (where the investigation of performance practice seeks to provide a guide to the theory and practice of interpretation) or in criticism (of which editing is a branch), is a strictly historical issue, but one that is equally rooted in the semiotic import of each sign. The interpreter must re-create, so far as it is possible, the historical context and conventions within which the text of the work was fixed in order to understand the meaning of each symbol.[73] Both Arthur Mendel and Philip Brett note that performers take the responsibility ever more seriously to investigate the historical conventions within which notational symbols are to be understood.[74]

These matters are especially important to editors of music because editing is centrally concerned with the text of a musical work, as noted above. In evaluating the sources of a musical work, and in establishing its edited text, editors confront the semiotic import of each notational symbol. They consider the conventions and circumstances that govern the meaning of each symbol in its historical context, and how those meanings can best be conveyed in the edition under preparation. At the same time, editors, too, bring their own set of conventions to the understanding of notation, and their awareness of their own historical context inevitably affects their interpretation of the work at hand. The third tenet of my approach to editing follows from these circumstances, and that is that the essence of editing is an investigation of the semiotic nature of musical notation, and that this investigation is also a historical undertaking.

[73] Feder, *Musikphilologie*, pp. 96–112, gives a sample of some semiotic problems in notation.

[74] Mendel, "The Purposes and Desirable Characteristics," p. 20; Brett, "Text, Context, and the Early Music Editor," pp. 98–99.

Editing and style

Within the context of a historical and semiotic investigation into a piece and its sources, the practice of editing depends in an elemental way on the editor's conception of the work's musical style. Taken together, the notational symbols and their semiotic meaning generate the stylistic attributes of a piece. Because editing amounts to the fixing of those symbols for a given piece, style ultimately governs many of the final editorial choices in that process. It is much easier to describe musical style than to define it. Jan LaRue gives the following:

> ...the style of a piece consists of the predominant choices of elements and procedures a composer makes in developing movement and shape (or perhaps, more recently, in denying movement or shape). By extension, we can perceive a distinguishing style in a group of pieces from the recurrent use of similar choices; and a composer's style as a whole can be described in terms of consistent and changing preferences in his use of musical elements and procedures. Even more broadly, common characteristics may individualize a whole school or chronological period. As these shared choices become increasingly general, of course, their application to any particular composer decreases. The only remedy for this statistical dilution is an increasingly thorough and perceptive style analysis.[75]

LaRue's definition starts from the premise that a musical work is the product of a discrete compositional act, and of course that paradigm is applicable for a great deal of Western art music.

The problem with the definition, though, stems from a point made above, that, no matter how precise the notation of a piece might be, there remains to the performer some discretion in the manner of execution. That discretion does not disappear even when the composer is also the performer. The performers' independence is guided and sometimes restricted by convention and context, but ultimately the decisions they make, from the possibilities for performance inherent in a musical work (as transmitted to them through a musical score), actively participate in the shaping of the work's style. The cadenza in a concerto from the late eighteenth century and the realization of the continuo part in a sonata from the beginning of the same century exemplify the material effect performance can exert on style. Style,

[75] LaRue, *Guidelines for Style Analysis*, p. ix. This book is a distinguished attempt to define and apply a concept of style. See also Adler, *Der Stil*, especially pp. 1–138; L. B. Meyer, *Emotion and Meaning in Music*, pp. 43–82; Meyer, *Style and Music*; Treitler, "Methods, Style, Analysis"; Westergaard, "On the Notion of Style"; and Wolff, "Towards a Methodology of Dialectic Style Consideration."

then, does not reside solely in the text of the work, but also in the plurality of performing options each work engenders.

It is essential to incorporate the intermediary stage of performance into the concept of style because of the semiotic nature of musical notation. The musical gestures that constitute style are inscribed in the symbols of musical notation that make up the work's text. These, in turn, direct the realization of the work in performance. But, as noted above, not all particulars of a performance are fixed by the text, and so the performer must bear the responsibility of deciding how to realize those particulars, according to precepts of convention. The nexus of the composer's instruction, as inscribed in the text of the work, and the performer's interpretation of that instruction creates the work's style.

A second issue in LaRue's definition requires comment, and that is the recurrence of common characteristics as the features of a particular style. This concept is the central concern of Leonard B. Meyer's formulation. "*Style is a replication of patterning, whether in human behavior or in the artifacts produced by human behavior, that results from a series of choices made within some set of constraints.*"[76] The addition of the indefinite article by LaRue, in the phrases "a distinguishing style" and "a composer's style," renders his statement all the more pointed, for, by collecting the typical gestures common to a group of pieces, we move from a definition of style, in general, to the definition of *a* style.[77] This distinction lies at the very heart of artistic endeavour and critical reaction to it, and that is the artist's striving for the unique gesture, and the critic's identification and appreciation of it. A prominent and important preoccupation of criticism is the kind of classification mentioned by both LaRue and Meyer, but equal to it, I believe, is the recognition of the artist's ability to redefine style with a single stroke. Editors must bring a special sensitivity to this capacity into their work because they make many decisions on the basis of stylistic criteria, as I explain below.

Style exists and operates within a historical context, and so its study is also, in the first instance, a historical undertaking. For style is influenced by function, genre, existing practice and feasibility of performance, as well as social, political and economic factors. Moreover, many elements contribute to style, which, of course, appear in an infi-

[76] L. B. Meyer, *Style and Music*, p. 3 (Meyer's emphasis).

[77] The structure of Adler, *Der Stil*, makes clear this distinction: "Stilprinzipien," pp. 1–138; and "Stilarten," pp. 139–272.

nite variety of combinations, changing with time, place, composer, genre, and even the individual piece. Any of these combinations, of course, constitutes a particular style, as noted above, but all possibilities must be entertained when we speak of style in general. All these considerations form a part of the historical investigation of the piece, as the example from Palestrina cited above demonstrates. The historical and liturgical context within which Palestrina worked affected the style of the music he wrote; elements of that style then became commonplace in liturgical music for the Catholic Church over the succeeding generations.

This historical view of style governs the editor's critical evaluation of readings in the text of the piece. Ultimately, editing boils down to the preference of one reading over another. Some readings are accepted, others rejected. All readings can be classified in one of three categories: good readings, reasonable competing readings, and clear errors. For the sake of economy, I shall call these categories 1, 2 and 3. The most important tool editors can bring to bear on these decisions is their awareness of style and its historical context. Where are editors supposed to obtain a notion of that style?

The simplicity of the answer reveals the circularity of the process: from the text of the work. If the text of the work, as transmitted in its witnesses, contains corruptions, or places where there is at least ambiguity as to which reading is correct, how is the editor to discern the style of the work? Feder terms this paradox the hermeneutic circle.[78] Clearly those who would seek definitive answers to these questions should abandon the task of editing at this point for the simple reason that this process is indeed circular. Readings are evaluated on the basis of conceptions of style that arise from the readings themselves. Nevertheless a point of entry to the problem does exist, and it depends on the critical acumen of editors and their sensitivity to issues of style.

That starting point is a critical study of works that stand in proximity to it in time, place, genre and function. These form a pool of parallel passages that may be used to test the validity of a given reading. Our knowledge of these works must ever be incomplete, and, what is more, our evaluation of that knowledge is sure to be in a continual state of change, as new critical judgements of style unfold. Style, like editing, is a moving target, and so a flexibility of approach is obliga-

[78] Feder, *Musikphilologie*, pp. 67, 90–91. See also Querbach, "Der konstruierte Ursprung," p. 16.

tory for editorial and all critical activities. Critics should marshal all their knowledge, erudition and insight in order to practise their craft, to criticize, but, because knowledge, erudition and insight are, one hopes, always deepening and growing, the vantage point from which criticism issues is always changing. Nevertheless, a start must be made somewhere, and in editing, it is with the sources and their texts (what philologists call the witnesses of a tradition), in whatever condition they may be, and the editor's knowledge of the work's historical context.

The following discussion is necessarily somewhat compartmentalized, but it intends to represent an ongoing re-evaluation of all readings and their place in the work's tradition. As editors define the elements of the work's style, the position of individual readings within the developing conception of the work's style continually changes, and so the status of a particular reading might well change as the process ensues. All readings are good readings until they are shown to be false on stylistic grounds. Because conceptions of style are constantly in flux, judgements of this type are never definitive or unequivocal. Moreover, there is no such thing as an "obvious error." Some readings will be deemed impossible within the stylistic boundaries of the piece. These are "clear" errors; "clear," because, on stylistic grounds, they cannot qualify as reasonable readings. The difference between clear and obvious errors is more than semantic: the latter apparently require no explanation, whereas the former do. Moreover, all these terms are relative, and what is a clear error for one editor can easily be a good reading for another. Such judgements patently depend on the editor's stylistic conception of the piece.

The editor begins by separating all readings into those for which the witnesses transmit competing readings, and those which are uncontested. From the latter group, readings found to be plausible enter the first category, good readings. Here begins the circular argument. Plausible readings are those which fall within the perceived boundaries of the work's style, as those boundaries and the editor's perceptions of them develop. Inevitably, however, readings from category 1 form the basis of an evaluation of the work's style. Because of the implicit circularity of the process, any judgements made here constitute a potentially fallible basis and therefore one in constant need of critical reappraisal. Upon the basis of these shifting criteria depend, in turn, all decisions regarding the placement of readings in the other two categories.

One test for the validity of a reading is a comparison with parallel readings. Alas, not all difficulties can be resolved by such means. Not without justification are textual critics called the dullest people in the world, because they insist that everything be said at least twice. Critics must be prepared to strike out beyond the safety of the parallel reading to consider the validity of the unique reading, for they must remain open to the possibility that a composer is capable of redefining style with a single note or gesture that is singular and unparalleled. Therefore, mere unanimity among witnesses is not sufficient for inclusion in this category: the reading must be judged to accord with its work's stylistic context.

Once editors have developed a preliminary conception of style, they can proceed to the definition of category 3, clear errors. Such readings fall outside the boundaries of the editors' adopted conception of style. Because editors are constantly refining and redefining that conception, they must be scrupulous about re-evaluating which readings fall outside it. Moreover, context plays an equally important role in the flexible interpretation of these boundaries. In the repertory of *uersus* from twelfth-century Aquitaine, for example, the polyphonic settings exhibit a preference for contrary motion. Therefore, when parallel motion occurs, as it does at a cadence in two of the witnesses that transmit *Omnis curet homo*, it could well have resulted from a copying error (see Example 1–2, where the parallel motion is marked **m**).[79]

Two passages from another *uersus*, *Senescente mundano filio*, show that not all instances of parallel motion in this repertory can be summarily deemed copying errors. (See Example 1–3.) Example 1–3a gives a passage that bears great similarity to that just cited from *Omnis curet homo*. The two voices proceed in parallel thirds throughout, including the final cadential sonority (marked **m** in the Example). And it is quite possible that this reading arose in exactly the same way as that in *Omnis curet homo*: the scribe copied the lower voice from his exemplar into the upper voice in the surviving copy, 3549, transposing by a third. The passage in Example 1–3b, however, exhibits an integration of contrary and parallel motion, again in thirds, that is unlikely to have arisen from miscopying. The use of parallel thirds in this second

[79] Sigla in Example 1–2: 3719b = Paris, Bibliothèque Nationale, fonds latin (hereafter Pa), MS 3719, fols. 23–32; 1139a = Pa 1139, fols. 32–39, 48–79; 3719d = Pa 3719, fols. 45–92; 3549 = Pa 3549, fols. 149–69; 36881a = London, British Library (hereafter Lo), Additional Manuscript 36881, fols. 1–16. For commentary, see Grier, "The Stemma," pp. 265–66.

Example 1–2: *Omnis curet homo* stanza 2

passage, therefore, might suggest that the parallels in Example 1–3a also did not result from scribal error. These two examples show that stylistic norms can help to identify copying errors, but that context sometimes causes those norms to be reinterpreted.

The establishment of stylistic criteria by which the editor can adjudge certain readings to be errors permits, in turn, a re-evaluation of category 1. Hitherto it consisted solely of uncontested, plausible

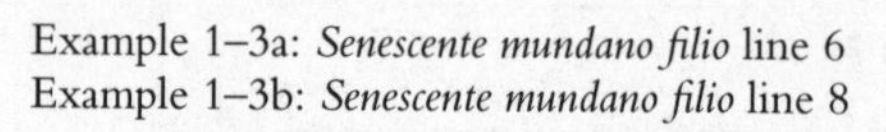
Example 1–3a: *Senescente mundano filio* line 6
Example 1–3b: *Senescente mundano filio* line 8

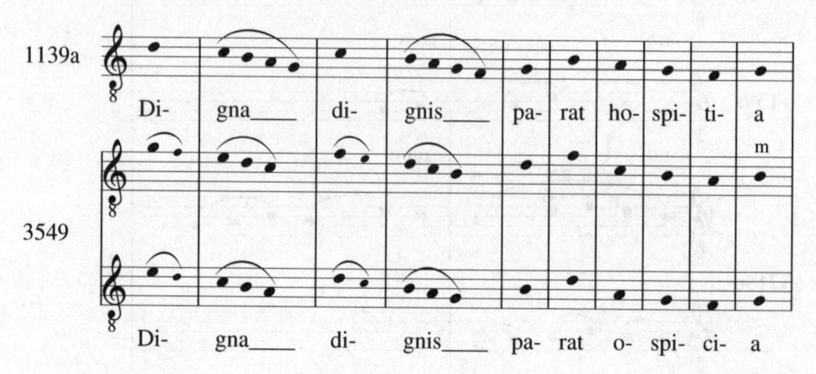

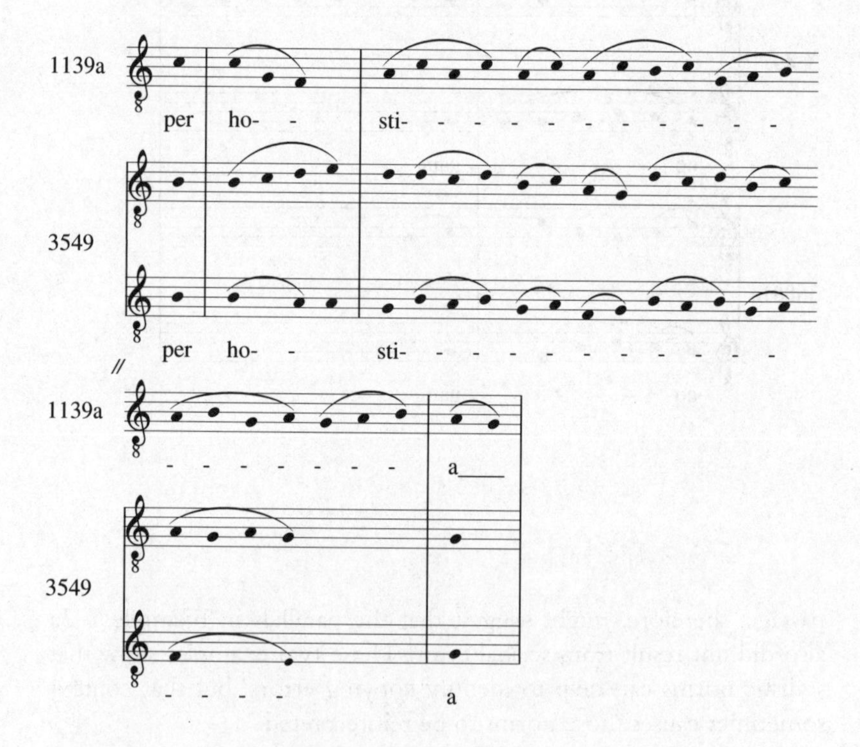

Example 1–4: J. S. Bach, Suite No. 3 for Violoncello Solo BWV 1009, Bourrée II, bars 1–8

readings. Now, all plausible readings that have, as their only competition, category 3 readings are recognized as good readings. Moreover, the basis for deciding which uncontested readings in fact belong to category 3 is sure to be firmer. We can now proceed to the definition of category 2, which contains reasonable competing readings. Textual critics, in their zeal to establish an original or authorial text, with the consequence that all other readings become unoriginal, non-authorial and therefore errors, have largely ignored this category.[80] Karl Lachmann recognized its importance early when he steadfastly refused to adopt a "method of criticism that depends on interpretation."[81] I define category 2 to contain all competing readings that fall within the boundaries of the work's style. A reading from the Solo Suite for Violoncello by J. S. Bach, BWV 1009, illustrates the problem (see Example 1–4).

A variant occurs at the end of bar 4 of the Bourrée II: the sources divide between A and A♭.[82] The former preserves the harmonic sense of C minor, the movement's tonic, with the Dorian modal orientation suggested by the key signature. The A♭, however, anticipates the move to E♭ major that immediately follows. Even though all editions agree in printing A♮, neither reading is stylistically superior to the other, and so neither can, in good conscience, be deemed an error.

[80] Notable exceptions are the discussions in Westcott and Hort, eds., *The New Testament*, II, 22–30; Eklund, "On Errors and Contamination"; and *idem*, "The Traditional or the Stemmatic Editorial Technique."

[81] "Die auf inneren Gründen beruhende Kritik"; Lachmann, "Rechenschaft über seine Ausgabe des Neuen Testaments," p. 820.

[82] Only the copy of Johann Peter Kellner (Berlin, Staatsbibliothek Preußischer Kulturbesitz, Mus. ms. Bach P 804) gives A♭; the other principal sources, including Anna Magdalena Bach's copy (Berlin, Staatsbibliothek Preußischer Kulturbesitz, Mus. ms. Bach P 269), transmit A♮. See Eppstein, *Sechs Suiten für Violoncello solo: Kritischer Bericht*, p. 64.

The editorial treatment of category 2 readings is vexing indeed. The common-error method of stemmatic filiation was introduced with the express purpose of providing a means to eliminate at least some of them, as I discuss in Chapter 3 below. In many cases, editors will simply have to choose between them, relying on their conception of the piece and the relationship between it and its sources.

In conclusion, four constituent principles shape my view of editing.
(1) Editing is a branch of criticism.
(2) All forms of criticism are historical undertakings.
(3) Editing starts from the critical and historical investigation of the semiotic import of the musical text.
(4) The editor's critical understanding of musical style, in its historical context, provides the final criterion for the determination of the musical text.

It is within the context of these four principles that the task of the editor is defined. Because each work is a unique artifact and will require a distinctive approach, any prescriptive methodology would unnecessarily restrict or confine the editor. The method to be used in any edition grows out of the evidence gathered in the preparation for it; the material itself leads the way. It is not possible to define the task of the editor in specific terms for each piece, composer or repertory in need of an edition. In fact two editors, each undertaking an edition of the same piece, might well define their tasks differently. That situation is only to be applauded, for no work of art is quantifiable, and so no study of it, including an edition, can be definitive. Therefore two competing editions, each manifesting a different and unique conception of the piece, can only be in the best interests of the audience, who, in any case, are striving to attain their own conception of the work. This discussion attempts to establish a theoretical position from which each editor can define the method and approach suitable for the editorial project at hand, while establishing a firm critical and historical foundation for the finished edition.

The final product of any edition is a text. The exact nature of that text, what it represents in relation to the work and its various sources, depends entirely on the editor's conception of the work, a conception reached through a critical evaluation of the work and its sources. And that critical evaluation persists throughout the process of editing. It might, therefore, lead to a rethinking of the editor's conception of the work at one or more stages, when the accumulated evidence indicates that a re-evaluation of the work is necessary. Editors who bring a preconceived notion of the piece to the task of editorship and who retain it throughout the preparation of the edition are more likely to produce an edition that fulfils that notion instead of one that responsibly and critically represents the evidence on which the edition is based.

And so the task of the editor is to establish and present a text that most fully represents the editor's conception of the work, as determined by a critical examination of the work, its sources, historical context and style. That task stands at the centre of all musical activity. Before anything can be done to a piece, performance, analysis, historical studies, its text must be made known to those who would pursue these undertakings. And the presentation of the text is the editor's job. Nevertheless, it is not so much a tool, leading to higher ends, as an active, critical participant in those ends, fostering further critical study and the ultimate goal, one hopes, of all types of musical endeavour, the animation of the music in performance.

2

The nature of the musical source

Most critical editions are founded on a thorough knowledge of the source materials. The accomplishments achieved by the recent Collected Editions of the works of Bach, Haydn and Mozart, among others, attest to the value of source studies and at the same time confirm that further research in this area will only enhance our understanding of the music, its creators and practitioners. No edition, existing, projected or future, including those lauded in the previous sentence, is definitive. New investigations of well-known sources will continue to yield new insights into the works they transmit in direct proportion to the imagination and erudition of the investigators. Moreover, although few startling discoveries remain to be made, many known sources suffer from unjust neglect or underappreciation.

Cliff Eisen, for example, has rehabilitated a corpus of sources from Salzburg that contain the music of Leopold and Wolfgang Mozart.[1] The NMA ignored these sources because they are not autograph. Eisen shows, however, that they carry authority as copies made under the supervision of the Mozarts by scribes in their employ. Critical studies like this one illustrate the importance of the continued examination and evaluation of music sources, even those already familiar. For beyond a recitation of facts about the sources, their age, condition or readings, the critical interpretation of the physical evidence of the sources contributes significantly to an assessment of their value in establishing the text of the edition. A well-planned edition, then, begins with detailed critical research into the sources.

All sources present two interrelated aspects: as historical documents and as the repositories of readings. Each source, as a physical artifact,

[1] Eisen, "The Mozarts' Salzburg Copyists."

originated in a particular historical context. As the Salzburg Mozart sources show, those historical circumstances directly affect the value and significance of the source for the history of the work or works they transmit. The newly recognized authenticity of the Salzburg copies requires that they play a more prominent role in future editorial considerations of these pieces, and, in at least one case (the *Linz* Symphony), overturns previous notions about the most authoritative source.[2] The authenticity of individual readings, however, still needs verification, regardless of the authenticity of the source, in establishing the text of the edition: every reading in a given source does not carry equal merit. In the illustration at hand, a whole class of sources, with their readings, was dismissed because the editors of the NMA did not fully appreciate their historical context. Yet once their historical importance is recognized, the readings they contain must undergo a process of critical examination before they enter the established text.

Source and text

A source transmits the text of a work. The relationship between text and work is treated in Chapter 1 above, where the text, and its physical manifestation, the source, is identified as the medium by which a work is communicated to the performer. Source and text can, however, occupy varying positions within that process of communication. Some composers create sketches and drafts intended for their eyes only. Complete scores in manuscript sometimes function as performing materials, or, since the advent of printing, as a pre-publication state. The autographs of Mozart, who saw very few of his works in print, and Beethoven, who, especially in his later years, wrote principally for publication, present a useful contrast. Many sources, particularly before 1700, have no direct association with the composer. Here the investigation seeks the motivation, personal, musical, national, institutional, that led to the creation of the source.

In many cases, the act of composition extends over time, and sometimes involves collaboration. Different sources, or distinct layers of the same source, record the stages of the work's evolution as it passes through revision and refinement.[3] Sometimes these processes occur in

[2] Eisen, *ibid.*, pp. 273–78 (with examples extending to p. 283); and "New Light."

[3] For two examples of Schumann manuscripts that preserve multiple layers, see L. C. Roesner, "The Autograph of Schumann's Piano Sonata in F Minor, Opus 14"; and Finson, "Schumann, Popularity, and the *Ouverture, Scherzo, und Finale*, Opus 52."

public, as is frequently the case in opera, where the work undergoes revision in response to varying circumstances of performance; individual sources might, then, represent a particular performance.[4] Other works change during their transmission as scribes (and, presumably, performers) assume the responsibility of altering the text in accord with their musical, aesthetic and practical needs.[5] This survey obviously does not cover all possibilities, but it serves to show the variability of the relationship between work and text. The significance of the source, as the physical abode of the text, within the history of the work depends on the precise definition of that relationship. That definition depends upon a historical investigation of the source's context coupled with a qualitative examination of the readings it transmits.

The course of such an investigation is influenced by two features of musical sources. First, almost all musical sources are practical, functional documents, and second, the production of musical sources, whether manuscript or printed, requires specialized, technical knowledge of musical notation. Musical scores enable performance. Most sources are created for direct use as performing materials, or, when publication is envisaged, to function as an intermediate stage in the production of printed sources that then serve as performing materials. There are contrary examples, such as the presentation manuscripts prepared under the supervision of Guillaume de Machaut, which contain his collected works, or, some would say, the series of Collected Editions undertaken in the second half of the nineteenth century.[6] But these are few in number beside the vast majority of sources produced with performance in mind. The functional nature of musical sources, as opposed to other types of books (literary, historical or philosophical, for example), is demonstrated by their impermanence. Scraps of music frequently turn up as binding material and end-papers in non-music books. When these sources outlived their usefulness, when their repertories became so outdated or expanded so much that a new book was needed, the obsolete books were destroyed and recycled as binding material.[7]

[4] For one famous example, see Abbate, "The Parisian 'Vénus' and the 'Paris' *Tannhäuser*."

[5] See Grier, "Scribal Practices," especially p. 410 n. 65, where scholarly work on several such repertories is cited. [6] On Machaut, see Earp, "Machaut's Role."

[7] For examples, see Lefferts and Bent, compilers, "New Sources of English Thirteenth- and Fourteenth-Century Polyphony"; Bowers and Wathey, compilers, "New Sources of English Fourteenth- and Fifteenth-Century Polyphony"; and Bowers and Wathey, compilers, "New Sources of English Fifteenth- and Sixteenth-Century Polyphony." Many of these are now collected in Wathey, *Manuscripts of Polyphonic Music*. On fragments of music manuscripts from the monastery of Lambach, see Babcock, *Reconstructing a Medieval Library*, especially pp. 15a–33b, 43a–48a.

The function of the source depends on its ability to communicate via its semiotic conventions, and those conventions can change with time. Even composers, as observers or performers, might understand their own texts in a different way after the moment of composition. Robert Pascall documents several instances where Brahms continued to experiment with published works, sometimes producing substantive revisions.[8] Most interesting is the oboe passage from the opening of the Andante of the First Symphony, Op. 68 (bars 17–21), to which Brahms added slurs in his personal copy of the print. Pascall suggests that this modification should not be understood "simply as a reinforcement of *espress* because it is more particular."[9] Brahms seems to have felt, in retrospect, that his original indication required further specification.

The interrelationship between notation and convention becomes crucial during the transmission of a piece. Each person involved in the process, scribe, engraver, editor, publisher, brings a unique set of conventions to the interpretation of the symbols in the text. Moreover, in many cases, the motivation to produce a new copy of a piece, in whatever medium, is the creation of a usable text for performance, rather than the accurate preservation of the symbols in the exemplar at hand. Consequently the act of copying often involves the imposition of the conventions of the scribe or engraver and thus the reinterpretation of the notational symbols that constitute the text of the work. A witness created under these circumstances, therefore, transmits the text that copyists or engravers feel carries the greatest meaning for their purposes or audience.

Philologists might consider this type of intervention to constitute scribal corruption, or at least licence. But the semiotic nature of musical notation requires that the critic adopt a much more flexible approach to the situation. Many sources present what amounts to a translation of the text from one set of notational practices and conventions to another. The most obvious example is a modern edition of a piece of early music, in which the editor has transcribed, or translated, the original notation into a modern idiom. But that extreme case, practised, presumably, under scholarly conditions, does not obscure the fact that practical, performing musicians, throughout the history of Western notation, have continually adapted the texts before them

[8] Pascall, "Brahms and the Definitive Text."

[9] *Ibid.*, facsimile of print on p. 64; discussion on p. 75.

to suit their needs. The development of plainsong notation, in which a stable repertory was inscribed in a variety of regional notational dialects, and the use of instrumental tablatures, where different instruments employ different notational systems, present just two instances of adaptation.

Moreover, the processes by which musical sources are created also affect the texts they transmit. Copying by hand, typesetting and engraving all occasion particular types of errors. The printing process also generates materials that exist solely for the benefit of the process, and not as performing materials: the fair copy used by the printer, proofs, second and subsequent editions. Each type of source exhibits distinctive characteristics that affect the evaluation of textual evidence. In the future, the influence of computer technology on the creative process will become a factor for critics, just as an understanding of the techniques of copying and printing and their effects on the source forms a part of current textual criticism. Different types of sources require different treatment on the part of editors, who seek to identify the place of each source in the history of the work under consideration, and then treat it accordingly.

Some textual alterations do not change the substance of the symbol: Example 2–1 gives a common pair of equivalents. Even greater changes in appearance can carry no substantive difference in meaning. Example 2–2 presents the opening of the tenor solo from J. S. Bach's Cantata *Christ lag in Todesbanden.* In both illustrations, no musically literate observer would have difficulty in comprehending the equivalency between the two versions. The use of either alternative follows purely from convention and does not threaten the integrity of the symbol's semiotic implications. Not all notational symbols, however, are equally unproblematic, as the example from Brahms, noted above, shows. Therefore the understanding of each witness of the work depends upon the observer's appreciation of the historical context and conventions within which it was produced.

A more specific example illustrates the problem. No autograph of the Suites for Violoncello Solo by J. S. Bach survives. The copy made by the composer's wife, Anna Magdalena Bach, transmits a slurring that differs from the other sources in many passages.[10] (See Example

[10] Sigla in Example 2–3: A = Berlin, Staatsbibliothek Preußischer Kulturbesitz, Mus. ms. Bach P 269 (the copy of Anna Magdalena Bach); B = Berlin, Staatsbibliothek Preußischer Kulturbesitz, Mus. ms. Bach P 804; C = Berlin, Staatsbibliothek Preußischer Kulturbesitz, Mus. ms. Bach P 289; D = Vienna, Österreichische Nationalbibliothek, Mus. Hs. 5007.

Example 2–1

Example 2–2: J. S. Bach, *Christ lag in Todesbanden* BWV 4, Versus III, tenor solo, bars 5–7

Example 2–3: J. S. Bach, Suite No. 1 for Violoncello Solo BWV 1007, Prelude, bar 1

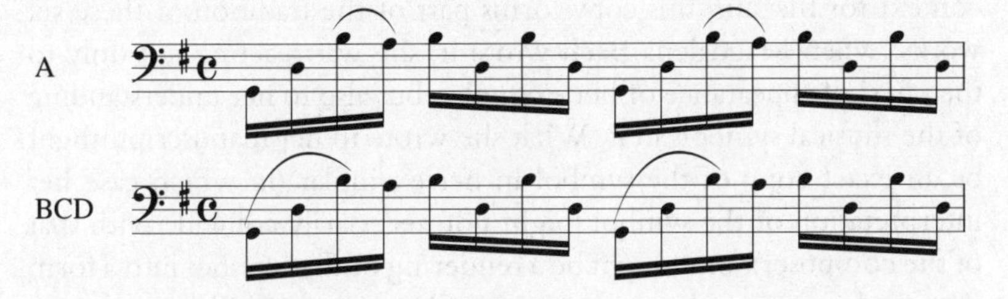

2–3.) Modern editors reject her reading in favour of the unanimity of the other sources.[11] Critics point to similar discrepancies between her copy of the Sonatas and Partitas for Solo Violin and her husband's autograph, which many take to be particularly precise and detailed in this regard.[12] The rejection of Magdalena Bach's slurring may well be justified, but it does not resolve all problems with the passage or the witness. To dismiss her markings, in either set of suites, as scribal error does not confront the semiotic issue raised by her version. The disagreement given in Example 2–3 is typical of many such readings throughout the Violoncello Suites. Although her slurring may be

[11] E.g., *Sechs Suiten für Violoncello solo BWV 1007–1012*, ed. Eppstein.

[12] Autograph of the Violin Sonatas and Partitas: Berlin, Staatsbibliothek Preußischer Kulturbesitz, Mus. ms. Bach P 967. Anna Magdalena Bach's copy: Berlin, Staatsbibliothek Preußischer Kulturbesitz, Mus. ms. Bach P 268. See Rönnau, "Bemerkungen zum 'Urtext' der Violinsoli J. S. Bachs"; and Eppstein, *Sechs Suiten für Violoncello solo: Kritischer Bericht*, pp. 27–30. On the precision of Bach's autograph, see Butt, *Bach Interpretation*, pp. 186–206. On articulation in general in the works of Bach, see Dadelsen, "Die Crux der Nebensache"; Dadelsen, "Zur Geltung der Legatobögen bei Bach"; and Butt, *Bach Interpretation*.

"inauthentic" in the sense that it does not graphically reproduce what was in the autograph (in the absence of which we can never be sure), nevertheless the very fact that the witnesses disagree suggests that her understanding of the semiotic import of the slurs differed from that of the other scribes, and perhaps even that of the composer. The implications of such a situation are that the meaning of every symbol can change with every new historical context.

This issue is of more than casual interest to the textual critic. When dealing with a derivative source, like Magdalena Bach's manuscript of the Cello Suites, the critic must seek to understand its meaning first *per se* and then within the work's transmission. That is, the scribe, Magdalena Bach here, had in mind a certain meaning, compatible with her understanding of slurs, when she wrote it. And our understanding of her action in writing it depends on our knowledge of the historical context in which she worked. But beyond this immediate context for the slur, this copy forms part of the tradition of these six works: when Magdalena Bach wrote it, she was reacting not only to the physical appearance of her exemplar, but also to her understanding of the musical symbols in it. What she wrote in her manuscript might be an exact copy of the symbol in her exemplar (in which case her interpretation of the symbol might not necessarily coincide with that of the composer), or it might be a rendering of that symbol into a form that, for her, gave it the same meaning. Another possibility, one not to be discounted, is that she simply changed the symbol to accord with her own aesthetic conception of the piece, in much the same way as modern editors of so-called performing editions.

Behaviour of this type on the part of scribes and performers does not necessarily indicate a lack of respect for the authority of the composer. On the contrary, most music in the Western art tradition requires the creative participation of the performer, as I discussed in Chapter 1 above. The conception of the music envisages, even fosters, a certain amount of freedom on the part of the performer to change the text of the work without changing the work itself. Many details are realized or determined only in performance, and this flexibility of interpretation is built into the constitution of the work. The composer understands and even requires that performers will seek their own solutions.

The text, then, remains in a continual state of flux, varying with each performance. When a written version of the piece comes into existence, it embodies the notational choices of the particular scribe responsible for the written version, and reflects that person's individual conception of the work. Variants introduced in such a copy usually correspond to aspects of a performance, real or virtual; that is, performers modify the text of the piece in accordance with either an actual performance or one that is envisaged. Textual critics in literature have observed a similar relationship between work, text and performance in drama.[13]

How critics sort through these possibilities is a matter of their erudition, insight and good taste, but what is important here is the recognition that the semiotic meaning of a notational symbol defines its interpretation in both the performing and textual tradition of a work. When two witnesses differ, the semiotic import of each reading determines whether they differ substantively. It is possible that two scribes, working independently in different contexts, could copy the same passage using differing styles of notation, but each version might retain, in substance, the identity of the passage because of the use of semiotic equivalents. Even more important, however, is the opposite situation: two witnesses with what appears to be the same notation might differ substantively because the historical context of each could give a contrasting semiotic meaning to the same notational symbols.

The interpretation of musical notation, therefore, the understanding of its semiotic import within a particular context and set of conventions, depends on the user's technical knowledge and competence. From the introduction of notation in Western art music, the production of musical sources has been entrusted to professional scribes, typesetters or engravers, who have achieved mastery of the notational system.[14] Trained musicians, who read music as fluently as text, may take this for granted, but successful copying requires as much command over notation and its conventions as performing does. And anyone who has performed from poorly prepared copy can confirm that assertion. The significance of this situation is twofold. The first

[13] Brett, "Text, Context, and the Early Music Editor," pp. 105–7. The controversy around the text of Shakespeare's *King Lear*, on which there is a voluminous literature, illustrates the problem. See Taylor and Warren, eds., *The Division of the Kingdoms*; Carroll, "New Plays vs. Old Readings"; and A. R. Meyer, "Shakespeare's Art and the Texts of *King Lear*." On Shakespeare's revisions in general, see Honigmann, *The Stability of Shakespeare's Text*; Bentley, *The Profession of Dramatist in Shakespeare's Time 1590–1642*, pp. 197–263; Taylor, "Revising Shakespeare"; Wells, "Revision in Shakespeare's Plays"; and McLeod, ed., *Crisis in Editing*. On revisions in the texts of two plays by Tom Stoppard, see Gaskell, *From Writer to Reader*, pp. 245–62, and "Night and Day: The Development of a Play Text."

[14] On the professional status of music scribes at the beginning of Western notation, see Fassler, "The Office of the Cantor."

consideration is noted above, namely that scribes often translate a text into the conventions with which they feel most comfortable, sometimes subconsciously. Plainsong presents perhaps the best example of this procedure, but it also occurs in other early repertories.[15] Second, professional scribes, charged with the business of preparing copy usable in performance, are inclined to replace manifest corruptions with feasible readings that do not necessarily reproduce the composer's text. The professional milieu within which the production of most musical sources takes place, therefore, profoundly affects their interpretation and evaluation.

Sources and history

The historical context of a source affects the evaluation of its readings, as the preceding discussion shows, in the matter of notational conventions, for example. Investigations of dating and provenance smack of dusty positivism, but a critical application of the results of such an investigation can dramatically influence the weight of a source. Recent controversies about the dating of sources for the music of Charles Ives reveal the consequences of such studies. Maynard Solomon suggests that Ives materially contributed to his own mythological image as musical innovator by falsifying dates in his autographs.[16] In particular Ives revised several works and apparently suppressed the dates of the revision so that earlier works would appear to incorporate more modern idioms.[17] Carol K. Baron defends Ives' revisions to a number of works by showing not only that the revisions do not, in fact, increase the level of dissonance in the piece, but also that, within Ives' atonal milieu, the degree of dissonance is irrelevant.[18] Baron then proposes a firmer methodology for dating Ives' autographs on the basis of handwriting analysis.[19]

Gayle Sherwood expands on Baron's results by combining a more thorough study of Ives' music handwriting with an exhaustive study of the manuscript paper used by him and other contemporary composers.[20] Her results show that many of the dates recorded by Ives and proposed by his cataloguer John Kirkpatrick require only slight

[15] Bent, "Some Criteria," pp. 304–17, especially 307–10.
[16] Solomon, "Charles Ives"; see also Lambert, "Communication," and Solomon's reply, "Communication." [17] Solomon, "Charles Ives," pp. 459–60, 465–66.
[18] Baron, "Dating Charles Ives's Music," especially pp. 26–32. [19] *Ibid.*, pp. 32–49.
[20] Sherwood, "Questions and Veracities." I am very grateful to Ms Sherwood for providing me with a copy of the article before publication.

revision. The primary importance of these studies for editors of Ives' music lies in the assessment of the chronological strata of revisions. Editors will decide how to treat these layers on the merits of each case, but the historical investigation of the sources places at their disposal the evidence for determining the chronological relationships between the various states of the piece.

The thirteenth-century repertory of polyphony associated with the cathedral of Notre Dame in Paris provides two further examples. Although opinions varied, W_1 (Wolfenbüttel, Herzog-August-Bibliothek, MS Helmstedt 628) was usually dated to the early fourteenth century.[21] Recent studies of the source's script and decoration have overturned this conclusion and posited a date in the 1240s.[22] Now that date has been revised to the previous decade through a re-evaluation of the codicological evidence in combination with the institutional history of the cathedral of Saint Andrews, where the book was used.[23]

Several deductions follow from these findings. The source was always recognized as transmitting the earliest form of notation among the principal sources of this repertory.[24] Scholars attributed that fact, however, to its peripheral origin. Mark Everist's findings show that it owes the early state of its notation to its date, and that, despite its provenance outside Paris, the connections of the patron who commissioned it (Guillaume Mauvoisin, Bishop of Saint Andrews 1202–38) provide close links with the central practice of the repertory. Thus, what was once a peripheral, apparently anachronistic fourteenth-century source now becomes the earliest principal record of the repertory, with solid claims to first-hand knowledge of the Parisian practice of the repertory.

The second example is the Notre Dame repertory's best-known source: F, the manuscript now in Florence. Scholars felt secure about the book's date (*c.* 1250), but Heinrich Husmann suggested that its content reflected two stages of development, one in the cathedral and the other in three urban Parisian churches, namely the Augustinian houses of Saint Victor and Sainte Geneviève (on the Left Bank) and the collegiate church of Saint Germain l'Auxerrois (on the Right

[21] For a survey of opinion on its date, see E. H. Roesner, "The Origins of W_1."

[22] J. Brown, Patterson and Hiley, "Further Observations on W_1."

[23] Everist, "From Paris to St. Andrews: The Origins of W_1."

[24] The other sources are F = Florence, Biblioteca Medicea-Laurenziana, MS Pluteo 29.1; Ma = Madrid, Biblioteca Nacional, MS 20486; and W_2 = Wolfenbüttel, Herzog-August-Bibliothek, MS Helmstedt 1099.

Bank).[25] Two studies have refuted his arguments. On the basis of the illuminations in F, Rebecca Baltzer attributes the production of the manuscript to an atelier close to the cathedral, and Craig Wright shows that its contents follow the cathedral's liturgical practice exactly.[26] Again the ramifications are great. The readings in F represent what was sung in the cathedral, the principal centre for the practice of the repertory, during the middle of the thirteenth century, and it is on this association, now newly reconfirmed by Baltzer and Wright, that its claims to authority rest.

Simply by adding three-quarters of a century to the age of W_1, or by placing F in the cathedral of Notre Dame, however, we do not improve the quality of the readings they contain. Scottish scribes of the 1230s, after all, are just as likely to err as their descendants at the beginning of the next century. The value of the readings in the source emerges only through critical scrutiny, with regard to the semiotic nature and import of the notation, and the perceived style of the repertory. But influencing that examination is the awareness that the scribes of W_1 may have been much closer to the living tradition of the repertory, both chronologically and institutionally, than we previously believed. Readings that may have appeared doubtful before might be closely connected to the central tradition. That judgement, however, depends upon the union of historical conclusions with the findings of a palaeographic and stylistic analysis of the readings.

The identity of the person or persons responsible for the production of the source can illuminate its history. Again, Eisen's arguments regarding the Mozart Salzburg copies rests, in part, on his attributing the sources to copyists normally in the employ of the Mozart family. The most important discovery of source material for the music of J. S. Bach in recent years is the composer's personal copy of the Nürnberg print of the *Goldberg Variations*, published by Balthasar Schmid probably in 1741.[27] In addition to fourteen canons, hitherto unknown, written in autograph on the inside back cover, the copy contains numerous autograph corrections, modifications and additions to the

[25] Husmann, "The Origin and Destination of the *Magnus liber organi*"; and "The Enlargement of the *Magnus liber organi*."

[26] Baltzer, "Thirteenth-Century Illuminated Miniatures"; Wright, *Music and Ceremony at Notre Dame of Paris*, pp. 243–67.

[27] Paris, Bibliothèque Nationale, Mus. MS 17669. On its discovery, see Alain, "Un supplément inédit"; and Wolff, "Bach's *Handexemplar*." On the date of the print, see Emery and Wolff, *Zweiter Teil der Klavierübung: Kritischer Bericht*, p. 94.

printed text of the *Goldberg Variations*.[28] Christoph Wolff, who edited the work for the Neue Bach-Ausgabe, accepts these entries as Bach's final thoughts on the piece, and incorporates them into his text.[29] The discovery of this source and its association with the composer have materially changed our understanding of the work and its history, as well as our perception of its text.

Collecting the data

Source research entails three discrete steps: gathering the evidence, classifying the sources, and evaluating the readings to establish the text. Below I devote separate chapters to each of the last two. The first of the three, in turn, divides into four stages, location, inspection, description and transcription. Each of these involves some mechanical tasks, and discussion of these occurs in the appendices. Here I review the critical issues that concern each phase. First, though, a comment on the order of their completion is appropriate. The realities of economics and the availability of the sources dictate that as much work as possible be completed in the editor's usual place of work or residence. Hence the initial work of transcription is undertaken from microfilm or some other form of photographic reproduction. Editing would simply be impossible without them.

Nevertheless photographic reproductions can never reproduce all the details required by an editor during the steps of inspecting, describing and transcribing the sources.[30] Therefore much of the detailed investigation, particularly in the categories of inspection and description, awaits an examination of the source itself in the library where it resides. A preliminary transcription, however, can usually be done from facsimiles, which the editor then confirms from the source itself. Thus time in the library is shortened and efficiency maximized. Consequently, the order in which I present the tasks here, the most logical order, is not necessarily the one that every, or perhaps any, editor would choose.

[28] The canons are published in *Zweiter Teil der Klavierübung*, ed. Emery and Wolff, pp. 117–28. On the autograph entries in the *Goldberg Variations*, see Wolff, "Bach's *Handexemplar*," pp. 226–29; and Emery and Wolff, *Zweiter Teil der Klavierübung: Kritischer Bericht*, pp. 95–96.

[29] *Zweiter Teil der Klavierübung*, ed. Emery and Wolff, pp. 67–115; see Emery and Wolff, *Zweiter Teil der Klavierübung: Kritischer Bericht*, pp. 113–18. The critical response to this edition by Schwandt, "Questions Concerning the Edition," concerns other alterations to the text by Wolff for which no justification is given.

[30] For a discussion of the hazards involved in working from photographic reproductions, see Tanselle, "Reproductions and Scholarship."

Locating sources

Modern bibliographic resources greatly facilitate the location of sources for the researcher, and the most important are cited below in Appendix A. Difficulties still exist, however, that require the assiduous application of imagination, ingenuity and industry, as the following brief anecdote reveals. Leonard E. Boyle, sometime Professor of Diplomatics at the Pontifical Institute of Mediaeval Studies in Toronto, was engaged, as a student, in the edition of a medieval text. "While I was working on it one day in the Bodleian Library, another scholar approached me and remarked that he had a graduate student who was working on the same text. 'How many manuscripts is he using?' I asked. 'Why there's only the one,' replied the elder scholar. At that time I knew of sixty-five." Careful and critical use of bibliographic resources may not turn up troves of previously unknown sources, but it may repay the editor by bringing to light materials whose full value was not appreciated, as in the case of the Mozart Salzburg copies.

Despite the noble and sometimes heroic efforts of bibliographers, many catalogue entries are inaccurate and incomplete. The chief problem is that all libraries cannot afford (either the funds or the time) to engage a specialist in every field to examine the collection's pertinent holdings; music is often one of the least well served disciplines in this regard because of the technical problems involved in reading music notation. Hence descriptions are sometimes misleading. Jeanice Brooks provides an example in her study of two sixteenth-century partbooks whose association had not previously been recognized, although they belong to the same collection.[31] They entered the Bibliothèque Nationale in Paris separately, became part of two different fonds within the manuscript, as opposed to the music, collection (fonds français and nouvelles acquisitions françaises), and were never catalogued properly.

Although this story is typical, I do not cite it to condemn bibliographers, cataloguers and the results of their labour. It is simply cautionary: catalogues enable research. Scholarship continues to advance, and the day a bibliographic resource is published it becomes obsolete. In 1939, the Département des Manuscrits of the Bibliothèque Nationale published the first volume of its *Catalogue général des manuscrits latins*. Among the manuscripts inventoried in the volume are several liturgi-

[31] Brooks, "Jean de Castro," especially pp. 136–37.

cal books that entered the collection from the library of the Abbey of Saint Martial. In many cases, the cataloguer identified that Abbey as the place of origin (e.g., Pa 1118, which is termed "Troparium et prosarium Sancti Martialis Lemovicensis"). Subsequent scholarship has determined that, although Pa 1118 did reside in the Abbey's library, it was not copied there but in southern Aquitaine, possibly in Toulouse.[32]

The library's cataloguer can hardly be blamed for not knowing the results of future research, research that may have been made possible, in some way, by the *Catalogue général* itself. Most scholars would recognize that the 1939 volume constituted a substantial improvement over its precursor, which was published in 1744.[33] Perhaps the 1939 cataloguer should have made inquiries of his or her own that might have led to a more accurate entry. There is a point of diminishing returns, however. Later volumes in the *Catalogue général* give fuller and more accurate information. They also take much longer to prepare. Today, more than a half-century after the appearance of the first volume, fewer than 4,000 of the 18,000 manuscripts in the collection are covered.

In contrast, the only catalogue that describes approximately 5,000 of the remaining books is that published in 1744; and another 10,000 or so manuscripts (mostly the holdings of Parisian libraries that were assumed into the Bibliothèque Nationale during the nineteenth century) are known to scholars through the inventories published by Léopold Delisle at the end of the nineteenth century, which contain descriptions one line in length for most manuscripts.[34] And the Bibliothèque Nationale, despite having its share of infuriating idiosyncrasies, is probably one of the best and easiest major research libraries to use. The situation, however, is far from desperate. Provided that the editor is sensitive to their potential shortcomings, published catalogues are a good place to start, if for no other reason than to get a sense of the holdings of a particular collection in order to determine whether further and more detailed investigation is warranted.

[32] Chailley, "Les anciens tropaires," pp. 177–79; Chailley, *L'école*, pp. 92–96; and Husmann, *Tropen- und Sequenzenhandschriften*, pp. 124–26.

[33] *Catalogus codicum manuscriptorum*, vols. III and IV.

[34] Delisle, "Inventaire des manuscrits conservés à la Bibliothèque impériale sous les nos 8823–11503"; "Inventaire des manuscrits latins de Saint-Germain-des-Prés"; "Inventaire des manuscrits latins de Saint-Victor"; "Inventaire des manuscrits latins de la Sorbonne"; "Inventaire des manuscrits latins de Notre-Dame." Printed in one volume as *Inventaire des manuscrits latins*.

After identifying and locating the sources of the text, the editor might wonder which ones deserve closer consideration. The more knowledge editors have of the text's tradition, the better informed their judgements will be at the stage of establishing the text. Do sources of the text that are significantly later in date than the composition deserve investigation by the editor? Giorgio Pasquali's dictum, *recentiores non deteriores* ("more recent, not worse"), concerns Classical texts that circulated in manuscript form for centuries after their composition, and whose earliest surviving witnesses are several centuries removed from the date of composition.[35] He argued that late manuscripts might faithfully preserve the readings of manuscripts that have perished but were perhaps as old as, or older than, the earliest surviving witnesses. Therefore these younger witnesses might be worthy of consideration when the text is established. In principle, of course, the tenet is valid for any text.

The example of Schubert's Adagio in D♭ major, D. 505, is a case in point. This is probably the slow movement (either second or third) of the Pianoforte Sonata in F minor, D. 625, whose autograph is lost.[36] The earliest sources are contemporary manuscripts, one of which contains the Adagio, the other the remaining three movements. The Adagio was published by Diabelli in 1848 as part of the Adagio and Rondo, Op. 145, altered to make it into a slow introduction for the Rondo, D. 506: it is transposed to E major, the key of the Rondo, and abbreviated.[37] Despite these mutilations, Diabelli's version transmits one bar that is missing from the contemporary manuscript.[38] And so, although it is *recentior* and in many other ways *deterior*, it is an absolutely essential source for this piece, as modern editors acknowledge.

The foregoing presupposes that the act of composition takes place at a clearly definable time and that all copies attempt to replicate as closely as possible the piece as it was fixed at that time. As discussed above, those circumstances do not accord with all processes of transmission. Some repertories changed considerably during their transmission, and each version of a piece has value as a record of that piece at the time the copy was made. In the case of plainsong, for example,

[35] Pasquali, *Storia della tradizione*, pp. 43–108.

[36] Deutsch, *Franz Schubert: Thematisches Verzeichnis*, pp. 296–97; and M. J. E. Brown, "Recent Schubert Discoveries."

[37] Diabelli's version is printed in *Phantasie, Impromptus und andere Stücke*, pp. 104–11 (D. 505, p. 104).

[38] Version in D♭ with extra bar incorporated from Diabelli's version printed in *Revisionsbericht*, no. 5, pp. 4–8.

variants can be identified with chronological periods, geographical areas or religious orders. No set of readings is necessarily superior to any other in respect to being faithful to some primordial (and probably hypothetical) act of composition. Each, however, is of value for the information it provides on the practice of plainsong in a particular period, region or order. In cases where the number of sources is unmanageable, a more restricted study, either as to time or place, is more valuable than a superficial survey of the entire corpus of sources.

The early editions of chant published by the monks of Solesmes suffer with this problem. They were never intended to function as scholarly editions of plainsong; rather they were to serve as practical editions for Catholic churches that wished to use plainsong in their liturgies. Nevertheless, Solesmes did claim that they were founded on scholarly method, and backed up the claim with a series of scholarly publications, including the series of manuscripts in photographic facsimile, Paléographie Musicale, and two journals, *Revue Grégorienne* and *Études Grégoriennes*.[39] And they still hope that the investigations that initially resulted in the current printed editions will eventually lead to a critical edition of the Gradual.[40]

Nowhere, however, do they indicate the specific sources used for the editions they have prepared.[41] Whatever the editors' intentions, then, the chant books give the appearance of being definitive statements about the text of medieval chant. More recent publications from Solesmes, like the *Graduale triplex* and the *Offertoriale triplex*, go some distance towards showing the scholarly derivation of the melodies.[42] In both volumes, neumations from early chant manuscripts are entered by hand above and below the printed text. These permit users to see the particular versions, regional and chronological, on which the printed melodies are based, and to judge the relationships for themselves.

Printed materials provide special problems in the matter of selecting sources for consultation. All copies of a press run are not necessarily identical in all details, never mind subsequent impressions or

[39] See Rousseau, *L'école grégorienne*; and Combe, *Histoire de la restauration*. See also Bergeron, "A Lifetime of Chants."

[40] Two volumes have appeared: *Le graduel romain*, II, *Les sources*; IV, *Le texte neumatique*, part 1, *Le groupement des manuscrits*, part 2, *Les relations généalogiques des manuscrits*. See Froger, "The Critical Edition of the Roman Gradual."

[41] Michel Huglo states that many of the readings in the *Graduale sacrosanctae romanae ecclesiae* derive from Montpellier, Bibliothèque de l'École de Médecine, MS H. 159; see his review of Hansen, *The Grammar of Gregorian Tonality*, p. 417.

[42] *Graduale triplex*; and *Offertoriale triplex*. See Jeffery, "The New Chantbooks from Solesmes."

editions.[43] Printers make stop-press corrections, engraved plates deteriorate with wear, and pieces of movable type shift or fall out. Therefore it is possible for significant variation to enter a printed text, even within a group of copies that were produced at the same time. Consequently, a full understanding of a print's value depends on an examination of as many copies as possible (some would say all available copies) to determine the exact bibliographical status of each, and to establish the variability of the text within a given impression or edition.

Obviously, one rapidly reaches a point of diminishing returns in such a quest, where the merit of consulting a large number of extant copies stands in opposition to the expenditure of time and effort. No theory can guide the scholar here. As copies are collated, the degree of variation will become evident and indicate how thorough the search should be. Of course, anytime one eliminates a source from consideration one runs the risk of ignoring important evidence. All scholarship is exposed to the same risk. Some scholars exercise more patience, thoroughness and diligence than others, but if all scholars waited until every library and archive were searched for that one last piece of evidence, nothing would ever be accomplished. Editors can depend only on their critical awareness of the sources. More information is better than less, but a limit exists beyond which lies the danger that the edition will never appear and no one will ever benefit from the energies already expended.

Inspection and description

Once the sources to be consulted are identified, the editor turns to the complementary tasks of inspection and description. What is discovered during inspection is presented in description. And both primarily concern the physical state of the source. This type of evidence is of great value because it often confirms specific historical facts about the source. These in turn can profoundly affect our estimation of the source. It is well known, for example, that the attribution of the *Jena* Symphony, once believed to have been composed by Beethoven, to Friedrich Witt depends on the positive identification of watermarks in the sources of the piece.[44] Another type of physical evidence that

[43] On Petrucci's printing practices, see Boorman, "The 'First' Edition of the *Odhecaton A*"; and "Petrucci's Type-Setters and the Process of Stemmatics."

[44] Landon, "The *Jena* Symphony."

can confirm the historical circumstances of a source's origin is rastrology. Jean K. and Eugene K. Wolf differentiate between eighteenth-century manuscripts from Mannheim and Munich by the disposition of the hand-ruled staves.[45] Again, affirmation of such historical details does not change the readings of a given source, but more precise data promote better-informed evaluations of the source and its readings.

It should be obvious that few of these details can be checked in photographic reproduction and hence the bulk of the inspection must take place in the library where the source resides. Watermarks, for example, do not appear in photographs, unless beta-radiography is used. And precise measurements, such as those necessary in rastrology, are not possible because the relationship between the reproduction and the original size of the document is not always known. Other matters can only be confirmed in person. In my research of twelfth-century Aquitanian music, for example, I was able to ascertain that two libelli, previously thought to be unrelated parts of the same codex, in fact form a single collection.[46] Two pieces of evidence supported this conclusion: ink of the same colour was used for certain additions in both libelli, and both libelli exhibited the same method of ruling. Neither detail was visible on microfilm.

Much of the information collected in this kind of detailed inspection might seem to be irrelevant, but one can never know when some seemingly insignificant observation might prove to be essential, either for one's own investigation, or for some related research. The examples cited above, from eleventh-century Aquitaine to Mozart, illustrate that the results sometimes more than justify the effort expended on what might be considered trifling and tedious matters. Equally significant results will not be achieved by every scholar in every case, but a meticulous examination of the edition's sources remains an important point of departure for most editions.

In the descriptions to be published as part of the edition's introduction, form follows function. The absolute minimum required is the positive identification of each source so that users can locate it for themselves. Locutions such as "the autograph in Berlin," or "the first edition of 1804" are simply inadequate. A full identification of manuscript sources includes the city and library where the source is held, and its shelfmark; printed sources require full bibliographic citation. In the case of rare

[45] E. K. Wolf and J. K. Wolf, "A Newly Identified Complex of Manuscripts"; and "Rastrology and Its Use."

[46] The source is Lo 36881; see Grier, "Some Codicological Observations," pp. 48–51.

printed materials (i.e., anything printed before 1800), the citation should indicate exactly which copies were consulted (identified by city, library and shelfmark); and, as noted above, it normally includes more than one copy unless the accidents of survival preclude that possibility. Beyond this minimum requirement, the context of the edition and its prospective audience determine the exact form of the description. It may be preferable, in some cases, to publish a full codicological or bibliographical description separately, especially if these data lead to thorough discussion of the source's historical circumstances. A briefer summary, then, may suffice for the edition, although most users would appreciate a succinct account of the historical position of the sources.

Some economy can be achieved by avoiding repetition of information that is already published in existing descriptions, unless it requires modification. Such descriptions would appear, in any case, in the bibliography of the source that forms part of the printed description in the edition's introduction. Many sources of early music are miscellanies in which non-musical materials have been joined by happenstance to music. An example is Pa 3549, which contains theological texts and sermons as well as a collection of twelfth-century song.[47] This combination probably resulted from a binding programme undertaken at the Abbey of Saint Martial during the thirteenth century, in which manuscripts of roughly the same size were bound into codices.[48] Most readers interested in the music transmitted in Pa 3549 have less need for detailed information about the other portions of the codex, and so they can be treated in summary fashion.

Some of the details collected during the inspection of the source may not carry obvious significance to the editor. Others may fall outside the editor's sphere of expertise. In either case, a brief reference or description might alert specialists in other fields to scrutinize the source. Most of the twelfth-century *uersaria* from Aquitaine passed through the monastic library at Saint Martial. I was able to suggest correlations between these manuscripts and surviving medieval catalogues of the library.[49] One of the codices, Lo 36881, never formed

[47] Bibliothèque Nationale, Département des Manuscrits, *Catalogue général des manuscrits latins*, VI (Paris, 1975), 52–69, gives a summary inventory of the codex. See also Grier, "Some Codicological Observations," pp. 35–37.

[48] Grier, "Some Codicological Observations," pp. 7–16.

[49] Four catalogues are published in Delisle, *Le cabinet de manuscrits*, II, 493–504, and Duplès-Agier, ed., *Chroniques de Saint-Martial*, pp. 323–55. For further bibliography, see Grier, "Some Codicological Observations," pp. 6–9. On the identification of the Aquitanian *uersaria* with items in the catalogues, see "Some Codicological Observations," pp. 10–14, 31–32, 35–38.

part of the library at Saint Martial, and its history prior to its acquisition by the British Museum in 1904 is unknown. It does, however, bear several shelfmarks from that previous history, whose meaning, otherwise, escaped me. Nevertheless, I printed them in my codicological study of the *uersaria* in the hope that someone would recognize them and illuminate this long, dark chapter in the manuscript's past.[50]

Transcription

We come now to the principal task when primary sources are used in editing: transcription. As I mentioned earlier, much of this work can be done from photographic reproductions and therefore it will probably be executed prior to the main inspection of the source, carried out *in situ.* At that time, all details can be confirmed with the originals. If the editor has done this work conscientiously and compiled a meticulous list of readings to be checked, the time spent in research at distant sites (and therefore the expense) is minimized. The difficulties that photographic reproductions can cause should not be underestimated. From a microfilm of one of the Aquitanian *uersaria,* I mistakenly transcribed a pin-prick as a note because the shadow it cast was exactly the same size and shape as notes in that source. In fact the error would have remained undetected even after a personal inspection of the source, had I not chanced to be looking at the hole when I turned the leaf, and happened to see daylight through what I had taken to be a note.

Bleed-through also causes difficulties in transcribing from reproductions. As distinguished a scholar as Higinio Anglès transcribed, from Pa 3549, portions of a decorated initial on one side of the leaf as notes in the piece on the opposite side.[51] A particularly good example of the potential problem bleed-through can cause is provided by the leaf from the manuscript, now in the Newberry Library, Chicago, that is reproduced in colour as the cover illustration of Richard H. Hoppin's *Medieval Music,* and his *Anthology of Medieval Music.*[52] Another difficulty is constituted by the ubiquitous holes through which the next (when looking at a recto) or previous (when looking at a verso) folio can be read, unless the photographer has had the pres-

[50] Grier, "Some Codicological Observations," pp. 48–49.
[51] Anglès, "La música del Ms. de Londres, Brit. Museum Add. 36881," pp. 307–8.
[52] Chicago, Newberry Library, MS 54.1, fol. 10r; Hoppin, *Medieval Music;* Hoppin, ed., *Anthology of Medieval Music.*

ence of mind to place a blank sheet under each folio as it was photographed. Of course inspection under ultra-violet light can only occur *in situ*, although beta-radiography facilitates the reading of erasures in photographic reproductions.

As troubling as these physical difficulties may be, they are surmountable with patience. More problematic is the issue of interpretation in transcription. No transcription is objective. Yet editors must maintain some distance between themselves and the music they are transcribing, or else the evidence of the source will have no chance to speak for itself. In fact, this dichotomy is exactly what Feder terms the hermeneutic circle.[53] We must know the meaning of the symbols before we can transcribe them in order to ascertain their meaning.

It is a common tendency for scholars to form and impose their interpretations as they transcribe, imputing sense, reason, logic, on the notational symbols before them. That imposition, however, regardless of its critical value, has the potential to distort the source's evidence and so make it that much more difficult to assess its importance at the stages of the classification of the sources and the establishment of the text. A diplomatic transcription (that is, one that records the information given in the source exactly as it appears with as many details as possible) would seem to solve the problem.

This procedure would separate most aspects of transcription into two stages: the inscription of the symbols, and their interpretation. In microcosm, that partition is analogous to the distinction between lower and higher criticism that haunts Feder's treatment of editing. As I argue in Chapter 1 above, however, it is impossible to make a rigid distinction between collecting and interpreting the evidence. Feder acknowledges that position, but then goes on to structure the central part of his book around that very distinction.[54]

The problem appears in high relief when we consider early sources whose notation differs considerably from modern practices. In mensural notation, for example, should modern rhythmic notation be used? Or should liquescents in plainsong be resolved into modern pitch values? Philip V. Bohlman notes the dangers involved in any kind of descriptive transcription, emphasizing the decontextualization that results.[55] In response to those dangers, original symbols could be

[53] Feder, *Musikphilologie*, pp. 67, 90–91.
[54] A rigid distinction impossible: Feder, *Musikphilologie*, pp. 38–40. Division of labour into lower and higher criticism: *ibid.*, pp. 56–82.
[55] Bohlman, "Musicology as a Political Act," pp. 420–27.

retained at this stage, particularly if contemporary or nearly contemporary sources are to be collated. This procedure allows the editor to make direct palaeographic comparisons between sources, which might afford heightened awareness of the problems facing the scribes of the repertory's sources. If transcriptions in modern notation, which involve at least a degree of interpretation, are compared, the editor will learn more about the problems of translating early notation into modern, than about how mensural notation was transmitted between scribes.

The same problem affects the treatment of sources in tablature. The most common use of tablature is in music for lute and keyboard, although it is employed for other instruments as well (e.g., flute and viol). Systems of tablature tend to run along national lines, and sources within the same notational type can be compared on a direct palaeographic basis. If, however, the sources cut across national lines or other classifications of notational types, or if the same piece occurs in tablature and mensural or rhythmic notation (as in the case of the intabulations of Josquin's motets), problems of collation multiply. The palaeographic dissimilarities between the notational types make the comparison of readings difficult, if not impossible. In order to make collation feasible, then, it may be necessary to sacrifice some of the palaeographic detail in the process of reducing the sources into modern, and therefore directly comparable, notation.[56] During the subsequent stages of classifying the sources and establishing the text, specific notational details can be confirmed by reference back to the original source (in facsimile or otherwise).

The practice of transcribing early music into modern notation at the stage of collecting the data stands in marked contrast with the treatment of modern experiments in musical notation. Throughout the twentieth century, composers have devised and continue to invent new symbols to represent specific instructions that cannot be conveyed by conventional notation.[57] Some individual signs, such as the Bartók pizzicato or the notation for *Sprechstimme*, have entered the standard vocabulary of

[56] Many guides exist on the transcription of older notations into modern. See, e.g., Rastall, *The Notation of Western Music*; and Caldwell, *Editing Early Music*.

[57] For bibliography on modern notation, see Warfield, *Writings on Contemporary Music Notation*. For general discussions, see Karkoschka, *Das Schriftbild der neuen Musik*; Cole, *Sounds and Signs*; Risatti, *New Music Vocabulary*; Boretz and Cone, eds., *Perspectives on Notation and Performance*; Lombardi, *Scrittura e suono*; and Stone, *Music Notation in the Twentieth Century*. Studies of notational practices for individual instruments exist, e.g., Salzedo, *Modern Study of the Harp*; and Penesco, *Les instruments à archet*.

modern notation, and can now be treated as conventional symbols. Even those which still require fuller explanation, however, are not replaced by more familiar equivalents, but are instead compared directly and eventually defined in the introduction of the edition. Similarly the graphic notations developed by modern composers do not normally admit transcription into conventional notation.[58] Scholars of twentieth-century music deal directly with the semiotic implications of the symbols, familiar and unfamiliar, that constitute the scores they study.

As this discussion shows, the semiotic nature of musical notation controls the situation. The notational symbols derive their meaning from context and convention, and, until the editor has fully investigated the historical circumstances, any semiotic interpretation of the notation is less than certain. Transcription, after all, is part of the process of gathering the evidence that will form the editor's conception of the work and its context. Ideally a dialogue takes place between scholar and sources. As editors gain experience with the sources, they become aware of new interpretations. All scholarship works this way: as new evidence enters, it affects the understanding of the entire study, and triggers an ongoing re-evaluation of the existing evidence and its interpretation.

Other types of sources

With the completion of the detailed inspection of the sources and the confirmation of transcriptions against the originals, the editor has gathered the bulk of the material necessary for the edition. Other types of sources, however, might provide additional evidence. Contemporary or near-contemporary theoretical treatises sometimes cite excerpts of the piece as examples, or offer discussions of it. The interpretation of the Notre Dame repertory of polyphony, for example, would be impossible without the discussions of thirteenth-century theorists like Garlandia and Anonymous IV, and the examples they supply. One issue in this repertory where these sources are indispensable is the copula. Jeremy Yudkin coordinates the evidence of the theorists with the passages they cite in the principal manuscript sources of the music to achieve a compelling synthesis.[59]

[58] E.g., Penderecki, *Threnody for the Victims of Hiroshima.* This score also contains a good example of a list of explanations provided by the composer for the unconventional symbols used in the work, p. 19.

[59] Yudkin, "The *Copula* According to Johannes de Garlandia"; and "The Anonymous of St. Emmeram and Anonymous IV on the *Copula*."

In the case of vocal music, independent non-musical sources of the literary text can offer illumination not available in the musical sources. The last three operas of Monteverdi exemplify the dependency of modern scholarship on literary sources. The key early sources of these works associated with Venice are manuscript libretti (for *Il ritorno d'Ulisse in patria*) and printed scenarios (in the case of *Le nozze d'Enea con Lavinia* and *L'incoronazione di Poppea*).[60] No music for *Le nozze* survives, and the extant scores for *Il ritorno* and *L'incoronazione* differ significantly from the Venetian literary sources. The two music sources for the latter were probably created for a revival in Naples in 1651, and that of the former has no demonstrable links with Venice. The literary sources, therefore, are our only evidence for the early creative stages of these operas in Venice.

Finally, the editor can turn to the correspondence or other writings of the composer, where the piece might be discussed, and contemporary critical reaction might be available. Even paintings surrender evidence for the text of a piece, as the work of H. Colin Slim shows.[61] And in the twentieth century, sound recordings and other mechanical reproductions have become important primary sources. All these materials might well provide valuable information for the editor. It is possible that they will not provide even a single valuable reading, but a greater understanding of the text will certainly be attained through their study, and that understanding might well affect the editor's judgement when it comes time to establish the text of the edition.

From the material gathered in locating, inspecting, describing and transcribing the sources, editors shape their texts. They need not delay over specialized tasks, like the search for previously unknown sources or the description of bindings, that may be outside their expertise. The principal job is to establish the text. If they can suggest to other specialists further avenues of research in the sources they have consulted, they have performed an admirable service. With this stage safely behind them, they can press on to the business of classifying the sources.

[60] Osthoff, "Zu den Quellen"; Osthoff, "Neue Beobachtungen zu Quellen und Geschichte"; Chiarelli, "*L'Incoronazione di Poppea* o *Il Nerone*"; Curtis, "*La Poppea Impasticciata*"; and Rosand, "The Bow of Ulysses."

[61] See, e.g., Slim, "Dosso Dossi's Allegory at Florence about Music."

3

Musical sources and stemmatic filiation

Ever since the philologist Karl Lachmann announced, in the last century, the startling results of his investigations into the texts of the New Testament and the Classical Latin poet Lucretius, textual critics have sought to apply his principle of common error to establish the genealogical relationships of the sources of a wide variety of texts.[1] The major advances in the common-error method and the most famous examples of its application have all occurred in the fields of classical, biblical and medieval philology, and involved the filiation of manuscript materials. Nevertheless, the technique holds much promise for application to music of all periods, whether preserved in manuscript or printed sources. A brief survey of the method's history in philology will serve to introduce its principal strengths and weaknesses, and form a background against which I can discuss how it may be adapted for use with music.

Lachmann devised his method in order to deal with a text that was central to the fabric of Western Civilization, the New Testament. In its witnesses, as in those of all texts, he found the three types of readings that I introduced in Chapter 1: category 1, good readings; category 2, places where the witnesses offered variant reasonable readings; and category 3, clear scribal errors. (The following discussion naturally pertains to both printed and manuscript sources. To avoid cumbersome locutions like scribal/typographical, or scribe/typesetter/engraver, I use "scribe" or "scribal" to stand for the various possibilities.) As dis-

[1] On the New Testament see Lachmann, "Rechenschaft über seine Ausgabe des Neuen Testaments," and his prefaces to each volume of the edition prepared with the assistance of Philip Buttmann, *Nouum Testamentum Graece et Latine*; on Lucretius see the preface to his celebrated edition, *In T. Lucretii Cari De rerum natura libros commentarius*. On the originality of Lachmann's contributions see Timpanaro, *La genesi*; Froger, *La critique*, pp. 38–42; Kenney, *The Classical Text*, pp. 105–29; and P. L. Schmidt, "Lachmann's Method."

cussed above, the classification of readings in these categories depends entirely on the critic's stylistic conception of the work.

Readings of the first and third categories did not long detain Lachmann: the former were directly incorporated into his edited text, and the latter were corrected, either by introducing better readings from the manuscript tradition (*ope codicum*) or by conjectural emendation (*ope ingenii*). But the usual method of judging between readings of the second category did trouble Lachmann. Hitherto editors had decided on the basis of interpretation, by evaluating the content of the passage and how well each of the competing readings accorded with it. Obviously, vastly different texts could be generated by the same set of readings through differing assessments of their meaning. For most works, such discrepancies would not occasion much comment outside scholarly circles. Does it matter that much what the exact wording of Lucretius or the *Nibelunglied* (another work edited by Lachmann) was?

Lachmann recognized, however, that the wording of the New Testament did make a difference, a theological difference that could affect basic historical, philosophical, cultural, moral and religious tenets that lie at the foundation of Western Civilization: heresy is not an accusation to be taken lightly. Hence he sought non-doctrinal grounds on which to base his decisions.

Shared error

In its simplest form, the common-error method is based on the assumption that it is more economical, historically, to postulate that, when several witnesses agree in the same error, it arose from a single common ancestor. That is, the error was committed once and then copied into surviving witnesses. It is more difficult to believe that the same error could have been made by several scribes independently. Here something that seems to be taken for granted by many textual critics must be given weighty emphasis, and that is that only readings from our third category above, clear scribal errors, are useful for determining filiation.[2] The sharing of good readings, no matter how rare,

[2] The earliest clear statement that errors must be used to make stemmatic judgements seems to be that of Westcott and Hort, eds., *The New Testament in the Original Greek*, II, 19–72, especially 53–54. Timpanaro, *La genesi*, pp. 58–61, and Froger, *La critique*, p. 42, both note the early use of the method without its express formulation. I was unable to verify Froger's assertion that Paul Lejay, in 1888, was the first to identify errors as the only evidence for filiation; he is, in any case, anticipated by Westcott and Hort. On the difficulties of positively identifying clear scribal errors see Boyle, "Optimist and Recensionist"; cf. Grier, "Lachmann, Bédier and the Bipartite Stemma," pp. 274–75, 278.

simply cannot show stemmatic relationships. There is only one ultimate source for good readings, the authorial original, and all witnesses that transmit good readings are simply faithful reproductions of that original, through any number of generations. Therefore, the most that can be said about two witnesses that share a good reading is that they descend from the original, and that deduction is of no value in a stemmatic assessment.

Errors, on the other hand, are most likely transmitted from the source in which they first occur, which usually appears below the authorial original in the stemma. And so shared error signifies, in most cases, common descent from that first source, a deduction that is central to stemmatic determinations because it can distinguish the ancestry of two (or more) witnesses that agree in error against another witness or witnesses; the witnesses that agree in error descend from an ancestor in which the shared error was made, and which was unknown to the other witnesses. The advantages of the method are obvious. On the basis of a few clear scribal errors the editor can draw a genealogical table of witnesses, a *stemma codicum* (family tree of sources), with the help of which many readings, including a good number in the troublesome second category, reasonable competing readings, can be eliminated from consideration, together with entire witnesses that can be shown to have been copied from a surviving witness; the latter process is called the *eliminatio codicum descriptorum* (the elimination of sources that are direct copies).

Not all problems are solved by a stemma, however. When there is an even number of branches at any division, there is the possibility that the witnesses will divide evenly between two reasonable competing readings (i.e., readings from category 2). In such a case, editors must steel themselves for the selection of one or the other, exactly the dilemma that Lachmann wished to avoid. In fact, many published stemmata divide into two branches, and the French philologist Joseph Bédier initiated a debate, now nearly a century old, by accusing adherents of the common-error method of deliberately arranging their stemmata in bipartite form so that more readings would be reserved for their judgement, just the reverse of Lachmann's intention.[3]

Bédier recognized that some of the readings he used for his stemmatic assessment of the *Lai de l'Ombre* could not reasonably be con-

[3] See the preface to Bédier's second edition of *Le Lai de L'Ombre*; and his further remarks in "La tradition manuscrite du Lai de l'Ombre." For a discussion of the controversy, see Grier, "Lachmann, Bédier and the Bipartite Stemma."

strued as errors. Instead of eliminating these readings from consideration, and restricting his stemmatic evidence to category 3 readings (clear scribal errors), he showed how readings from the second category could be used selectively to construct several competing stemmata. He concluded that these reasonable competing readings arose from authorial or scribal revision, and that the most profitable method of editing the text would be to use the text of one witness, correcting it only where it was manifestly corrupt; that is, expunging its clear scribal errors.[4] Philologists call this procedure the "best-text" method.

Other complications affect this seemingly simple and efficient method: first among them are contamination, which is the consultation by a scribe of more than one exemplar, and conjectural emendation, whereby scribes, unsatisfied with the reading of the exemplar, introduce a reading of their own invention. Furthermore, to define an error is not without difficulty. And finally, a simple fact of life is that, no matter how unlikely it is, it is possible for two scribes to make the same error independently. Hence any stemma based on textual evidence alone is built on a web of assumption and probability. It is an interpretative tool that depends on interpretation itself, starting with deciding what, exactly, constitutes an error. Errors are readings that are impossible within the stylistic conventions of the work. And defining the stylistic conventions of a work is clearly a hermeneutic task. Nevertheless, when the dangers of its possible misuse are recognized, and if the editor acknowledges that, in virtually all cases, the stemma does not represent absolute, objective truth, then stemmatic filiation provides a powerful tool for the textual critic.

The stemma allows the editor to work from readings about which there is more certainty (but whose evaluation is still interpretative) to those whose value is less certain. The whole operation depends, however, on the editor's critical understanding of the work and its style. The hermeneutic nature of the technique, when based solely on textual evidence, creates restrictions on its application, as I discuss below. Specifically, stemmata that eliminate complete witnesses or divide the tradition in such a way that individual readings can be eliminated because a majority of the branches at any division agree carry the possibility of elevating potentially erroneous readings to the archetype. These dangers pose a serious threat to the utility of the method. Sometimes, however, help is available in the form of physical evidence

[4] Bédier, ed., *Le Lai de L'Ombre*, pp. XXVIII–XLV.

from the witnesses, or circumstantial evidence from the history and geography of the text's tradition, that can assist the editor in making firmer genealogical assessments. In fact some of Lachmann's most startling discoveries about his texts arose from just such types of evidence.

The shortcomings of the common-error method have generated several attempts at improvements since the 1920s. Dom Henri Quentin, W. W. Greg and Vinton A. Dearing, each working independently on different types of texts, attempt to eliminate any subjectivity in the classification of texts by refusing to distinguish between errors and good readings for the purpose of that classification.[5] Instead, all three employ the statistical analysis of variants to determine the filiation of sources. Unfortunately such analysis is unduly influenced by the intermixture of good readings among those variants, and, as noted above, the sharing of good readings carries no weight in stemmatic judgements.[6]

George Kane and E. Talbot Donaldson, working together on the texts of William Langland's *Piers Plowman*, err on the other side by basing their stemmatic conclusions on readings from category 2, reasonable competing readings, that they judge to be errors on interpretative grounds (exactly the procedural difficulty that vexed Bédier in his editorial endeavours).[7] Starting from the observation that all stemmata are based on interpretation, Kane and Donaldson subjected all readings in the manuscript tradition to critical examination, adjudging each to be either authorial or scribal. From a practical standpoint, this procedure is defensible in consideration of the complexity of this text and its transmission. My objection arises purely from theoretical grounds and my conviction that a legitimate third category, category 2, exists between authorial readings and scribal corruptions, a category ignored by most textual critics, as I discuss in Chapter 1 above, and dismissed by Kane and Donaldson.

[5] Quentin, *Mémoire sur l'établissement*, and *Essais de critique textuelle*; Greg, *The Calculus of Variants*; Dearing, *A Manual of Textual Analysis*, and *Principles and Practice of Textual Analysis*.

[6] See Kenney, *The Classical Text*, pp. 134–38 (especially pp. 135–36 n. 3: "The fundamental flaw in Quentin's method, as Dr Timpanaro reminds me, is that it treats agreement in correct readings as significant for the determination of relationships"); and Metzger, *The Text of the New Testament*, pp. 163–69.

[7] See the prefaces to Kane, ed., *Piers Plowman*, especially I, *Piers Plowman: The A Version*, ed. Kane, 53–172; II, *Piers Plowman: The B Version*, ed. Kane and Donaldson, 16–97, 128–220; and Patterson, "The Logic of Textual Criticism." For criticisms, see Pearsall, "Editing Medieval Texts," pp. 98–106; Grier, "Lachmann, Bédier and the Bipartite Stemma," pp. 272, 278; and Brewer, "The Textual Principles of Kane's A Text." A balanced discussion of this method is given in Adams, "Editing *Piers Plowman B*."

The problem with using category 2 readings is that editors can only evaluate them on the basis of content and meaning. At this point, the nature of the text under consideration becomes an issue. If Bédier or Kane and Donaldson express a preference for one category 2 reading over another, they will probably not elicit a response from any group other than medieval philologists. Editors of the New Testament, on the other hand, or of other texts that form the foundation for the beliefs of a civilization (such as Homer for the Greeks), must address doctrinal matters in judging between category 2 readings, and their decisions could well give rise to controversy outside the academy or perhaps even to charges of heresy. Bédier, Kane and Donaldson, as editors of vernacular texts, felt no such pressure, and so elevated decisions about category 2 readings to the position of determining filiation.

Filiation and the reconstruction of an authorial original

The usual purpose of the method's application in philology is to determine, as closely as possible, the text of an authorial original. This goal presupposes the existence of such an original, a text, resulting from the act of composition, that could be construed as carrying the authority of its creator. At this point of creation, the work, as an artistic entity, and the text, as its physical manifestation, are virtually identical, to the degree that the author has been able to transfer the work, in its psychological state, to its physical manifestation as a text. Once the work achieves this physical state, it is then transmitted in various ways, and along the way it sustains various accidents. The task of textual criticism, aided by the method of stemmatic filiation, is to return to that authorial state, to peal back the layers of accident and reveal the text, the physical manifestation of the work that would have been known to the author.

Clearly many musical works fit this paradigm, and the reconstruction of the composer's text is an important and worthwhile task, one in which stemmatic filiation can assist. But the nature of the musical text and the ways in which it is transmitted demand a special application of the common-error method. As discussed in the preceding chapters, the musical score is a semiotic document whose meaning depends on context and convention. In such a situation, the graphic form of the text is subject to change whenever it is copied or otherwise transmitted, as new scribes bring their own set of conventions to the task of inscribing the text. The substance of the text, however, may remain unchanged during transmission because the scribe may have used a semiotic equivalent. Forearmed with the awareness that professional music scribes constantly evaluate the semiotic implications of the texts they are copying, editors of music can call upon the aid of the common-error method when dealing with pieces that originate in a definable compositional moment.

Filiation and a living tradition

For a great deal of music in the Western art tradition, however, it is impossible to restrict the definition of the work to a discrete compositional moment. Composers introduce some flexibility of interpretation, in the form of performance, into the constitution of the work. Each performance creates a new reading of the work based on the performer's understanding of it. In the process of transmission, some of these characteristics might enter the text. Neither performers nor scribes, after all, feel that they are altering the work, only its text; and even then, in the spirit of an ongoing cooperative and collaborative dialogue between composer and performer. A witness created under these circumstances, therefore, transmits one possible text that carries no greater or lesser authority than other possible texts of the same work. No text, even the composer's, is fully authoritative. Only the act of performance carries authority, because in it the mutual creative intent of composer and performer is realized. The text carries nothing more than an enabling set of instructions.

Is there any point in incorporating witnesses of this sort into a stemmatic assessment? In the first place, how can one distinguish between an error and a variant in these witnesses? Presumably the sources vary, one from another, because of the processes by which they were produced and by which they incorporated variants from the performing tradition. How, then, can any reading be judged an error? The same criteria apply to witnesses within this type of tradition as in any tradition. Errors fall outside the stylistic norms. The very nature of the tradition, however, tolerating or even fostering variation as it does, widens the category of possible readings and so requires even more caution when these norms are determined. Nevertheless, an editor sensitive to style and, especially, the context of the individual reading, can suggest some guidelines for these decisions.[8]

Even if a stemmatic assessment of such witnesses is thus possible, why bother to reconstruct, via the filiation of the witnesses, an authorial text that either does not exist (and never did) or is irrelevant as a result of the processes of transmission? The stemma, however, flows both ways. As a tool, it can eliminate readings from the perished witnesses at its top, and so assist in the reconstruction of an authorial original (should one have existed). But it can also isolate distinctive readings in surviving witnesses at the bottom of its branches. The stemma can help to identify those variants peculiar to individual witnesses and groups of witnesses, and often show when these variants entered the tradition.

This evidence illuminates not only the processes of transmission (that is, the techniques employed in the production of a particular witness) but also the musical practices that generated these distinctive variants. And it therefore opens a window on to at least some aspects of performance practice. (This evidence is always indirect, because we can never be sure to what extent a text represents actual, as opposed to ideal or virtual, performance.) Stemmatic filiation, then, provides insight into the history of a work and its transmission. It is not an autonomous method of editing: the stemma cannot determine the text in any definitive way. But it is a useful, even powerful, tool for understanding the historical descent of a work and its texts.

Filiation and music

And so there is nothing in the theory that limits its application to music. Indeed musicologists are now applying the method to a broad range of repertories across the chronological spectrum and are including printed sources in their stemmatic assessments.[9] The fundamental

[8] See Grier, "The Stemma," for an example. I develop the concept and typology of error in this repertory in a companion article, "Scribal Practices," pp. 388–400.

[9] On the general applications of stemmata to music sources, see Dadelsen, "Über den Wert musikalischer Textkritik"; Staehelin, "Bemerkungen zum Verhältnis von Werkcharakter und Filiation"; and Boorman, "The Uses of Filiation." For a list of musicological writings concerning the application of stemmatics, see Boorman, "Limitations and Extensions," pp. 344–46. See also Atlas, "Conflicting Attributions"; Bent, "Some Criteria"; Boorman, "Limitations and Extensions," "Petrucci's Type-Setters," and "Notational Spelling and Scribal Habit"; Noblitt, "Textual Criticism and Selected Works Published by Petrucci," and "Filiation vis-à-vis its Alternatives"; Hamm, "Interrelationships between Manuscript and Printed Sources"; H. M. Brown, "In Alamire's Workshop"; and Strohm, "Quellenkritische Untersuchungen an der Missa 'Caput'."

principles of the descent of errors, further corruption caused by the compounding of an existing error and their eradication through contamination and conjecture, are valid no matter what the medium of transmission. Printers and engravers are just as likely to fall prey to the hazards of copying, such as omissions caused by homoeoteleuton (words or, in music, notational units that end the same), as scribes and copyists. To be sure different processes generate different types of errors, but these do not jeopardize the validity of the method if the editor is sensitive to the idiosyncrasies of the process of transmission under consideration.

All the difficulties that confront the editor of a literary text who uses the common-error method can also confound an editor of music. Two in particular warrant mention here. First, many music sources contain several items or even groups of items. Because a source could have derived its repertory from more than one exemplar, the editor begins by considering the filiation of individual pieces before proceeding to conclusions about groups of pieces or the entire source. In the twelfth-century Aquitanian *uersus* repertory, for example, I was able to ascertain that the song *Ex Ade uitio* descended to one of its witnesses via a route different from that taken by some of its companions in the same witness.[10] The scribe of this witness, then, drew on at least two different exemplars in compiling his manuscript, and therefore it participates in at least two stemmata, one for *Ex Ade uitio* and one for the other pieces in the manuscript. This is the type of treatment accorded anthologies, of poetry for example, by philologists. The second difficulty is the question of revised editions issued by the composer (e.g., the revisions of Bruckner, Mahler and Hindemith).[11] This situation is, of course, very familiar in literature, and, with the provision that the editor can successfully distinguish between sources particular to the various editions, it need not disrupt the procedure of classifying those sources.

Substantive alterations

In addition, an editor of music must deal with some problems that arise from its status as a performing art. As discussed in Chapter 2 above, many music sources are practical, prepared for a specific performance

[10] Grier, "The Stemma," pp. 273–76. The witness is 3549.

[11] Anton Bruckner: Cooke, "The Bruckner Problem Simplified"; and the essays in Grasberger, ed., *Bruckner Symposion "Die Fassungen"*. Gustav Mahler: Mitchell, *Gustav Mahler: The Wunderhorn Years*. Paul Hindemith's revisions to *Das Marienleben*: Hindemith, *Das Marienleben*, pp. III–X; and Neumeyer, *The Music of Paul Hindemith*, pp. 137–67.

or for the professional use of a particular musician. Hence, the first requirement, when such a source is compiled, is not utmost fidelity to the text, but the professional needs of the compiler.[12] Therefore a piece might suffer many alterations in the course of entering a practical source: simplification or omission of an inner voice; elaboration of an exposed voice; deletion, addition or substitution of a movement; transposition to a more comfortable key; replacement of one instrument with another more readily available where the source is to be used, to name a few.[13]

Again, the twelfth-century *uersus* provides an example. Several monophonic songs were converted to polyphony by the addition of a second voice, for example *Omnis curet homo*.[14] Three witnesses preserve the polyphonic version, and the added second voice is close enough in all three to show that they descended from a common ancestor. As the repertory was transmitted during the course of the twelfth century, polyphony gradually superseded monophony in the sources.[15] Therefore scribes who had access to this polyphonic version would probably not copy in its stead the monophony, and so in all likelihood those witnesses that transmit the monophonic version did not know the common ancestor of the three polyphonic witnesses. Therefore that common ancestor, designated in Figure 3–1 as manuscript δ, appears on the stemma of this piece below the witnesses of the monophonic tradition. (In stemmata, Greek letters denote witnesses that no longer exist.) The addition of a second voice to this song is not, then, an error *per se;* errors are readings that are impossible on stylistic grounds. Variants of this type, however, are alternatives that appeared to be feasible, or perhaps even preferable, options to the source's compiler, and as such it is often difficult to isolate them as alterations of the composer's text for the purposes of stemmatic assessment. In the case of *Omnis curet homo,* the historical development of the repertory suggests the chronological priority of the monophonic version, and therefore the existence of manuscript δ, the common ancestor of the witnesses of the polyphonic version.

[12] Bent, "Some Criteria," pp. 307–10, suggests eight courses of action a music scribe might follow in the process of copying.

[13] Bent's fourth possibility, "Some Criteria," pp. 308–9.

[14] Grier, "The Stemma," pp. 262–67. The monophonic version is found in 3719b and 1139a; the three witnesses of the polyphonic version are 3719d, 3549 and 36881a.

[15] Grier, "Scribal Practices," pp. 417–18.

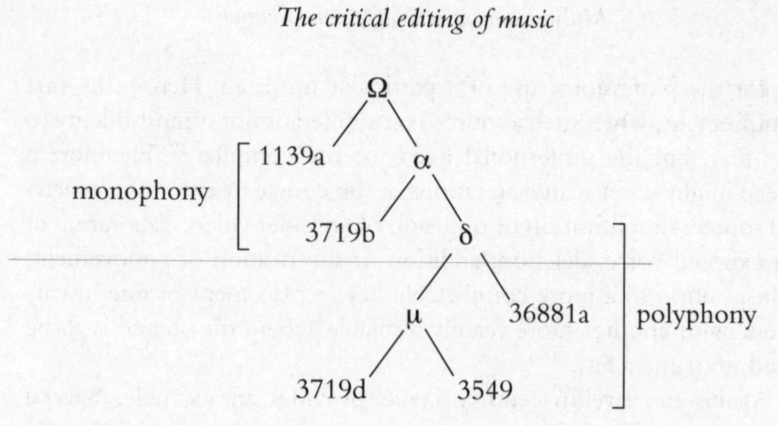

Figure 3–1

Conjectural emendation

Scribal editorial intervention can affect the text of a work in a second, more subtle way, and one much more difficult to discern: conjectural emendation.[16] This type of activity also arises from the professional milieu in which much music-copying takes place. When professional scribes confront a manifest corruption in the text from which they are copying, they are apt to replace it with another reading that is stylistically more feasible without necessarily restoring the composer's text. Now successful emendations, ones that accord with the work's perceived style, are invisible within the fabric of the piece. Only those alterations that move outside the stylistic boundaries of the work are discernible, and so they fall into category 3, as defined above, clear scribal errors.

The twelfth-century Aquitanian *uersus* provides examples of the kind of situation that could motivate scribal emendation. In *Noster cetus psallat letus*, a copying error at the beginning of a phrase eventually causes the scribe to rewrite the cadence with uncharacteristic parallel unisons.[17] A contrasting situation is presented in the prosa *Arce siderea.* Two harmonic seconds, which seem to belong to the original conception of the piece as we have it, led the scribe of one witness to alter the lower voice. Unfortunately he thereby introduced several additional harmonic seconds, and changed the lower voice from an independent line moving in contrary motion to the upper voice, to a clumsy doubling of it.[18] When these emendations fall into error, they

[16] Bent's second and third possibilities, "Some Criteria," pp. 307–8.
[17] Grier, "Scribal Practices," pp. 379–83; the witness is 3719b.
[18] Grier, "Scribal Practices," pp. 397–98; the witness is 3719d.

Example 3–1: Gloria trope *Rex apostolorum*

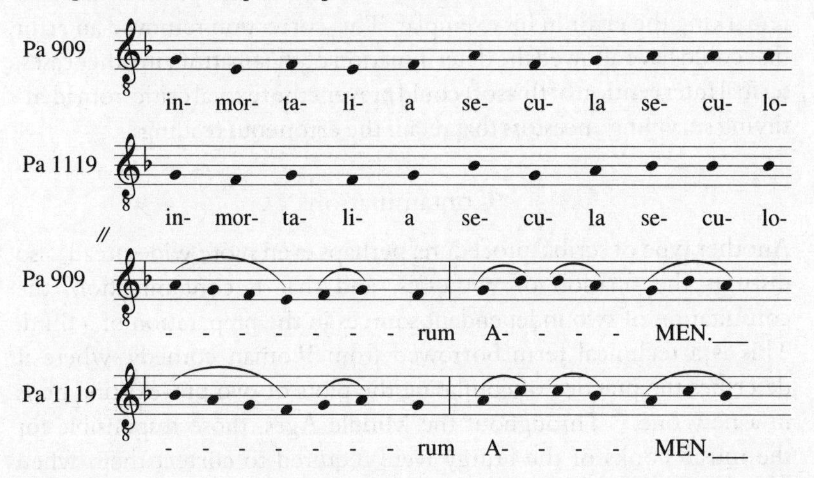

can be used to determine filiation. When they do not, they silently enter the work's text.

In some repertories, scribes are able to make corrections, not on the basis of conjecture, but out of their knowledge of the piece. Plainsong, in respect to both literary and musical texts, is perhaps the best example of such a tradition. The Bible is the source of many of the literary texts used in plainsong, and scribes could very easily correct errors in the exemplar from knowledge of the Bible; they might not even be aware of some corrections while making them.[19] Similar corrections, conscious or unconscious, might be effected during the copying of the melodies, certain to be well known to the scribes of music books for the liturgy, which were usually entrusted to the most learned and accomplished scribes.[20] A passage from an eleventh-century Gloria trope demonstrates the principle. (See Example 3–1.)

Codex Pa 1119 is a direct copy of Pa 909.[21] Yet the version in Pa 909, which gives the melody a second lower, is incorrect. As Example 3–1 shows, the passage concludes with a cue to the *Amen* that ends the Gloria melody. All other Aquitanian sources agree with Pa 1119 in starting this *Amen* on A.[22] When the scribe of Pa 1119 reached this passage, he copied

[19] Planchart, "The Transmission," p. 348 and n. 2.

[20] Evans, *The Early Trope Repertory*, pp. 33–34; Planchart, *The Repertory of Tropes*, I, 14–16, 32–33; Planchart, "The Transmission," pp. 355–57; and Fassler, "The Office of the Cantor," especially pp. 44–51.

[21] Grier, "*Ecce sanctum*," pp. 36–37.

[22] Other Aquitanian sources: Pa 1120, 1132, 1133, 1134, 1135, 1136, 1137, 1177, 1086 and 778.

the correct version of the melody from memory, possibly without remarking the error in his exemplar. This correction removed an error that could have allowed the determination of the filiation; in other cases, scribal intervention of this sort could prevent the textual critic from identifying surviving ancestors that retain the erroneous readings.

Contamination

Another type of scribal procedure, perhaps even more widespread, also disrupts the filiation of witnesses, and that is contamination, the consultation of two independent sources in the preparation of a third. This is a technical term borrowed from Roman comedy, where it describes the practice of conflating the plots of two pre-existing plays in a new one.[23] Throughout the Middle Ages, those responsible for the music books of the liturgy were required to correct them when they were found to be faulty.[24] As examples of the procedure, two of the tropers executed in the scriptorium of the Abbey of Saint Martial in Limoges during the eleventh century exhibit a double derivation from two other surviving tropers, and thus attest to the fact that their respective scribes had both tropers open on the desk while copying. Codex Pa 909, written AD 1028–29, combines elements of Pa 1120 and 1121.[25] In the next generation, Pa 1119, written between AD 1050 and 1063, was copied from Pa 1120 and 909.[26]

The usual result of contamination is the replacement of clear errors with reasonable readings that are not necessarily authorial, just as is the case with conjectural emendation.[27] In fact, readings that arose from

[23] The Roman comic playwright Terence uses the term in response to the critics of his method, *Andria*, 16, and *Heauton timorumenos*, 17.

[24] See, for example, the eleventh-century customary of Cluny, *Liber tramitis*, 2.26, ed. Dinter, p. 239; the twelfth-century customary of the Abbey of Saint Victor in Paris, *Liber ordinis sancti Victoris parisiensis*, 19, ed. Jocqué and Milis, pp. 81–82; and the thirteenth-century regulation for the Dominican order, Humbert of Romans, *Instructiones magistri Humberti de officiis ordinis*, 8, ed. Berthier, *Opera de uita regulari*, II, 238. See also Fassler, "The Office of the Cantor," pp. 46–51. The directions for the copying of music books issued in the mid-thirteenth century by both the Franciscan and Dominican orders require scribes to check their copies against corrected exemplars twice (in the case of the Dominicans) and three times (in the Franciscan order). See van Dijk, *Sources of the Modern Roman Liturgy*, I, 110–20; Dominican rule printed I, 118; Franciscan rule II, 361–62. See also Huglo, "Règlement du XIIIe siècle." Neither regulation, however, specifies that the scribe use different exemplars each time, and so it may not refer to a process that would constitute contamination.

[25] Grier, "*Ecce sanctum*," pp. 54–57.

[26] On its derivation from Pa 1120, see Husmann, *Tropen- und Sequenzenhandschriften*, p. 129; on its relation to Pa 909, see Grier, "*Ecce sanctum*," pp. 36–37.

[27] Collomp, *La critique des textes*, pp. 105–19; Pasquali, *Storia della tradizione*, pp. 146–83; West, *Textual Criticism and Editorial Technique*, pp. 35–47; Eklund, "On Errors and Contamination."

emendation or contamination are, in many cases, indistinguishable to the editor. Nevertheless, it is unlikely in the extreme that all characteristic errors would have been removed through scribal editing, and so the filiation of such witnesses is not beyond the realm of possibility. Such is the case with the ancestry of Pa 1119, as shown above. Its scribe was able to correct at least one error in its exemplar, Pa 909, on the basis of his knowledge of the melody, but its derivation from Pa 909 is attested by other evidence. The Aquitanian *uersus* repertory of the twelfth century also shows signs of at least limited conjectural emendation on the part of its scribes, although I am very doubtful that contamination is present, and yet enough distinctive errors remain to suggest a filiation of the witnesses.[28]

Supplementary evidence

The preceding paragraphs would appear to place significant obstacles in the way of determining the filiation of witnesses with any degree of certainty. Two types of evidence, however, can greatly facilitate the work, if used critically. Editors of vocal music have available to them the transmission of the literary text. If it is demonstrable that literary and musical text circulated together, then errors in the literary text are useful for indicating the filiation of the witnesses. The criteria for judging errors in literary texts are much better established than those applicable to music. Such evidence is essential for the stemma that I suggest for the Aquitanian *uersaria,* and also for my assessment of scribal procedures in these codices.[29] It is quite possible, however, that the literary text could descend by a different route from that taken by the musical text, and perhaps the best example of this mixed type of transmission would be plainsong, with its biblical texts, as discussed above. The circumstances of transmission will determine whether this evidence is admissible.

Occasionally documentary evidence can illuminate the stemmatic filiation. For example, until recently the most authoritative editions of Mozart's *Linz* Symphony, K. 425, were based on a set of parts that Mozart sold to the Fürstenberg court at Donaueschingen.[30]

[28] Grier, "The Stemma"; on the presence of emendation, see *idem*, "Scribal Practices," pp. 397–98.

[29] Grier, "The Stemma," especially p. 257, where I discuss the applicability of evidence from the literary text; and "Scribal Practices," pp. 375–77, on copying procedures in the literary text.

[30] Donaueschingen, Fürstlich Fürstenbergische Hofbibliothek, MSS S.B. 2/9.

Cliff Eisen shows that this set was copied from a faulty score of the work.[31] The use of a score, as opposed to a set of parts, for the exemplar is guaranteed by three passages in which readings from one part have entered another. In movement 1, bar 264, the second horn gives the reading of the first trumpet; the second violin in 3:22 gives C–B, which replicates the reading of the viola part (D-C, but, in alto clef, so that it lies in exactly the same position on the staff); and the first horn, in 4:365–66, presents the reading of the first trumpet.[32] In each case, the copyist's eye slipped down to the wrong part in the score, and so these are errors of intrusion.[33] These corruptions could not have arisen had the copyist been working from parts.

That the exemplar transmitted errors is verified by the agreements in error of two pairs of parts. At 3:24, both horn parts agree in an error on the first note; and at 4:384, both bassoon parts share an error on the second note. Because each pair of parts contains a significant amount of independent writing, the copyist would not have been able to copy one part from another (e.g., second horn from first horn). Each part, then, was copied in turn from the score; because it is extremely unlikely that the copyist would have made the same error twice independently when producing the pairs of parts, the two shared errors could only have entered the parts from the score. That score, therefore, could not have been Mozart's autograph, and so is at least one generation removed from it. Another set of parts exists, however, copied in the main by Joseph Richard Estlinger, who copied many works for the Mozart family between 1752 and the mid-1780s.[34] Eisen coordinates the documentary evidence of correspondence between Wolfgang and his father, and paper types in the Salzburg parts, to show that this set derives directly from the autograph, and therefore carries equal stemmatic weight to the Donaueschingen parts.

[31] Eisen, "New Light."

[32] Eisen, "New Light," Table 1, p. 83, gives the errors found in the Donaueschingen parts.

[33] On errors of intrusion, see Grier, "Scribal Practices," pp. 377–79, 396–97.

[34] Salzburg, Internationale Stiftung Mozarteum, MSS Rara 425/1; see Eisen, "New Light," pp. 84–85. On Estlinger's relationship with the Mozart family, see Eisen, "The Mozarts' Salzburg Copyists," pp. 259–65, and the Appendix, pp. 300–7, where the authentic Salzburg copies of works by Leopold and Wolfgang Mozart are listed.

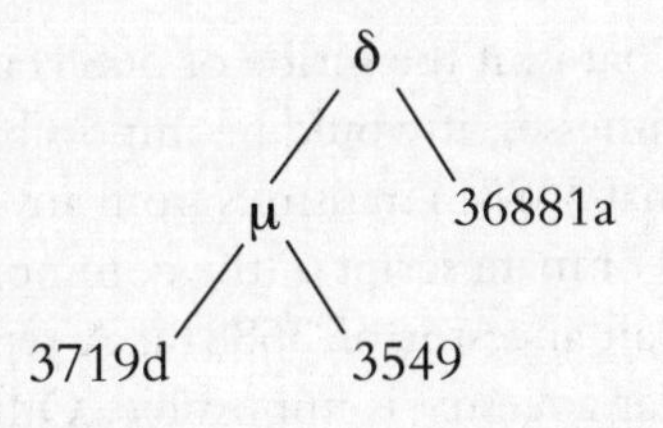

Figure 3–2

Technical matters: significative errors, archetypes and hyparchetypes

With all these reservations in mind the editor can then proceed to the actual business of drawing a stemma.[35] First a word on two troublesome technical terms is in order: separative and conjunctive errors. Two of the witnesses of the Aquitanian *uersus Omnis curet homo* agree in transmitting parallel motion between the two voices at a cadence, which, on stylistic grounds, I take to be an error.[36] This agreement, then, marks the error as conjunctive: that is, it is most likely that the two scribes simply copied it from a common ancestor, and less probable that both made the same error independently. Therefore, we can posit a common ancestor from which these two witnesses descend. Meanwhile, a third witness, 36881a, carries the correct reading, which it could only have copied from a witness above the common ancestor of 3719d and 3549, because all witnesses below that ancestor carry the conjunctive error common to 3719d and 3549 (see Figure 3–2). Therefore, a conjunctive error is one in which two (or more) witnesses agree, and it constitutes evidence of the parallel descent of those witnesses from a single common ancestor in which the error was originally committed. It is always possible that one of the witnesses conjoined by the error is the ancestor of the other, but that decision arises from a consideration of separative errors.

At the same time, the error in 3719d and 3549 is also separative, because the witness that transmits the correct reading, 36881a, could not have been copied from either of the erroneous witnesses, or their

[35] The following discussion draws on these works: Maas, *Textkritik*, pp. 5–9, 26–30; Collomp, *La critique des textes*, pp. 33–81; Pasquali, *Storia della tradizione*, pp. 3–12; Willis, *Latin Textual Criticism*, pp. 13–32; West, *Textual Criticism and Editorial Technique*, pp. 31–47; Kenney, *The Classical Text*, pp. 130–42; Blecua, *Manual de crítica textual*, pp. 47–122; and Reynolds and Wilson, *Scribes and Scholars*, pp. 211–16. For a theoretical discussion in a musical context, see Feder, *Musikphilologie*, pp. 61–67.

[36] Grier, "The Stemma," pp. 265–66; the two witnesses are 3719d and 3549.

common ancestor. That is, if the scribe of 36881a were copying from any of these three witnesses, it would be impossible for him to derive the correct reading that 36881a transmits from any of them. Therefore none of 3719d, 3549 or manuscript μ (the common ancestor of 3719d and 3549) could be an ancestor of 36881a. A separative error, then, shows that a particular ancestry is impossible. Other separative errors in 36881a demonstrate that it could not be an ancestor of either 3719d or 3549 (and therefore also of manuscript μ), and show that neither 3719d nor 3549 could be the ancestor of the other. Therefore I posit the stemma given in Figure 3–2. Conjunctive and separative errors are, as a group, called significative errors.

Furthermore each type of significative error must demonstrate specific characteristics. A separative error must not be susceptible to conjectural emendation or correction through contamination. That is, for the error shared by 3719d and 3549 (and therefore their ancestor, manuscript μ) to be considered a separative error, it must be unlikely that the scribe of 36881a could have restored the correct reading through conjecture or consultation of another exemplar. Otherwise it is possible that 36881a descended from one of these three witnesses. Conjunctive errors, on the other hand, are unlikely to be made independently. The error that links 3719d and 3549 is so distinctive (music from the bottom voice is copied into the upper voice so that the voices move in parallel thirds) that it is improbable that each scribe could have committed it independently. If they could have made the error separately, it would carry no conjunctive force.

An important corollary to this discussion, taken up in more detail below, is that the absence of either type of error does not permit any stemmatic deduction. For example, if 36881a contained no separative error that would prevent it from being the ancestor of 3719d and 3549, it would not necessarily follow that it was, in fact, their ancestor. As I demonstrate below, much more concrete evidence is required to prove such a relationship.

As noted above, Greek letters indicate lost witnesses. Capital Ω is used to indicate the archetype, the latest witness from which all extant witnesses descended.[37] In many cases, of course, the archetype survives, either in the form of the composer's autograph or some such similarly authoritative source. Here, the editor should designate it by its ordinary siglum. Only perished sources should be allocated Greek

[37] Reeve, "Archetypes."

letters. Other lost witnesses are indicated by lowercase Greek letters, such as manuscripts δ and μ in the stemma given above. These are hyparchetypes because only some of the surviving witnesses descend from them.

Here it is useful to restate that only clear scribal errors are useful for establishing stemmatic relationships. As discussed above, editors place readings in that category on the basis of stylistic criteria, publishing the selection of errors used to determine the stemma, with a detailed explanation of their reasoning, for scholarly scrutiny. A crucial point in defending the validity of the stemma is the distinction between the firm errors on which they base the stemma and reasonable competing readings, those in category 2. Readings in category 2 could be errors, but, more important, they are conceivable readings within the stylistic context of the piece under consideration, whereas category 3 readings are not conceivable. How many significative errors will suffice to establish the relationship of two witnesses? The answer is directly related to the length of the piece. Naturally the greater the number, the more certain the relationship, but in shorter pieces even a single significative error can indicate the relationship. Finally I cannot lay enough stress on the fact that errors, not good readings, are the only evidence admissible in stemmatic discussions.

Filiation based on textual evidence

Let us begin with the relationships that can be determined on the basis of textual evidence alone. Above I mentioned that such a stemma normally does not eliminate any complete witness, or any reading because of the agreement of a majority of the branches at any particular division. The reason for this restriction is that both types of elimination depend on the absence of evidence, the *argumentum ex silentio.*[38] The usual requirement for the elimination of a witness (*eliminatio codicum descriptorum*) is that it contain all of the errors of its exemplar plus one or more unique errors. (See Figure 3–3.) B contains all the errors present in A, and some of its own. These unique errors are separative and so prevent the hypothesis that A was copied from B. On the other hand the hypothesis that B was

[38] On the *eliminatio codicum descriptorum*, see Palmer, *The Logic of Gospel Criticism*, pp. 67–75, and "Proving Uniqueness." On multipartite stemmata, see Blecua, *Manual de crítica textual*, pp. 74–77, and Eklund, "On Errors and Contamination," p. 82 and n. 16. See also Grier, "Lachmann, Bédier and the Bipartite Stemma."

Figure 3–3

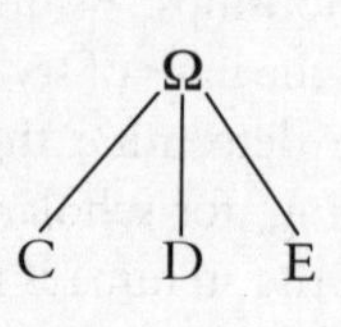

Figure 3–4

copied from A depends not so much on the presence of separative errors in B as on their absence from A. The same problem vexes the division of the stemma into more than two branches. (See Figure 3–4.) CDE all contain separative errors against one another, but the only evidence of their parallel descent from **Ω** is the absence of a conjunctive error that would establish the presence of a common ancestor below **Ω** known to only two of the witnesses. In this stemma, the agreement of any of CD, DE or CE eliminates the reading of the third witness on purely numerical grounds. In the preceding stemma, the entire witness B is eliminated because it is copied from a surviving witness.

In both cases the elimination is consequent to the absence of evidence, and here the distinction between readings in categories 2 and 3, reasonable competing readings and clear scribal errors, respectively, is of the utmost importance. The absence of clear scribal errors in either case, a separative error in A in the first stemma and a conjunctive error that links any pair of witnesses in the second stemma, does not prove conclusively the stemmata that we have proposed above. Nevertheless, some would say that witness B, above, is a *codex inutilis*: it contains no good readings not found in A, and a few more corruptions of its own.[39] Even if it were not a direct copy of A, it contributes nothing to the text's tradition that cannot be obtained from A. A similar argument could be advanced about the multipartite stemma. If no conjunctive error attests to the existence of a hyparchetype, one could assume that all shared readings are good, and should therefore ascend to the archetype. The dangers of accepting either a multipartite

[39] The term was coined by Timpanaro; see "*Recentiores e deteriores*," especially pp. 187–88.

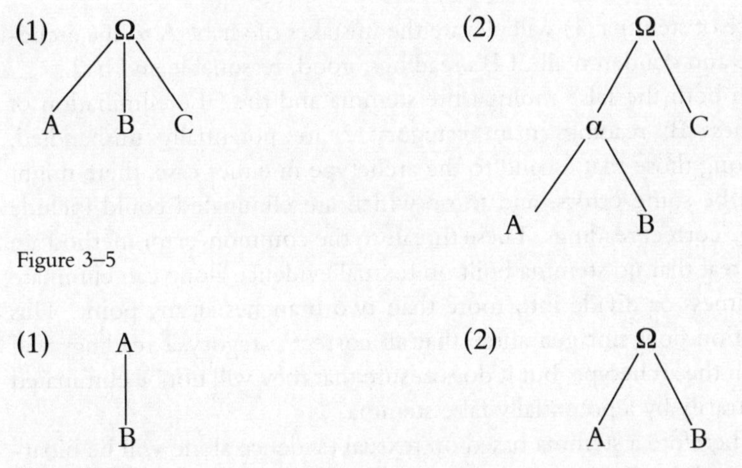

Figure 3–5

Figure 3–6

division of the stemma or the *eliminatio codicum descriptorum* will emerge from the following examples.

In the first (Figure 3–5), there are three surviving witnesses. In the first instance the tripartite stemma is correct, but the scribes of AB chanced to err in exactly the same way independently. Editors would posit stemma (2) and eliminate the readings of B when AC agree and those of A when BC agree. All these readings would be eliminated were the correct filiation ascertainable. In the second instance, however, the bipartite stemma is correct, but the scribe of α committed no clear scribal error. Consequently most editors would choose stemma (1) and eliminate the reading of the third witness in the event of the agreement of any pair. Hence, where the scribe of α erred, but the resulting reading is reasonable, that erroneous reading will ascend to the archetype on stemmatic grounds because of the absence of a firm conjunctive error in AB that would indicate the presence of a hyparchetype.

The same danger is to be found in the second example (Figure 3–6), where two witnesses have survived. In the first instance stemma (1) is correct but the scribe of B corrected some of the obvious errors in A. Editors would choose stemma (2) and eliminate no readings. In the second instance the bipartite stemma is correct, but the scribe of A committed no clear scribal errors, while B's scribe did. Stemma (1) would present itself as the correct filiation and B would be eliminated. Again the scribe of A might have erred but in erring produced reasonable readings where B retained the correct readings. The acceptance of stemma (1) will elevate the mistakes of scribe A to the archetype and condemn all of B's readings, good, reasonable and bad.

In both the false multipartite stemma and the false elimination of witness B, readings from category 2 are potentially mishandled. Among those that ascend to the archetype in either case, there might well be some errors, and those which are eliminated could include some correct readings. These threats to the common-error method are so great that no stemma built on textual evidence alone can eliminate a witness or divide into more than two branches at any point. This solution does not guarantee that all correct category 2 readings will reach the archetype, but it does ensure that they will not be eliminated arbitrarily by a potentially false stemma.

Therefore a stemma based on textual evidence alone will be bipartite in all its divisions and no source will be eliminated as a *descriptus*. This type of stemma automatically requires a relatively large number of hyparchetypes because no surviving witness has as its ancestor another surviving witnesses. They all appear at the ends of branches, whereas hyparchetypes occur at every junction of the stemma. Obviously this stemma does not depict the genealogical relationship of the sources; rather it charts the descent of the piece to various hyparchetypes whence it was transmitted to the surviving sources. Philologists use the term *stemma textuum* instead of *stemma codicum* for a stemma based on this type of evidence.

Example: J. S. Bach, Six Suites for Violoncello Solo BWV 1007–12

These pieces are transmitted in four principal manuscript sources, mentioned in Chapter 2 above, whose filiation raises some typical problems.[40] Manuscript A, Anna Magdalena Bach's copy, is thought to have been made from the autograph (now lost) in approximately 1730, whereas Johann Peter Kellner's copy, manuscript B, is derived from another exemplar, possibly a different autograph, and was probably copied in the first half of 1726.[41] These observations carry significant ramifications for understanding the transmission of the Suites. The

[40] For the manuscript sigla, see p. 42 n. 10 above.

[41] Eppstein, *Sechs Suiten für Violoncello solo: Kritischer Bericht*, pp. 18–19. On Kellner's copy, see Stinson, *The Bach Manuscripts of Johann Peter Kellner*, pp. 23, 60–61; and on Magdalena Bach's copy, which may have been commissioned by the violinist Georg Heinrich Ludwig Schwanberg, see Schulze, *Studien zur Bach-Überlieferung*, pp. 95–101.

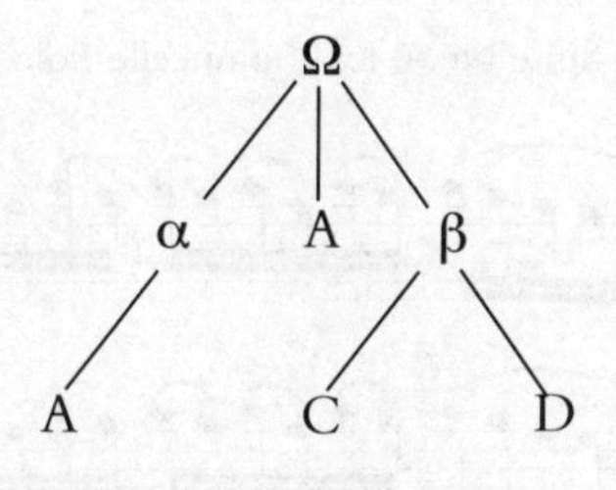

Figure 3–7

Example 3–2: J. S. Bach, Suite No. 2 for Violoncello Solo BWV 1008, Allemande, bar 9

other two copies, C and D, are somewhat later and share several errors that permit Hans Eppstein to posit a hyparchetype in their ancestry, unknown to the other two sources. Because of the absence of firm conjunctive errors linking A and B, Eppstein further proposes, without printing it, a tripartite stemma.[42] (See Figure 3–7.) Manuscript A, however, agrees in error with CD in several places. In the Allemande of the Second Suite, ACD agree in omitting a note from the upper voice in bar 9. (See Example 3–2.) The anticipation at the end of the second beat in the upper voice requires its fulfilment at the start of the third beat. In the Sixth Suite, ACD agree in two errors of perseveration (an error of assimilation by which a reading that occurs later is altered to conform with one that occurs earlier). (See Examples 3–3 and 3–4.) In bar 95 of the Prelude, the figure that occurs on the second and third beats is repeated in ACD for the fourth beat (marked **m** in Example 3–3). Two factors suggest this reading is an error. First, the lower voice is moving in sequence through bars 94–95 under the inverted pedal on E. And second, the voice leading is smoother if the lower voice continues down to A in preparation for the F♯ that begins the next bar. The error in bar 14 of the Courante

[42] Eppstein, *Sechs Suiten für Violoncello solo: Kritischer Bericht*, pp. 20–26.

Example 3–3: J. S. Bach, Suite No. 6 for Violoncello Solo BWV 1012, Prelude, bars 94–96

Example 3–4: J. S. Bach, Suite No. 6 for Violoncello Solo BWV 1012, Courante, bars 13–14

arises from a failure to recognize that the lowest voice provides a pedal (on the dominant of the dominant) instead of participating with the other voice or voices in a sequential progression. It is not altogether impossible that two copyists (Magdalena Bach and the copyist of manuscript β) made these three errors independently, although the nature of each suggests strongly to me that it is unlikely.

For the Fifth Suite, however, an additional source survives, namely the autograph of the composer's own arrangement for lute, BWV

995.[43] This manuscript is assigned the same approximate date as Anna Magdalena Bach's copy of the Suites, and so it post-dates Kellner's copy.[44] In this Suite, ACD agree in error four times where B, Kellner's copy, agrees with the lute transcription.[45] If Eppstein's tripartite stemma is correct, then manuscript Ω, Bach's autograph, contained the readings in ACD. How did B come to incorporate the correct readings? There seem to be only two possible explanations. Either Kellner emended his copy through conjecture, or his exemplar, manuscript α, contained corrections that originated with the composer, and which the composer subsequently entered into the lute arrangement. In view of Russell Stinson's analysis of Kellner's copying in his manuscript of the Sonatas and Partitas for Solo Violin by Bach, BWV 1001–6, I find it hard to believe that he could have emended successfully four times in this piece.[46] It is much more likely that Bach himself made corrections to the work, either in a copy or a second autograph, which is manuscript α, the ancestor of Kellner's copy. And from this revised version, Bach produced the lute transcription after Kellner made his copy.

Is it possible to explain the errors shared by ACD through a closer association of the three sources? Here, the assumption that A is a direct copy of the autograph becomes a problem. If we retain that assumption, then the only way in which errors made in A could have entered CD would be through direct descent from A. (See Figure 3–8.) But Eppstein notes several separative errors (i.e., errors present in A but not in CD) that prevent A from being an ancestor of CD.[47] These include two omissions that could not possibly have been remedied in CD through conjectural emendation. Therefore the only other conceivable explanation is that A was not copied from the autograph, but from a copy in which the errors common to ACD were committed. (See Figure 3–9.)

The two most likely explanations both involve historical circumstances that would seem to contradict conventional wisdom. If the bipartite stemma proposed above is correct, then Anna Magdalena Bach did not copy directly from her husband's autograph. If, on the other hand, Eppstein's tripartite stemma is correct, then manuscript α

[43] Brussels, Bibliothèque Royale, MS II.4085.

[44] Eichberg and Kohlhase, *Einzeln überlieferte Klavierwerke II: Kritischer Bericht*, pp. 105, 109.

[45] Courante, bars 3 and 5; Gavotte I, bar 13; and Gavotte II, bar 10.

[46] Stinson, *The Bach Manuscripts of Johann Peter Kellner*, pp. 55–70.

[47] Eppstein, *Sechs Suiten für Violoncello solo: Kritischer Bericht*, p. 22.

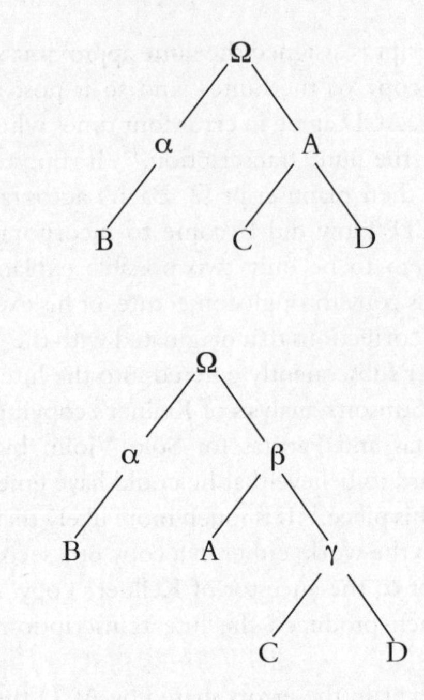

Figure 3–8

Figure 3–9

contained corrections by Bach, some of which he retained in his lute arrangement of the Fifth Suite, that were incorporated into Kellner's copy. Why were these revisions not made available to Magdalena Bach when she prepared her copy at approximately the same time as her husband was preparing the lute transcription of the Fifth Suite? Both explanations require that Magdalena Bach did not have access to sources that we might conventionally assume she did.

The simplest solution to the problem is flatly contradicted by the chronology of the sources. That solution would be to propose that Bach himself made several errors in the autograph of the Fifth Suite, which then entered Magdalena Bach's copy and the ancestor of CD. When the composer undertook the lute arrangement of this Suite, he found and corrected several of the errors in the autograph and introduced the corrections into the lute arrangement. At this point manuscript α was created, incorporating Bach's corrections, and from which Kellner made his copy. The problem with this theory is that our best information, which is at least somewhat tenuous, dates Kellner's copy before Magdalena Bach's and the autograph of the lute transcription, and so Kellner knew an earlier state of the autograph, not a later, revised state. Consequently, we revert back to the

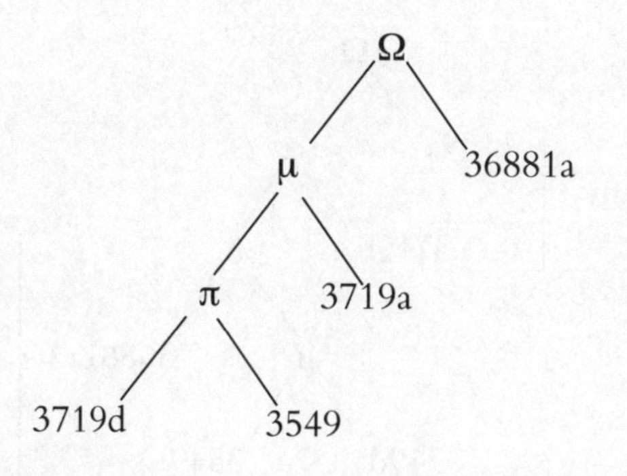

Figure 3–10

hypotheses advanced above: either Kellner had access to a corrected version of the Fifth Suite that was not made available to Magdalena Bach, even though her husband was using it at about the same time in the preparation of the lute transcription, or she did not copy directly from the autograph.

Example: *Veri solis radius*

The filiation of the twelfth-century Aquitanian *uersaria* provides further illustrations of the procedure. First, the stemma of the *uersus Veri solis radius* shows how conjunctive errors demonstrate the relationships between witnesses (see Figure 3–10).[48] Two errors in the poetic text are shared by 3719a, 3719d and 3549, and so they descend from a witness (manuscript μ), in which the errors were made, unknown to 36881a, which transmits the correct reading in each case. Further copying errors in both the literary and musical text are shared by 3719d and 3549, in passages where 3719a gives the correct reading in agreement with 36881a. Two deductions follow: first that 3719d and 3549 descend from a common ancestor unknown to 3719a, which could only have copied the correct readings from a source above the common ancestor of 3719d and 3549 on the stemma; and second that agreement in good readings, as between 3719a and 36881a here, proves nothing about common descent. Errors that are shared by two or more witnesses against another witness or witnesses permit the establishment of the filiation given in Figure 3–10.

[48] Grier, "The Stemma," pp. 258–62; in the sigla below, 3719a = Pa 3719, fols. 15r–22v.

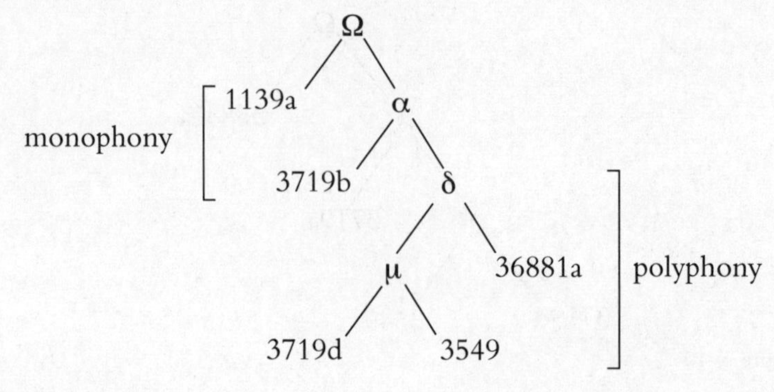

Figure 3–11

Example: *Omnis curet homo*

Evidence other than conjunctive error can determine filiation, as the stemma of the twelfth-century Aquitanian *uersus Omnis curet homo* shows.[49] As I pointed out above, the presence of a polyphonic version in 3719d, 3549 and 36881a distinguishes them from the other two witnesses, and indicates that they descend from a common ancestor unknown to either 1139a or 3719b. That ancestor is the hyparchetype δ, which therefore contained the polyphonic version that occurs in its three extant descendants. Furthermore, 3719d and 3549 agree in a conjunctive error, mentioned above: the use of parallel motion at a cadence. This agreement guarantees that they descend from a hyparchetype unknown to 36881a, manuscript μ.

No clear conjunctive error associates either 1139a or 3719b with the polyphonic versions, but the treatment of embellishment and melodic sequence in 3719b shows very close similarities with the three polyphonic versions. Therefore, I judge it to descend from an ancestor that was also known to them, manuscript α. (See Figure 3–11.) In two cases, then, readings that are not clear errors can nevertheless show shared descent. Copies of manuscript α evince treatment of melodic sequence not found in 1139a, and the polyphonic version, which originated in δ, distinguishes the three witnesses that transmit it from the two monophonic witnesses.

[49] Grier, "The Stemma," pp. 262–67.

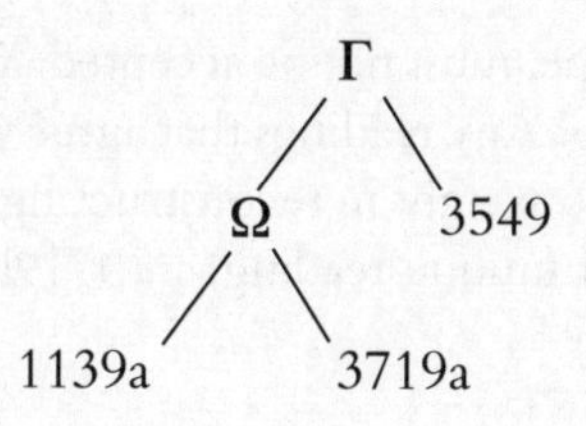

Figure 3–12

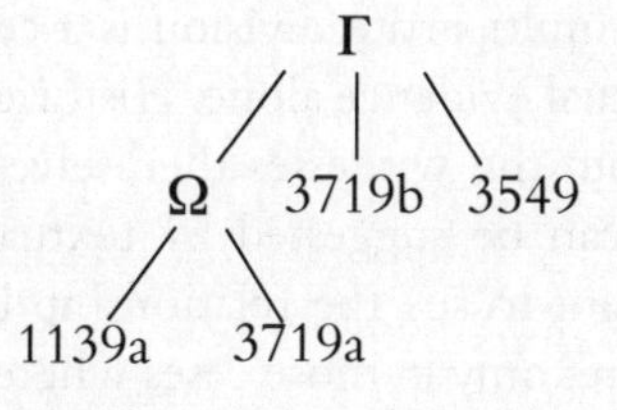

Figure 3–13

Example: *Ex Ade uitio*

Where the absence of conjunctive error does not permit the grouping of witnesses in a bipartite arrangement, the editor should not resort to a multipartite division, as the stemma of *Ex Ade uitio* shows.[50] A firm conjunctive error in the text associates 1139a and 3719a against 3549 (see Figure 3–12). This is the error, mentioned above, that shows that this song descended to 3549 via a different route from that which other *uersus,* such as *Omnis curet homo* and *Veri solis radius,* followed. No conjunctive error allows 3719b, however, to be linked with any other witness. According to the strictest stemmatic theory, then, a tripartite division should be posited immediately below the archetype. (See Figure 3–13.) As mentioned above, the absence of error does not prove descent. The danger of accepting this stemma is that any agreement between 3719b and any other witness automatically elevates that reading to the archetype. Because this filiation is not proved, it is possible that some of these agreements might be category 2 readings, reasonable readings, that are in fact errors. This potentially false stemma, then, could elevate some errors to the status of archetypal readings. Therefore, this stemma, with its unproved tripartite division immedi-

[50] Grier, "The Stemma," pp. 273–76. In Figure 3-12 I use Ω for the hyparchetype because it is the same witness as the archetype of the stemma of the central tradition of Aquitanian *uersaria*, as found in the stemmata of *Omnis curet homo* and *Veri solis radius*. Uppercase Greek letters, like Γ in this stemma, denote relationships outside the central stemma.

ately below the archetype, must not be accepted. What should be done about readings in 3719b? Any readings that agree with any of the other three witnesses are of no weight in reconstructing the hyparchetype Ω or the archetype Γ. All unique readings in 3719b are reserved to the final stage of *examinatio.*

Multipartite division and *eliminatio codicum descriptorum*

In some cases, a true multipartite division is ascertainable, but never on the grounds of textual evidence alone. Historical, geographical and physical testimony from the witnesses themselves can show multiple parallel descent that can be suggested by textual evidence, but not proved.[51] It is important to see the relationship between textual and historical evidence here: only in those cases where the state of the text indicates a multipartite division, can historical evidence be used to confirm or reject that division. A case in point is the stemma of *Ex Ade uitio*, discussed above, where 3719b seems to have no place. Unfortunately, no evidence from the manuscript is forthcoming that would affirm its position on the stemma, and so its readings contribute nothing to the stemmatic assessment of the text.

Historical evidence can also assist in the detection of *codices descripti*, copies of extant witnesses.[52] A striking example is offered by two of the eleventh-century tropers from Saint Martial de Limoges. As I mentioned above, Pa 1119, compiled *c.* AD 1050–63, is a direct copy, a *codex descriptus*, of parts of Pa 909 written by Adémar de Chabannes in AD 1028–29.[53] In the Epilogue below I detail how Adémar replaced portions of Pa 909 with newly copied material that transmits the apostolic liturgy for the feast of Saint Martial. One of the parts so replaced is a single quaternio from the libellus of proper tropes, the central contents of which are the troped items for the Mass of Saint Martial (fols. 41r–48v). Because this gathering had to fit into an existing context, Adémar was obliged to ensure that the final piece in the gathering meshed smoothly with the beginning of the next gathering.

The next gathering begins with the word *mortis*, which occurs midway through an Introit trope (*Quia naturam*) for the Mass of Assumption.

[51] Reeve, "Stemmatic Method," pp. 59–61, 63–64, gives examples of verifiable multipartite stemmata from classical literature.

[52] Timpanaro, "*Recentiores e deteriores,*" pp. 165–69; Irigoin, "Accidents matériels et critique des textes"; and Reeve, "*Eliminatio codicum descriptorum.*"

[53] Grier, "*Ecce sanctum,*" pp. 35–37.

When Adémar reached the last line of his replacement gathering, there remained just slightly too little text for the available room. First he greatly elongated the *n* of *ascendit*, which precedes *mortis*, and then, to justify the right margin, he wrote *mortis*. Thus the transition from the end of Adémar's replacement gathering to the beginning of the gathering from the original layer that follows presents an intentional dittography (i.e., something that should be written once is written twice), *mortis* (last word on fol. 48v) *mortis* (first word on fol. 49r). This dittography is then repeated in the version of *Quia naturam* that appears in Pa 1119 (fol. 69r). The music scribe was aware of the problem, because he wrote the musical setting of *mortis* only once, above its first presentation. This corruption could only have entered Pa 1119 from Pa 909, and so we have firm evidence of direct copying from the latter to the former.[54]

In the strictest application of the common-error method to editing, this relationship should eliminate Pa 1119 from consideration in the establishment of any texts that can be shown to have been copied into it from Pa 909. I note above, however, that it contains at least one important emendation (in the Gloria trope for the Mass of Saint Martial) that corrects an error in Pa 909. This situation is typical of the transmission of music sources. Music scribes are, by and large, professional musicians who create their sources for professional, practical purposes. Therefore, they continually subject the texts they are copying to critical scrutiny, not with any text-critical aim in mind other than the production of a useful copy. This procedure does not guarantee that scribes will not err, but it does result in sources that contain well-considered readings that might not return the text to a compositional original (if such a thing ever existed) but constitute significant improvements over the errors in an exemplar.

Reconstruction of archetypes and hyparchetypes

The stemma, once determined, allows the texts, both musical and literary, of the hyparchetypes and archetypes to be reconstructed. That

[54] Similar evidence enabled Margaret Bent to show that the fifteenth-century codex Trent, Museo Provinciale d'Arte, Castello del Buon Consiglio, MS 90 was copied from Trent, Museo Diocesano, MS BL (commonly known as Trent 93), and that, in the manuscript tradition of Machaut's works, manuscript B (Paris, Bibliothèque Nationale, fonds français, MS 1585) was copied from manuscript Vg (New York, Wildenstein Galleries, no shelfmark; *olim* private collection of the Marquis de Vogüé), and that portions of manuscript E (Paris, Bibliothèque Nationale, fonds français, MS 9221) were copied from B. On the Trent codices, see *Fifteenth-Century Liturgical Music*, II, *Four Anonymous Masses*, ed. Bent, pp. x–xi, 180–83; and "Trent 93 and Trent 90"; and, on the Machaut tradition, "The Machaut Manuscripts *Vg*, *B* and *E*."

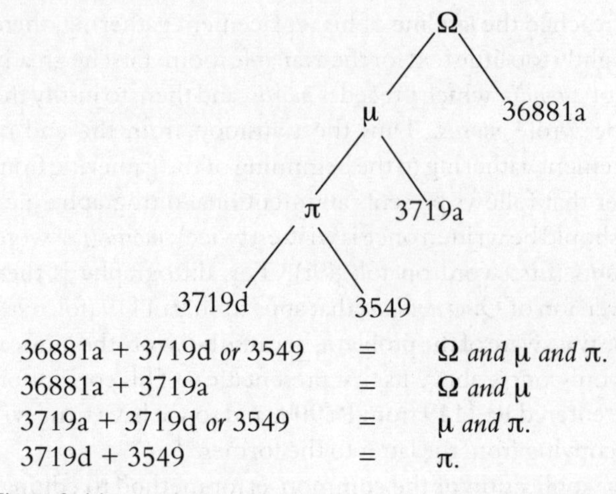

Figure 3–14

of *Veri solis radius* demonstrates the procedure. (See Figure 3–14.) The agreement of 36881a with any of the other three extant witnesses guarantees the reading of Ω and eliminates any variant readings. For example, if 36881a and 3719d agree against the other two witnesses, that agreement gives the reading of Ω, μ and π, and the reading or readings of 3719a and 3549 are eliminated. If 36881a disagrees with all of 3719a, 3719d and 3549, then its reading must be compared with that of μ to determine which was more likely to have been in Ω. This is the stage of *examinatio* in the terminology of classical textual criticism. Similar elimination or *examinatio* will determine the reading of μ and π, as necessary. The process of *examinatio*, wherein two or more readings of identical stemmatic weight are judged in order to select the readings of a hyparchetype or the archetype, is the very stuff of editing. As such, it requires further discussion in Chapter 4. Here it is sufficient to note that critical knowledge of the text, the sources, their transmission and the style of the composer is essential even at the seemingly mechanical stage of stemmatic determination.

Stemmatophiles will note that the arrangement of this stemma (a very common one, indeed), with a single witness (here 36881a) on one side, is tantamount to proposing 36881a as the best witness, a procedure that is often represented as the opposite of the common-error method. In the "best-witness" method, an editor selects one witness as the best (for such reasons as, it is the oldest extant witness, or, in the opinion of the editor, it preserves the least corrupt version of the text), which is then followed in all details except where it is manifestly corrupt. There the editor has recourse to the other witnesses or conjectural emendation to establish the text. In the sample stemma given in Figure 3–14, 36881a is virtually the best witness because all its readings ascend to the archetype except where 3719a, 3719d and 3549 all disagree with it. Even then, these three agree in at least one error against 36881a, an error that descended to them from μ and in fact establishes the existence of μ, and so the corresponding reading of 36881a here again ascends to the archetype. Moreover, the worst status that any reading of 36881a can achieve is to compete with the reading of μ for elevation to the archetype. Therefore 36881a, unless it contains many unique and obvious corruptions, will contribute more readings to the archetype than any other witness and so is virtually the best witness.

Of course the most carefully constructed stemma can collapse like a card house through the effects of contamination or conjectural emendation, as mentioned above. An assessment and discussion of these factors, drawn from the editor's knowledge of the processes of transmission in the repertory, will orientate the edition's user to the likelihood of their presence. Was the text of such importance that a scribe would have consulted more than one exemplar, or was it unlikely that a scribe would have access to more than one? Are there instances of relatively easily correctable errors that have not been emended, or places where one scribal error has generated further corruption? Or, on the other hand, did the scribe or publisher work in an environment where emendation was tolerated or even encouraged? In general both contamination and conjectural emendation tend to replace errors with correct or at least reasonable readings, and are therefore difficult to detect. Nevertheless, in a piece of any length, it is extremely unlikely that all significative errors will be removed through contamination or emendation. Consequently, sources that agree in some but not all such errors may be the results of these two processes.

The results of the method and their application

In the traditional application of the common-error method, the text of the archetype, which is thus reconstructed by a combination of *eliminatio* and *examinatio*, is then, itself, examined to determine whether readings that are unlikely to have been in the authorial original remain. The editor then subjects any such readings to emendation in order to arrive at the final edited text. The exact use that music editors will make of this procedure depends entirely on the nature of the piece's transmission. Some editors will decide that such a thing as a composer's original text existed and that it is worth reconstructing as far as the extant evidence will permit.[55] Lothar Hoffmann-Erbrecht followed this procedure in his edition of the psalm motets of Thomas Stoltzer, which he claims as the first edition of music to do so. He created individual stemmata for several of the pieces, and used them to determine the text of the archetype, which then became the point of departure for the final edited text.[56]

In other cases, the text of the archetype contributes not so much to the establishment of the final edited text as it does to the illumination of the history of the text's transmission. For example, through my own stemmatic assessment of the twelfth-century Aquitanian *uersaria*, I was able to identify and isolate substantive variants in the musical text that were added by the individual scribes of the repertory.[57] The identification of these variants led, in turn, to an appreciation of the scribes' active participation in the dynamic processes by which the repertory was transmitted and disseminated. In two studies of the late fifteenth-century chanson, Allan W. Atlas used stemmatic filiation to illuminate the historical circumstances under which that repertory was transmitted, and to associate variants in the tradition with conflicting attributions in the sources that carry the variants.[58] Sometimes substantive variants can be localized and used to discern regional traditions. The motet repertory of Josquin des Prez gives two examples: Lothar Hoffmann-Erbrecht identifies a German tradition of the piece *Domine, ne in furore tuo arguas me*, separate from that transmitted in Italy and stemming from Petrucci's print; and similar findings about the transmission of *Aue Maria . . . uirgo serena* are presented by Thomas Noblitt.[59] Such

[55] Bent, "Some Criteria," pp. 311–13.

[56] Stoltzer, *Ausgewählte Werke*, II, *Sämtliche Psalmmotetten*, ed. Hoffmann-Erbrecht, stemmata on pp. 174–82; see, on the chronological priority of his edition, Hoffmann-Erbrecht, "Problems in the Interdependence of Josquin Sources," pp. 288–89.

[57] Grier, "The Stemma," and "Scribal Practices."

[58] Atlas, *The Cappella Giulia Chansonnier*, especially I, 233–58; and "Conflicting Attributions."

[59] Hoffmann-Erbrecht, "Problems in the Interdependence of Josquin Sources," pp. 291–92; and Noblitt, "Textual Criticism," pp. 208, 234–35. See also Kirsch, "Josquin's Motets in the German Tradition." In his assessment of *Domine, ne in furore tuo arguas me*, Hoffmann-Erbrecht places the alto partbook London, British Library, Additional MS 19583 in the German tradition on the basis of shared error, and another partbook, Modena, Biblioteca Estense, MS α F 2.29, with the Italian tradition. Edward E. Lowinsky, however, shows that the Modena source belongs to the same set of partbooks as the London manuscript (Lowinsky, ed., *The Medici Codex of 1518*, I, 117–18). Hoffmann-Erbrecht cites no evidence from the Modena source to justify his conclusion, nor are any readings from it given by Lowinsky or in the edition of Smijers, Josquin des Prez, *Werken*, XXI, in *Motteten*, II, Bundel, 8 (Amsterdam, 1942), p. XVI. Therefore, Hoffmann-Erbrecht's classification of the Modena source is uncertain at best.

conclusions illuminate not only the reception of these works in various geographical regions, but also lead to deductions about individual scribal and performing practices in those areas.[60]

The common-error method and its creation, the stemma, do not constitute a mechanical procedure that results in the automated production of the final edited text. The stemma is, rather, a tool that can illustrate relationships between witnesses, illuminate the processes of transmission by which those witnesses were created, and provide guidance in sorting through the competing readings that make up the work's tradition. It is only as good, however, as the readings on which it is based, and a faulty stemmatic conclusion can do irreparable damage to the edition it is supposed to help. Nevertheless, the stemma constitutes a very powerful tool in the preparation of an edition that is based on a truly critical appraisal of the work and its sources.

[60] Boorman, "The Uses of Filiation," pp. 176–78.

4

Errors, variants and editorial judgement: the establishment of the text

At this stage of the editorial procedure, editors summon all the knowledge they have accumulated from the study of the sources, the repertory and its composer, as well as their historical context, in order to fix the text of the edition. The decisions editors make here are as difficult as any they face in the entire process and their erudition serves as their chief guide. The dangers, too, that await the editor at this stage of the journey are perhaps greater than at any other: to improve the composer, to impose an arbitrary stylistic standard, or to follow either source materials or previous editors without revision or critical comment; in short either to assert editorial authority without restraint, or to decline to exercise it at all. How editors will avoid these dangers is largely a matter of the way they view the relationship between themselves and the texts they are editing, a matter for discussion in Chapter 6 of this book.

The steps outlined in the previous two chapters provide the editor with a large mass of material from which the text of the piece is now extracted. The gathering of evidence employs critical judgement throughout its constituent steps, a fact that substantively influences the way in which it is used at this stage of determining the text. That is, the evidence collected is not simply a set of neutral facts, but it has been shaped by the processes involved in its collection, from the selection of sources for consultation, to the methods of transcription and the classification of the sources. These are all critical activities whose validity depends solely on the acumen of the editor, who now continues to exercise that judgement in evaluating not only the evidence but the critical decisions that shaped it during its collection.

An example from my edition of the music copied by Adémar de

Chabannes illustrates the problem. In a plainsong Mass, the Introit consists of an antiphon, one or more verses and a statement of the Lesser Doxology that is treated as another verse. The antiphon serves as a refrain to the verses, which are sung to recitation formulae. A typical arrangement is antiphon, verse, antiphon, Doxology, antiphon. All antiphons are classified, on the basis of final note, melodic range and other melodic characteristics, in one of the eight ecclesiastical modes in order to determine which recitation formula is to be used for the accompanying verse. Each mode supplies a single formula for the singing of Introit verses. To save space, most medieval chant books give the formulae for all modes together in the tonary, instead of providing them separately for each Introit.

Adémar, in his autograph of the troped apostolic Mass for the feast of Saint Martial (Pa 909, fols. 42r–46v), lists nine verses to be sung as part of the Introit. For eight of them, he gives the incipit only, as is usually the case, but for one, *Ecce sanctum* (which Adémar in fact composed), he writes out the entire verse with the full musical setting.[1] It took no great effort to apply this formula to the other eight verses, but a thornier problem arose regarding the treatment of the Doxology. Codex Pa 909 contains a tonary (fols. 251r–257v) that was compiled in part by Adémar: he wrote the musical notation in the tonary, and made several revisions to its literary text.[2] It includes formulaic settings for the Doxology when sung as part of the Introit, and that for mode 1 (the mode of *Probauit eum*, the Introit for this feast) differs slightly from the version Adémar gives for *Ecce sanctum* in the troped Mass. (See Example 4–1.) The difference is not great, to be sure, but it poses a real question as to which one is to be printed. Adémar clearly knew both, as he wrote the musical notation in each case. In the end I elected to print the version from the tonary for the Doxology on the grounds that it might represent a special application of the formula for that text.

The eventual choice of the tonary's version in this case arose from an ongoing critical dialogue between the editor and the sources. No decision is absolute and resistant to modification on the basis of new evidence or a careful reconsideration of existing testimony. Previous critical assessments undergo a continuous process of re-evaluation as the editor works through the stages of the edition. Therefore the establishment of the text depends on the nature of the material thus

[1] Grier, "*Ecce sanctum,*" pp. 38–43.

[2] On the tonary, see Merkley, *Modal Assignments in Northern Tonaries*, pp. 50–53.

Example 4–1: Psalm Tones for Mode 1

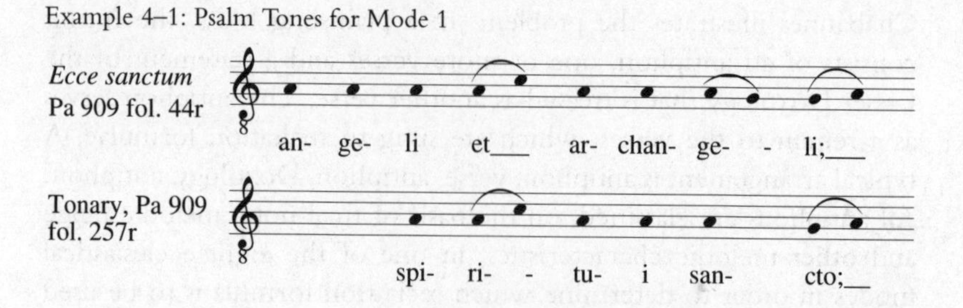

gathered, the critical methods used in collecting it, and the editor's ongoing appraisal of it. The historical relationship between the work and the source or sources that preserve its text (or texts) determines, on the one hand, the editor's procedure and, on the other, the limits of possibility and certainty that can be achieved. Conclusions about that relationship stand among the most important results obtained from the source studies described in the previous two chapters.[3]

All sources, no matter what their origin, contain only three types of readings: good readings, reasonable competing readings and clear scribal errors, as defined in Chapter 1 above, where the importance of style in determining the classification of readings is stressed. The editor's task is to place each reading in one of the three categories. I have already mentioned the difficulties involved in defining an error in music, but here the editor confronts the problem head on and establishes defensible criteria for making such judgements. If the piece survives in a unique source, the second category, reasonable competing readings, will be considerably diminished; it will not necessarily disappear because a unique source may still contain variant readings for some passages. Once the classification of readings into the three categories is completed, the even more difficult task of dealing with those which landed in category 2 must be tackled. In some cases a stemma affords some or even a great deal of help, but in all cases the editor will have some very difficult choices indeed.

Editorial theory

Because the relationship between the act of composition and the subsequent transmission of the product of that act (the piece) is infinitely

[3] See Feder, *Musikphilologie*, pp. 42–56, for a discussion of the critical issues involved in gathering evidence for the edition.

variable, the procedure to be followed in treating the sources and their readings will vary according to the editor's perception of that relationship. Accordingly I make no attempt here to treat every possibility. Every piece is a special case, as I stated in Chapter 1, and every piece will tolerate more than one editorial solution. Moreover, no single editorial theory can satisfactorily accommodate the multiplicity of situations that arise in editing, even though each of the proposed theories of textual criticism has some value in particular contexts. Therefore it is necessary to begin by investigating those theories and their applicability to music.

In Chapter 3 above I give a full account of the common-error, or recensionist method. As stated there, stemmatic filiation provides a useful and powerful tool for the elimination of some readings from category 2, reasonable completing readings, but it does not automatically and mechanically generate a fully edited text. It is simply a critical aid in sorting through some of the readings. In addition, it can assist in the historical evaluation of the descent of readings from the original moment of composition to the surviving sources. In the twelfth-century Aquitanian *uersaria*, for example, I was able to ascertain the moment at which score notation of two-voice polyphony was introduced, namely in manuscript δ (see the stemma of *Omnis curet homo* [Figure 3–11] in Chapter 3).[4]

This conclusion may have no direct bearing on the evaluation of specific readings, but it may inform the editor about the copying environment and possible influences it may hold on the results. Two witnesses of the *uersus Veri solis radius* contain an error of intrusion (see Example 4–2, where it is marked **m**).[5] The error was originally committed by the scribe of manuscript π, the ancestor common to 3719d and 3549, and could only have been made in the process of copying from score. Exactly the same problem afflicted the copyist of the Donaueschingen parts of the *Linz* Symphony, as discussed above in Chapter 3: the scribe's eye slipped to the wrong line in the score when transferring the passage in question. In neither case does this information alter our evaluation of the problematic reading, but it does help us to understand how the errors came about.

In the *uersus*, moreover, the stemma allows us to eradicate the error. The agreement of 3719a and 36881a at this point shows that the contrary motion they present occurred in their ancestors, manuscripts δ

[4] Grier, "The Stemma," pp. 276–80. [5] See Grier, "The Stemma," pp. 259–60.

Example 4–2: *Veri solis radius* stanza 5

and μ. Both these latter are also ancestors of manuscript π, the ancestor of 3719d and 3549, and so the error they share, which entered the tradition at manuscript π, is a corruption of the reading common to 3719a and 36881a. Were I to edit this *uersus*, I would under no circumstances print the reading of 3719d and 3549; I would replace it with that which can be reconstructed from the agreement of 3719a and 36881a. The decision to classify the reading of 3719d and 3549 as an error is based on a critical assessment of the repertory's style, and the stemma, as a tool that shows the historical descent of readings, indicates how that error came about, and the reading of which it is a corruption.

Example 4–2: (continued)

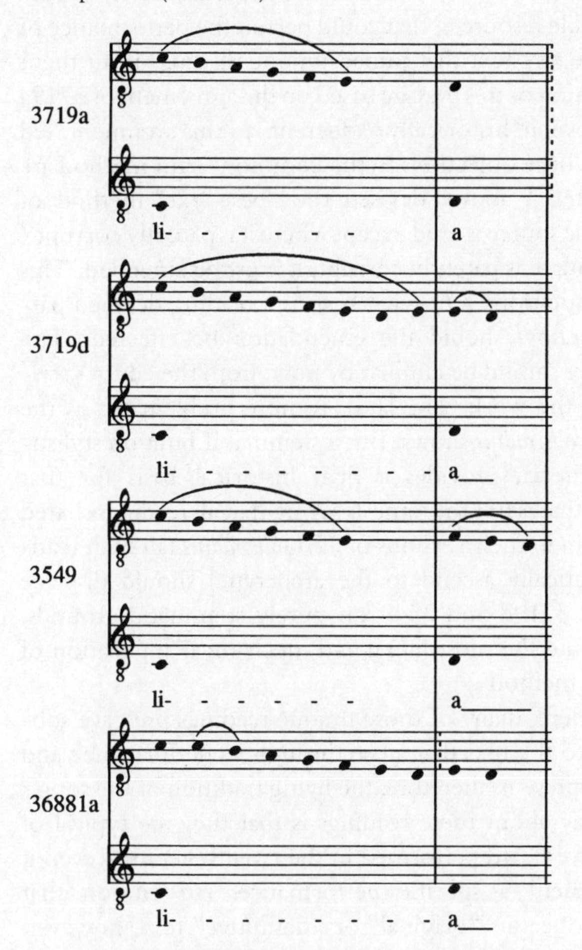

Some would argue that this type of reconstruction creates a text that never existed, that a so-called eclectic text, which combines readings from more than one source, is a historical impossibility. And in this case, it is extremely unlikely, I would agree, that the scribe of either 3719d or 3549 would have been able, through text-critical means, to determine the correct reading.[6] Their main concern, and that of most music

[6] This is the conclusion of Bryan Gillingham in his edition of the *uersus* from both witnesses, *Saint-Martial Mehrstimmigkeit*, pp. 61–65 (3719d), 97–101 (3549), where he emends to parallel unisons, a type of part-writing which is uncharacteristic of this repertory, but which nevertheless comes closest to the preserved readings in the witnesses. Karp, *The Polyphony of Saint Martial*, II, 3–7 (3549), 107–11 (3719d), retains the reading of the manuscripts but arranges the rhythm to avoid the consecutive seconds. Van der Werf, *The Oldest Extant Part Music*, II, 32–50, retains the manuscript reading and the parallel seconds.

scribes, copyists and editors, was to produce a text, as accurately as possible from the available resources, that could permit the performance of the song. Therefore any text that joined unique readings from them with the reconstruction of this passage based on the agreement of 3719a and 36881a is impossible historically. Adherents to this argument, led by Joseph Bédier, whose objections to the common-error method are discussed in Chapter 3 above, devised the "best-text" method of editing, in which one source is used except where it is patently corrupt.[7]

But where the source is patently corrupt, it must be emended. This dictum raises two questions. On what basis is a reading deemed patently corrupt, and how should the emendation be effected? The answer to the former should be familiar by now: from the editor's stylistic conception of the work. The latter is more problematic, as the example from *Veri solis radius* shows. But a stemma, if built on stylistically defensible criteria, provides a firm historical basis for that emendation. Now, that is not the same as saying that all readings shared by 3719a and 36881a in their versions of *Veri solis radius* (all such readings would automatically ascend to the archetype) should displace unique readings in 3719d and 3549 on purely stemmatic grounds. That would constitute the most literal and mechanical application of the common-error method.

As I argue elsewhere, many of those unique readings preserve substantive alterations to the text that arose through its performance and transmission, and represent, therefore, the living tradition of the song.[8] The least we can say about these readings is that they are typical of what one would have heard performed in the twelfth century, even if they do not represent a specific performance. An edition that attempted to reproduce an "original" or "definitive" text, however, would have to ignore these unique readings in favour of the reconstructed text of the archetype. And that text would simply not reflect the musical practice associated with this repertory, in which the idiosyncratic style of the individual singer seems not only to be permitted, but perhaps even encouraged.

The only tenable way to edit this repertory, I believe, is to consider each version of each song separately, exactly the position endorsed by all its recent editors.[9] This could be construed as a form of the "best-

[7] On its application to musical works, see Brown, "Editing," p. 840a; and Feder, *Musikphilologie*, pp. 58–59. [8] Grier, "Scribal Practices," especially pp. 400–20.

[9] Gillingham, ed., *Saint-Martial Mehrstimmigkeit*; Karp, *The Polyphony of Saint Martial*, vol. II; and van der Werf, *The Oldest Extant Part Music*, vol. II.

text" method, although the editor treats each version as its own best text, instead of picking one to the exclusion of the others. The unique substantive variants of each version form part of the text of the appropriate edition, and corruptions can be eradicated with help of the stemma. And how does one distinguish between substantive variants, which are to be retained, and errors, which require emendation? Style. Example 4–3 shows the edited texts of this passage from *Veri solis radius* when based on 3719d and 3549. Thus, neither the "best-text" method nor stemmatic filiation suffices, on its own, to produce a satisfactory edition of *Veri solis radius*. The former comes closest to replicating the text as it might have been performed in the twelfth century, but the correction of scribal errors remains problematic unless the historical evidence of the stemma is used to provide guidance in emending them.

Nevertheless there remains the historical problem of printing readings that the scribe did not and could not have known. If we really believe that each version has a substantive existence of its own, then the introduction of readings from other parts of the tradition is a historical impossibility. My rationale for endorsing this procedure, despite its logical absurdity, rests on an unflagging trust in human nature to aspire towards accuracy whenever possible. That is, had the correct reading of this passage from *Veri solis radius* been available to the scribes of 3719d and 3549, or had the scribe of manuscript π, who first committed the error, noticed it, they all would have copied it correctly. This is not to say that scribes are incapable of error. To err, after all, is human. But I do believe that they are entirely capable of copying correctly, and that they would insist that that is their intention and goal.

Now with this statement, we seem to be approaching some kind of theory of scribal intention, but its goals are modest and fully dependent on the editor's critical perspective of the work. And that is because we do not infer intention in the substance of what the scribe is copying, only in the scribe's desire to copy what he or she believes to be correct. We can only judge whether a scribe has copied incorrectly through our own critical inquiry into the style of the work and copying procedures, not through a presumed, and necessarily false, knowledge of scribal intention. In other words, we can never know with certainty what a given scribe would recognize as an error, although we can safely assume that he or she attempted and intended to copy correctly. Thus the decision of what is erroneous and what

Example 4–3: *Veri solis radius* stanza 5

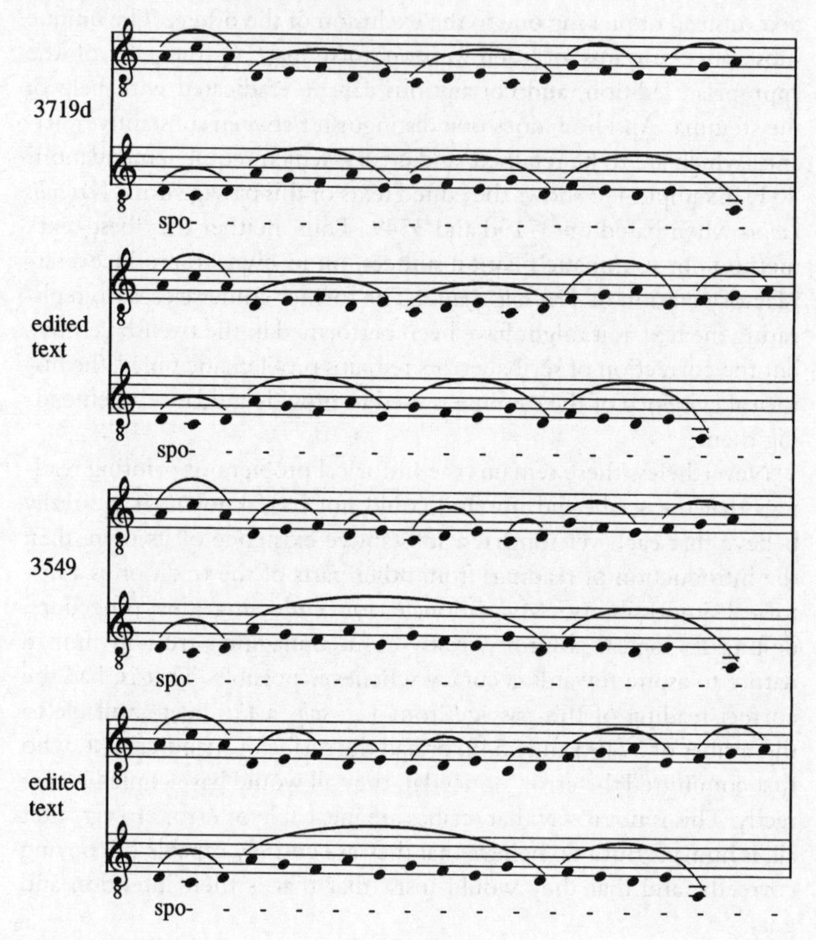

correct is entirely in the province of the editor and arises solely from the editor's critical acumen and knowledge of the piece and its context.

Similarly, the theory of the copy-text, a method developed principally in modern English philology, does not generate a fully independent method of editing.[10] The most familiar form of the theory is

[10] First proposed by Greg, "The Rationale of Copy-Text." See also Bowers, "Current Theories of Copy-Text"; Bowers, "Greg's 'Rationale of Copy-Text' Revisited"; and Tanselle, "Greg's Theory of Copy-Text."

Example 4–3: (continued)

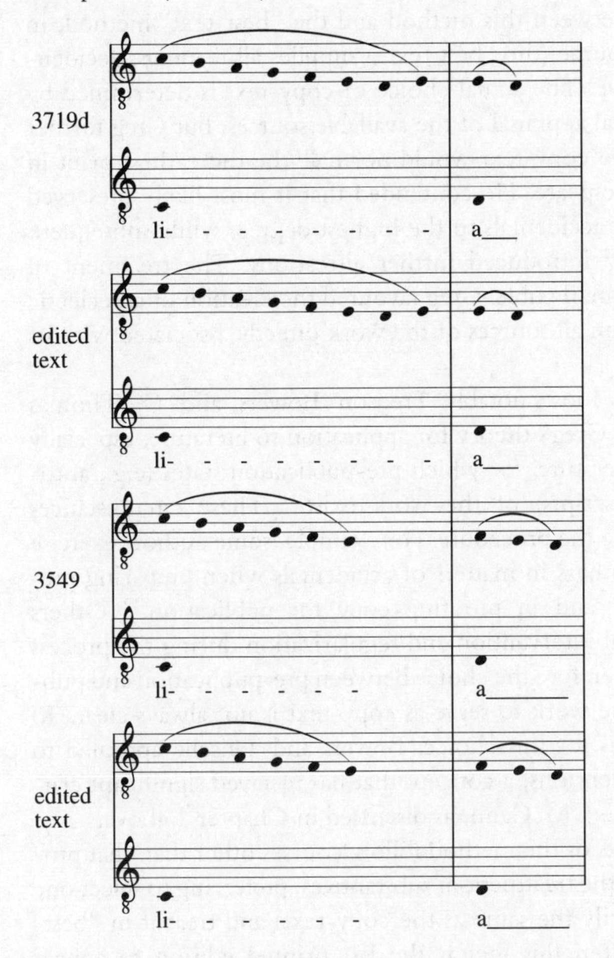

that proposed by W. W. Greg in order to deal with editing problems in Shakespeare, where virtually all sources are printed. Greg divided the transmitted readings into their substantive and accidental components. Substantives carry meaning, as, for example, the words of a text. Accidentals include such matters as spelling, punctuation and capitalization, qualities that may not, in themselves, carry meaning. Greg reasoned that, in publication, Shakespeare did not retain absolute control over accidentals, as printers imposed their own style and otherwise altered the text.

Consequently, Greg suggested that the editor choose one text of the work as the copy-text, and follow its accidentals faithfully. And here is the distinction between this method and the "best-text" method, in which a single source (the "best text") supplies all readings, accidental and substantive. The actual choice of copy-text is determined by the editor's critical appraisal of the available sources, but Greg further suggested that the copy-text would normally be the earliest print in the case of Shakespeare. He contended that it most likely preserved the author's own accidentals to the highest degree, while subsequent editions probably introduced further alterations. The treatment of substantives is more flexible. Greg favoured the creation of an eclectic text by drawing on all sources of the work directly associated with its author.

Other critics, most notably Fredson Bowers and G. Thomas Tanselle, adapted Greg's theory for application to literature, especially more modern literature, for which pre-publication states (e.g., autographs and typescripts) of the work exist.[11] These circumstances greatly complicate the procedure. For example, some authors exercise more care than others in matters of accidentals when preparing pre-publication copy and in proofing copy for publication.[12] Others welcome editorial intervention and regularization during the process of publishing. Therefore the choice between pre-publication and published states of the work to serve as copy-text is not always clear. To provide guidelines for this choice, Bowers and Tanselle appealed to final authorial intentions, a concept that has received significant criticism from Jerome J. McGann, as discussed in Chapter 1 above.

Other adherents of the method follow courses other than that proposed by Greg in the treatment of substantives, preferring to select one text (not necessarily the same as the copy-text) and treat it in "best-text" fashion. Often this text is the last printed edition to appear during the author's lifetime because it probably preserves final authorial intention with regard to the substantives of the work. Whichever the procedure chosen for dealing with substantives, editors have a broad scope for the exercise of critical judgement, either in the choice of readings that constitute an eclectic text, or in the selection of a text for "best-text" treatment.

Despite the virtues of its attempting to deal with the historical cir-

[11] But now see Tanselle, "Editing without a Copy-Text," in which he reaches a position of which traces are visible in his earlier articles "Greg's Theory of Copy-Text," and "Recent Editorial Discussion," namely that editorial judgement, not a copy-text, is the principal means for establishing a text. [12] For examples, see Thorpe, *Principles of Textual Criticism*, pp. 131–70.

cumstances of publication, the method fails as a theory for one simple reason: the difficulty in creating an unequivocal definition of substantive and accidental. Jerome McGann shows that the physical presentation, the bibliographic codes, of the work and text can carry significant meaning. He cites an example from Byron that illustrates how the changing bibliographic context of *Don Juan*, even when the text remained relatively stable, profoundly affected its meaning. And, at the extreme, both William Blake and Ezra Pound consciously controlled all aspects of the appearance of their printed works, Blake by executing the printing himself, Pound by supervising the production.[13] In these contexts it is impossible to make a meaningful distinction between accidental and substantive. But McGann argues that this is true of all works that enter the public domain. Their bibliographic guise, or bibliographic codes, some of whose qualities might be identified by supporters of the copy-text method as accidentals, affect their meaning and interpretation.

The problems are exacerbated when we try to transfer the concepts of substantive and accidental to music.[14] Apart from the unfortunate coincidence of the term accidental, on which Ronald Broude puns in the title of his article, the semiotic nature of musical notation makes the distinction all the more difficult. Any and all graphic aspects of notation can convey meaning. In Chapter 2 above, I discuss the question of semiotic equivalents, that is, symbols that have the same significance in certain contexts. But the qualities of notation that make semiotic equivalents possible are not necessarily accidental. My second example involved the transcription of a vocal part originally written in tenor C-clef to the transposing treble clef (see Example 2–2). But some semiotic information is lost in the transcription, for example, the indication of what vocal range the composer specifies for this part. Because the two versions do not differ substantively, they can be considered semiotic equivalents. The notion of substantives, then, is a useful one in discussing musical notation, and determining when specific symbols do carry equivalent meaning. But the transcription does differ semiotically from J. S. Bach's notation, and in a way that is more than "accidental." Therefore the idea of selecting a copy-text whose accidentals are to be incorporated into the edited text (already problematic in literature) becomes virtually meaningless in music.

[13] On Byron, see McGann, "The Text, the Poem, and the Problem of Historical Method." Blake: McGann, *The Textual Condition*, pp. 39–59. Pound: McGann, *The Textual Condition*, pp. 101–76.

[14] See Broude, "When Accidentals Are Substantive." See also Feder, *Musikphilologie*, p. 59.

Finally, should the composer's autograph or a first edition printed during the composer's lifetime stand as the principal source of a work?[15] Obviously the question arises in only those cases where both sources survive, and so is irrelevant for almost all music before 1700; but for much since then it has generated some debate. Both sources can be misleading. Composers are fully capable of changing their minds at any stage during the preparation of pre-publication and published states, and both sources can transmit errors. Neither, then, is infallible, as Max Friedländer recognized early in the twentieth century, and others since him.[16] Therefore, on purely theoretical grounds, it is impossible to posit a preference for the autograph over the first edition or vice versa.

We come now to the one theory that I believe holds promise for editing either literature or music, and that is the understanding of the work in its social and historical context. As discussed in Chapter 1, my exposure to this approach began with the writings of Jerome McGann, whose views are discussed above. The clearest exposition of the theory in the field of music was, curiously enough, published in a philological journal, the article by Klaus Harro Hilzinger.[17] Above, I mention the relationship between Hilzinger's account and theories of genetic editing, as well as the critique of Carl Dahlhaus.[18] There, too, are given my principal reasons for endorsing the approach. Here I would only add that, in a sense, it is an anti-method. Its theoretical content ends with the recognition of a work of art as a social and historical artifact. Once that point is reached, the historical context and circumstances of survival guide the editor instead of any single theory.

Indeed, each of the theories discussed above supplies some useful concepts for producing a critical edition based on historical principles. The idea of identifying substantive elements of musical notation, borrowed from the copy-text method, can facilitate the evaluation of semiotic equivalents, although its companion concept, the accidental, is not similarly applicable. Stemmatic filiation illuminates the historical relationships between the texts, and sometimes the sources, of a work. In many cases, however, the reconstruction of an archetype holds no significance for the understanding of the musical practices

[15] Altmann, "Ist die Originalhandschrift oder der Erstdruck maßgebend?" and Schmieder, "Nochmals: Originalhandschrift oder Erstdruck?"

[16] Friedländer, *Ueber musikalische Herausgeberarbeit.* See also Henle, "Über die Herausgabe von Urtexten."

[17] Hilzinger, "Über kritische Edition."

[18] Dahlhaus, "Philologie und Rezeptionsgeschichte."

that form the living tradition of the work. Most helpful among the theoretical methodologies is the notion of the "best text."

Individual sources preserve musical texts that are faithful to the circumstances in which they were created and used: they are historical documents. Their unique variants represent the way the work was performed, or might have been performed when the source in question was used. Consequently, for many works, each source is a viable record of one form of the work, and so can be treated as a possible "best text." All sources, however, have the potential to contain errors, readings that are impossible within the stylistic conventions of the repertory, as understood by the editor. These can only be identified and mended through the editor's intimate knowledge of style, processes of transmission and the work's history. Therefore no theory provides a fully self-contained method for editing, but, within the historical approach, each contributes some valuable concepts and procedures.

Sources that originated with the composer

The following discussion raises some of the typical problems that occur with different types of sources and works. The selection of examples cited here is intended to address the principles behind editorial action in a variety of contexts. In broad terms, it is possible to classify sources in two categories: those directly associated with the composer and those not.[19] All sources require consideration in their unique historical context, but this coarse differentiation provides a useful starting point. When sources associated with the composer, such as the autograph, or a printed edition published under the supervision of the composer, survive, it is possible to speak of a composer's text. The survival of such sources does not eliminate all problems, as we shall see, nor does it mean that the composer's text is the only one worth considering or even printing in a modern edition.

When such sources do not survive, the possible courses of action multiply because the evidence for the work's text is inextricably linked with the work's reception. In many cases the editor can reconstruct a text that probably agrees in many details with the composer's text, although that goal generally becomes more difficult to realize as the age of the work increases. And again texts other than the composer's may be of equal or greater interest or importance. It bears repeating

[19] Feder, *Musikphilologie*, pp. 51–52.

that music sources are almost always functional, and so the prime concern of the copyist or printer is not necessarily to replicate the text of the piece with exactitude, but often to create a usable text for the purpose at hand. Therefore, for many pieces no such thing as a composer's text has, or ever had, any real existence.

When documents that can be associated with the composer survive, they normally form the focus of the editor's attention. These are the stuff of editors' dreams: sketches, autograph drafts and fair copies, other manuscript copies produced under the composer's supervision, proofs corrected in autograph, editions printed under the Master's watchful scrutiny, and printed copies (as opposed to proofs) with autograph corrections. In the presence of even a single complete source that can be associated with the composer, the importance of those not so associated is diminished. Nevertheless careful consideration of sources from the latter group can yield important information. Sometimes posthumous editions or later copies used sources from the first category that are now lost (i.e., *recentior non deterior*), as the example of Schubert's Adagio in D♭ major D. 505, discussed in Chapter 2 above, illustrates. In other cases a later editor or scribe might have resolved problems in a source associated with the composer by conjecture. Also in Chapter 3 above, I discuss how the scribe of Pa 1119, when copying the troped Mass for the feast of Saint Martial from Adémar de Chabannes' autograph (Pa 909), silently, and perhaps subconsciously, corrected an error in the Gloria trope. This example shows that sources not associated with the composer, when considered critically, can offer the editor much useful testimony.

Each type of source can yield various sorts of information. Let us begin with the start of the compositional process. Sketch study has become a discipline in its own right. Can sketches, however, illuminate the final text as the composer intended it?[20] Sketches record what a composer might have written, and, in most cases where they differ from the finished score, they show how and where the composer changed his or her mind. Therefore the sketches will probably not yield a single useful reading unavailable in other sources. A possible exception is the sketch of the *Hammerklavier* Sonata discussed in Chapter 1 above. Paul Badura-Skoda's arguments in favour of the reading of the sketches, A♮, seem convincing, especially because this

[20] See the thoughtful and controversial article by Johnson, "Beethoven Scholars and Beethoven's Sketches"; and the commentary in Brandenburg, Drabkin and Johnson, "On Beethoven Scholars and Beethoven Sketches"; see also Kropfinger, "Von der Werkstatt zur Aufführung."

Example 4–4: Ludwig van Beethoven, *Hammerklavier* Sonata, Op. 106, first movement, bars 223–25

reading provides a dominant for the retransition back to the tonic, B♭ (see Example 4–4).[21]

It is not entirely satisfactory, however, because of the preceding open fifth, A–E, that results. The sketch implies that C♯ is to be understood, suggesting the dominant of D, the significance of which is, at best, obscure. The reading of the print, on the other hand, keeps the passage in B major until the enharmonic shift from A♯ to B♭, which raises two problems. First, as Badura-Skoda notes, the notation of the perfect fifth B♭–F as A♯–F is unusual in Beethoven, and the arrival of the tonic through an enharmonic transformation seems too weak to serve as the pivotal progression leading to the recapitulation. All these arguments depend on a conception of Beethoven's style and what is possible or probable within that conception.

Although sketches do not, in most cases, materially affect the text of the edition, they can contain some very useful information for the editor. They provide evidence of the compositional thinking that led to the final version, and this evidence might well affect how the editor reconciles, for example, conflicting evidence from two sources further along in the compositional process. Drafts, some of which will probably appear in the same sources as the sketches, render the same sort of service. A full and detailed investigation of the sketches will, in many cases, constitute a separate and independent study because of the

[21] P. Badura-Skoda, "Noch einmal zur Frage Ais oder A."

specialized nature of the work. Reliable studies and editions do exist of some sketches, and so, although it is certainly better to know as much as possible about the entire body of sources and optimal for editors to do the research themselves, it may not be absolutely necessary to duplicate these efforts. Here is another of those issues that requires sensitive and sensible judgement on the part of the editor.

With the autograph, the editor tackles the earliest principal source in the compositional process.[22] When it is the only surviving source associated with the composer, as is the case with many of the works of J. S. Bach and Mozart, for example, which were not published during their respective lifetimes, editors will accord it the first place in their deliberations, and its readings the most weight. Some autographs record more than one layer of compositional activity, like Schumann's score of the orchestral piece, Op. 52, discussed in Chapter 1 above. These layers constitute evidence of compositional revision. No theory or general policy is able to account for all the possibilities that the editor will entertain in dealing with this issue.

At any stage in the compositional process, the composer can have second thoughts; conversely, those responsible for the text at any stage, including composers in their autographs, might make copying errors; and copying errors can be detected and emended by the composer or others involved in the copying and preparation of the text for performance or publication. Furthermore, it is unlikely in the extreme that all errors in a previous edition will be eradicated in a subsequent one and just as likely that new corruptions will occur. Confronted with a complex history of transmission during the composer's lifetime, the editor might decide that more than one layer or version of a work is worthy of publication. Neither the theory of final authorial intentions nor the priority of first thoughts adequately accommodates all possible situations.

The process of revision, beginning with alterations to the autograph, documents the transformation of the work from a psychological state, existing only in the mind of the composer, to a social state, in which the composer attempts to communicate the work to the public, however that might be defined. In the process, the composer undoubtedly re-evaluates the work and in consequence often introduces changes. Other alterations, however, may come about because

[22] On the use of compositional autographs in editing, see Feder, "Das Autograph als Quelle wissenschaftlicher Edition"; and Herttrich, "Autograph–Edition–Interpretation."

of suggestions or pressures from other areas: publishers, patrons, critics, friends, colleagues or performers. If a composer has responded to the audience in some concrete way, such as by a revision of a work, those revisions should be given every bit as serious consideration as those introduced by the composer independently. It is true that some alterations might be made entirely against the wishes of the composer, but even then changes executed unwillingly by composers (or by another without their consent) might help to define the public state of the piece and so deserve consideration for inclusion, in some form, in the edition.

The composer may be exposed to these influences already at the stage of the autograph. The context of every correction and alteration must be considered in an attempt to judge its origin. Linda Correll Roesner documents the alterations that Schumann made in the autograph of his F Minor Piano Sonata, Op. 14.[23] Schumann undertook some significant revisions to the work between 3 February 1836, when he first submitted the Sonata to Tobias Haslinger in Vienna for publication, and 5 June 1836, the date of completion entered at the end of the Finale.[24] These included the suppression of the two Scherzos (the second and third movements within the original five-movement scheme), the replacement of the original Finale with a newly composed movement (completed 5 June) that may, in fact, relate to Schumann's first thoughts for the Finale, and a new coda for the opening movement.

Roesner posits that these revisions may have resulted from suggestions and comments by the publisher. Here again, as in the case of Schumann's Op. 52, the composer is responding to the commercial requirements of a publisher with compositional revision. And in the Sonata, too, it is apparently impossible to return to the state of the piece when it was first submitted to Haslinger in February 1836 because Schumann discarded the original Finale. Therefore, whatever Schumann's regard was for that Finale, he preserved only the new movement, of June 1836.

Schumann did not, however, abandon other aspects of that original state of the piece with the publication of the Sonata by Haslinger in 1836. Soon after, he seems to have pursued a second set of revisions among which were a rehabilitation of the second Scherzo

[23] L. C. Roesner, "The Autograph of Schumann's Piano Sonata."
[24] *Ibid.*, pp. 100–11.

(which thus became the second of four movements) and the reinstatement of several passages that had been covered with paste-overs, presumably during the first period of revision.[25] Not all of these alterations entered the second edition, which did not appear until 1853, issued by Julius Schuberth of Hamburg. From this evidence, Roesner deduces that the autograph of the Sonata did not serve as the exemplar for the engraving of the second edition, but that a third revision, which incorporated some of the changes from the second group of alterations, immediately preceded the print of 1853. This account shows that Schumann's actions reflect a balance, not always optimal in his own mind, between commercial and artistic motivation.

When more than one source associated with the composer survives, the situation becomes more complicated, but does not, in essence, differ. Such sources might include, for example, the autograph, an apograph prepared by a professional copyist to serve as the copy for engraving, proofs corrected in autograph, an edition printed under the supervision of the composer, and a printed copy with autograph corrections. As in the case of variants in the autograph, any disagreement within this constellation of sources could have arisen from a copying error or an authentic revision from the composer. Sometimes a piece exists in two concretely identifiable versions, such as Hindemith's *Das Marienleben*, each of which deserves editorial attention as a separate work. Documentary evidence, such as correspondence, diary entries, memoirs, and contemporary journalism and other printed sources, may illuminate issues of authenticity regarding these sources and their readings, as Cliff Eisen shows in his study of the Mozart Salzburg sources.

Apographs present particular difficulties of assessment. They are authentic copies, prepared under the direct supervision of the composer, but it is not always possible to verify their authenticity. Sometimes the apograph bears autograph corrections or annotations; others can be identified through documentary evidence, such as correspondence or invoices for professional copying services rendered; finally circumstantial evidence, like the identification in the source of the hand of a scribe whose work is elsewhere known to be associated with the composer, can assist the researcher in recognizing a copy as an apograph. But, with the authentication of the source, we do not

[25] *Ibid.*, pp. 111–21.

necessarily confirm the authenticity of its readings.[26] Where the composer has entered a correction in autograph, we can verify that the reading is authentic, but those readings that are not changed do not signify that the composer proofread them carefully and ascertained that they were correct.

This distinction is of importance because, in the absence of the autograph, these copies take the place of the most authoritative sources, and, if the identification is firm, they should be given the same weight, in matters such as attribution as well as authority of readings, as a copy in the composer's own hand. Even if the autograph survives, an apograph can be useful for corroborating readings; in some cases it might even supersede the authority of the autograph, when, for example, the composer has taken advantage of the preparation of an apograph to make revisions. Again documentary evidence and supporting testimony from subsequent editions known to be published with the composer's approval would confirm the authenticity of these revisions.

Performing materials that are contemporary with the composer can be problematic. Often they contain a variety of marks, alterations and corrections through which editors will have to sift in order to isolate the information that is important for their work. Can any of these performing materials be proven to be associated with a performance given under the supervision of the composer? If the answer is no, they are not without interest as I shall discuss below. If they can be associated with the composer, the marks can probably be divided into two classes: supplementary performing indications and substantive changes to the text. The first is familiar to all practising musicians: fingerings, bowings, pedalling, breathing indications, tempo marks, dynamics, accents and other marks of articulation, and other expression marks the performer might require. As is the case with sketches, the editor is likely to learn a great deal about the history of the text and the environment in which it was performed (again information that will be of great importance in assessing the style of the piece) without necessarily extracting any readings that will improve the edition in substance.

The second category of marks to be found in performing materials, substantive changes to the text, requires more consideration. Which of these are genuine second thoughts of the composer, perhaps

[26] Feder, *Musikphilologie*, pp. 52–53.

inspired by the composer's hearing the piece in rehearsal, and which ones have been entered on the initiative of the performers? Schubert's Mass in F major, D. 105, provides a good example. In addition to an autograph score, autograph parts, which were prepared for the first performance in 1814, survive.[27] In the score, Schubert altered the harmonic scheme near the beginning of the Kyrie to arrive on A major, V of D minor, instead of the tonic (bars 20–24).[28] The revised version appears above an erasure in the parts for the second and third desks of both first and second violins, and so it would seem that he copied the earlier version into these parts first, and then replaced it with the revision. The parts for the first desks of both sections, however, show no sign of correction.

Schubert, then, undertook the revision during the copying of the parts after he had completed two copies for each of the violin sections. He subsequently copied an additional part for each section, which was eventually assigned to the first desks, presumably because it incorporated the revision without erasure. And only later did he enter the revision in the score. Here, and in many other places, Talia Pecker Berio, the editor of the work for the Neue Schubert-Ausgabe, accepts the reading of the performing materials. Where the original version can be reconstructed, as in the example from the Kyrie, the editor will have to decide whether these two states constitute independent versions, each worthy of an independent edition, or that one or the other state deserves preference.

Sources not directly associated with the composer

When sources that are associated with the composer survive, what is the value of sources that are not? If they contain variants that cannot be directly attributed to the composer, how should the editor treat them? An assessment of the degree to which the text of the work was fixed by the composer will determine an editorial course of action. Did he or she understand the relationship between composer and performer as one that permitted, or even encouraged, certain freedoms with the text? Each composer, and perhaps every piece, will require a

[27] Score: Vienna, Stadt- und Landesbibliothek, MS MH 13. Parts: New York, Pierpont Morgan Library, Cary Music Collection; two second violin parts in private hands. See Deutsch, *Franz Schubert: Thematisches Verzeichnis*, p. 76; and Schubert, *Messe in F*, ed. Berio, p. 231b.

[28] For the original reading of the score, see Schubert, *Messe in F*, ed. Berio, p. 252; see also *ibid.*, pp. 231c–32a.

re-evaluation of this issue. As discussed above, it is conventional in the musical environment within which many composers work to delegate at least some discretion about certain aspects of the text to the performer; one such area, obviously, is ornamentation.

When ornaments have been written out in full by a composer, should we accept that there is only this one way of performing them? For example, when Arcangelo Corelli's Sonatas, Op. 5, were reprinted in 1710, decorations attributed to the composer were added to the slow movements of the six sonatas that form its first part.[29] If the attribution to Corelli is correct, should his version be considered as definitive? The answer will involve a thorough understanding of the performance practice associated with the piece. Should the editor find that the composer intended the performer to take certain freedoms with the text, what would be the status of two sources that give differing versions of the ornamentation? In theory, each would carry equal weight, regardless of how close either stood to the composer's own ideas of ornamenting. Moreover, a full realization by the composer, like that attributed to Corelli for his Op. 5, would not necessarily possess greater authority, although it would, of course, hold a great deal of interest for the work's audience.

Any source that provides written-out ornaments attests to the reception of the work on the part of performers or scribes, and, as such, can offer valuable guidance to modern performers and critics. The eighteenth-century music historian, John Hawkins, published a decorated version of Corelli's Sonata, Op. 5 no. 9 (not, incidentally, one of the sonatas provided with ornaments in the 1710 reprint), which he claimed to represent the performing practice of Francesco Geminiani.[30] In most cases, however, these realizations do not constitute a fixed part of the work's text, even when they come from the pen of the composer. They simply represent various ways of filling out the ornaments that the composer indicated in the text or understood would be supplied in performance.[31] To be sure, many users of a modern edition will require some assistance in understanding the style and conventions of the ornamentation, and the available source materials can be enlisted to render that service. How the editor might

[29] Corelli, *Les Œuvres de Arcangelo Corelli*, III, part 1, *VI Sonate ... Op. 5, I*, ed. Joachim and Chrysander. See Boyden, "The Corelli 'Solo' Sonatas."

[30] Geminiani's version printed in Hawkins, *A General History*, II, 904–7; cf. Corelli, *Les Œuvres*, III, part 2, *Preludii, Allemande ... Op. 5, II*, ed. Joachim and Chrysander, 80–84.

[31] See Meister, "Die Praxis der 'gelenkten Improvisation' und der 'Urtext'."

provide access to those materials is a matter for discussion in the next chapter.

The example of ornamentation demonstrates, however, that sources not associated with the composer can significantly amplify our knowledge of the text and how it was treated in performance, even when sources that derive from the composer exist. This knowledge illuminates, for the editor, the musical practices of the milieu in which the piece was composed and circulated. These sources will not necessarily provide any useful readings for the final edited text, like much of the evidence the editor will consult, but they may suggest how the readings in the composer's own sources might be evaluated. A similar situation obtains with other types of secondary sources, such as later editions and scholarly treatments of the work. The English editions of several of Beethoven's works for pianoforte, in particular the Sonatas Opp. 106, 110 and 111, the Bagatelles Op. 119, and the Variations Op. 121a, were issued somewhat later than the Vienna editions, and Beethoven profited from the interval to correct some corruptions that had crept into the Viennese prints. Some of these English editions (Opp. 110, 111 and 119), moreover, were brought out under the supervision of Muzio Clementi, whose editorial scrutiny resulted in some other textual improvements over the first editions. The English editions, therefore, are truly *recentiores non deteriores*, and are essential sources for these pieces.[32]

Of course this second group of sources, those not associated with the composer, takes on paramount importance when no source from the other group survives. For a great deal of music (almost everything up to 1600 and a large amount after that date), this is the only type of source available to the editor. If the source is not directly associated with the composer, at what remove does it stand? The answer to this question will in turn lead to a consideration of why the source in question was created and why this piece (the one being edited) forms part of its contents.[33] The motivation, liturgical, musical, social and political, for incorporating a Mass by Josquin into two codices widely separated in time and place might be very different.

For example, among the sources for his *Missa Malheur me bat* are two that differ significantly in date and place of origin. One (Rome, Biblioteca Apostolica Vaticana, Cappella Sistina, MS 23), was copied

[32] Tyson, *The Authentic English Editions of Beethoven*, pp. 28–34, especially 33, and 102–7 (Op. 106), 110–13 (Op. 111), 114–16 (Op. 119), 117–20 (Op. 110), 121–25 (Op. 121a).

[33] See Feder, *Musikphilologie*, pp. 52–56.

in Rome for the Sistine Chapel in the first decade or so of the sixteenth century; the other (Rostock, Bibliothek der Wilhelm-Pieck-Universität, MS Mus. Saec. XVI-40 [1–5]) is a set of five partbooks copied during the second half of the sixteenth century, probably in Rostock.[34] What performing forces were available in the institutions for which the codices were created, what were the institutions' liturgical needs, and what effect did Josquin's status, his nationality and his professional activities (or lack thereof) in the two regions in question have on the codices' compilers? These factors could well provoke quite a different response to the piece in each instance, and so affect the editor's appraisal of the source and its testimony. In fact, Smijers, Josquin's editor, reports many slight melodic and orthographic variants in the Rostock partbooks that could well be the result of the more distant origin of the source from the central performing tradition of the piece.[35]

This example demonstrates that a central issue in dealing with sources not produced under the composer's direct supervision is the editor's control of scribal initiative. How much freedom did a scribe, engraver or editor assume when copying a work? It would seem to be in inverse proportion to the level of specificity to be found in the composer's score. One appealing paradigm for understanding the course of Western music history is that of an ever increasing precision in notation, from pitch in the eleventh century, and rhythm in the thirteenth, to dynamics in the works of Giovanni Gabrieli, tempi fixed by metronome marks in the nineteenth century, and continual inflation in the number of expression marks, up to the works of composers like Schoenberg and Stockhausen, in whose works nearly every note (sometimes in very complex scores, indeed) carries a specific instruction that governs volume, timbre and expression.[36] The ultimate manifestation of this tendency to date is the work of some composers in electronic music, who record the sounds or instructions directly on

[34] Josquin, *Werken*, XIX, in *Missen*, II, ed. Smijers (Amsterdam, 1939), p. VII. See also *Census-Catalogue of Manuscript Sources*, III, 121 (Rostock), and IV, 36–37 (Vatican).

[35] Josquin, *Werken*, XIX, ed. Smijers, pp. XIII–XIV.

[36] E.g., Schönberg, *Fünf Orchesterstücke Opus 16*, in *Orchesterwerke I*, ed. Kokkinis, 1–69; see especially Schoenberg's instruction regarding dynamics at the beginning of the third piece, *Farben (Sommermorgen am See)*, *ibid.*, p. 35. Stockhausen, *Nr. 2 Klavierstücke I–IV*, requires the pianist to perform chords in which each note has a different dynamic. For a discussion of this trend in musical notation, see Feder, *Musikphilologie*, pp. 97–98. Cf. Goehr, *The Imaginary Museum*, pp. 187–89, 224–27, who sees a dramatic change in the density of notational devices beginning around 1800; and Butt, *Music Education and the Art of Performance*, pp. 121–65, who observes that on occasion the composer assumes the responsibility for fully noting ornaments.

to electro-magnetic tape or computer disk, bypassing the middleman of the performer altogether, although not achieving complete control of performance, as noted above in Chapter 1.

Somewhere along the line, the discretion of the performer all but disappeared. My discussion above shows, however, that, for a great deal of music in the Western art tradition, perhaps even the majority, significant liberties were tolerated and even encouraged in performance. The score or text becomes the starting point for a dialogue between composer and performer, a dialogue that is renewed with each performance. The nature of the liberties that can be taken is determined by the performers' experience with and knowledge of the stylistic boundaries of the piece or repertory, as well as their technical abilities. In some repertories, especially those recorded with less specific notation, it is entirely possible for the stylistic boundaries to be defined in performance, rather than in the text. Unfortunately we can never recapture the full scope of that performing tradition.

Some traces of it might remain, however, in the written tradition. The example cited above from Corelli's violin sonatas is particularly instructive because we have good evidence of the composer's original text as well as his own conception of how the slow movements might be ornamented in performance (or at least a conception attributed to him, which would still constitute evidence of the reception of the piece). In older repertories, it is less likely that the surviving documents record the composer's text. Scribes and compilers exercised their independent initiative to alter the text in line with their aesthetic and musical sense. In so doing, they could very well record aspects of the performing tradition. That is, when they chose to inscribe a particular reading, they might have responded to their aural recollection of specific performances of the piece, perhaps by themselves. They also might be influenced by the range of possibilities inherent in the cultural milieu in which the piece was performed; they write down a virtual, instead of an actual, performance.

The creators of the written sources, then, appropriate to themselves the liberties envisaged to be the province of performers. It is up to the editor to judge, in specific cases, the degree to which this appropriation has occurred.[37] In many cases, the written versions are only the tip of the iceberg in relation to the wealth of performing variants that

[37] I cite, as an example, my discussion of the twelfth-century Aquitanian *uersus* repertory, "Scribal Practices."

surrounded these pieces. They do, however, reflect the type of variants the performing environment permitted or encouraged to be added to the repertory. Therefore each surviving version potentially possesses equal validity as a representation of the performing possibilities intrinsic to the tradition of the piece and as such is worthy of an independent edition. Each is its own "best text."

The application of stemmatic filiation

Because of the varying circumstances under which sources of the same piece might have been produced, the editor may enlist the technique of stemmatic filiation here to good effect. If contamination and conjectural emendation are controllable, the editor should be able to determine the text of the archetype. In not all cases, however, will the text of the archetype appear in the edition, nor does it necessarily have any primeval position of authority beside which the extant versions are defective shadows. Critically employed, however, the archetype's text, even though it may never have been performed, or perhaps even existed in a concrete sense, can illuminate the relationships between those extant versions and help to isolate the contributions to the history of the piece exhibited in them. Some of these idiosyncrasies are sure to be corruptions and the editor should attempt to eliminate them from consideration. Others, however, are the unique substantive variants from the performing tradition that have been captured in the process of writing the piece out. Hence developments in sources at the bottom of the stemma often carry just as great an import to the final shape of the edited text as readings in the archetype.

Above I discussed the dangers and virtues of using this approach, but here it will be instructive to see how it assists our efforts with two repertories, each of which raises unique problems. The first is the tradition of Josquin's motets, discussed above in Chapter 3, specifically *Domine, ne in furore*, whose transmission splits along regional lines.[38] It is possible that none of the extant sources completely represents Josquin's own text of the work, but it may be possible to reconstruct certain elements of it via the stemma published by Hoffmann-Erbrecht. The stemma splits into two principal branches, and so the agreement of any source from the Italian branch with any source on the transalpine branch guarantees the reading of the archetype.

[38] Hoffmann-Erbrecht, "Problems in the Interdependence of Josquin Sources," pp. 291–92.

Example 4–5: Josquin Desprez, *Domine, ne in furore* alto and tenor, bars 142–46

The difficulty with this approach is that it ignores the kind of scribal initiatives common in music sources of the sixteenth century.[39] In those cases where the editor must reconcile two or more readings of equal stemmatic weight, they all may obscure the composer's reading in some way. Therefore it might be impossible to eradicate readings that originated with the scribes altogether, with the result that the editor will probably not want to print the eclectic text generated by the stemma. Smijers, for example, chooses to publish the text given by Petrucci in his 1519 print, which he follows in places where the Italian and German traditions provide readings of equal stemmatic and stylistic weight.[40] At bars 142–46, for example, alto and tenor engage in an imitative passage. One of the traditions, and it is by no means clear which, has reversed the two parts (see Example 4–5).[41] Smijers prints Petrucci's version. Nevertheless, the stemma does provide useful information, principally the regional division of the sources. It also isolates those variants that distinguish the regional traditions. These can, in turn, illuminate copying and performing practices that affected the transmission of the motet, and subsequently affect our evaluation of sources produced under similar circumstances.

Quite a different situation is presented by the Haydn String Quartets Op. 33, whose autograph is lost. Two of the principal sources, however, can be connected with the composer: the manu-

[39] See, e.g., Blackburn, "Josquin's Chansons."

[40] Josquin, *Werken*, XXI, in *Motteten*, II, Bundel, 8, ed. Smijers (Amsterdam, 1942), no. 39, pp. 81–87. [41] See Josquin, *Werken*, XXI, ed. Smijers, p. XVI.

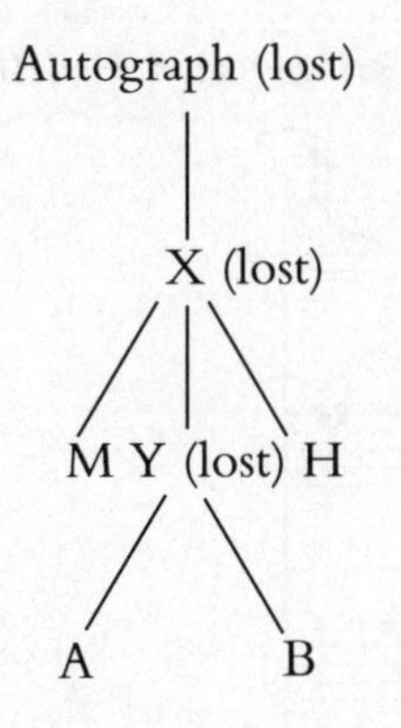

Figure 4–1

script parts now in Melk (Benediktinerstift, Musikarchiv, MSS VI, 736–39; hereafter M) and the first publication, by Artaria in Vienna, dated April 1782 (hereafter A).[42] They contain shared errors that indicate they derive from a common source. Two other sources, the print by Hummel (Berlin and Amsterdam, May 1782; hereafter H) and the manuscript in Budapest (Országos Széchényi Könyvtár, MS K 1148; hereafter B), also agree in error with AM, showing that they derive from the same source. Despite Feder's contention that Haydn almost never made scribal errors, it is possible that this common source was Haydn's autograph.[43] Nevertheless Feder and Gerlach posit an intermediary copy of the autograph as the source common to AMBH. Moreover, AB agree against MH in error, and so they depend on a second intermediary source unknown to the other witnesses. Witnesses MH do not agree in error, and so Feder and Gerlach propose a tripartite stemma. (See Figure 4–1.) The threefold division depends entirely on the absence of shared error in MH, an argument from silence, as discussed in Chapter 3 above. It is possible that, in any of the passages where MH agree in giving a reasonable competing reading, they may err, a possibility that Feder and Gerlach ignore.

In application, then, any agreement of AB, or of A or B with either of M or H, guarantees the reading of Y, and any agreement of MY (that is, MA or MB), YH (similarly, AH or BH) or MH determines the reading of X, the copy of the autograph posited by Feder and Gerlach. For example, in the opening movement of Hob. III:41, the

[42] See Feder and Gerlach, *Streichquartette "opus 20" und "opus 33": Kritischer Bericht*, pp. 19, 20, 22, 24 (on the sources), and 29–31 (on their relationship). See also Feder, "Textkritische Methoden," pp. 95–96.

[43] "Haydn hat selten eine falsche Note geschrieben." Feder, "Textkritische Methoden," p. 85.

Example 4–6: Joseph Haydn, String Quartet, Hob. III:41, first movement, bar 251

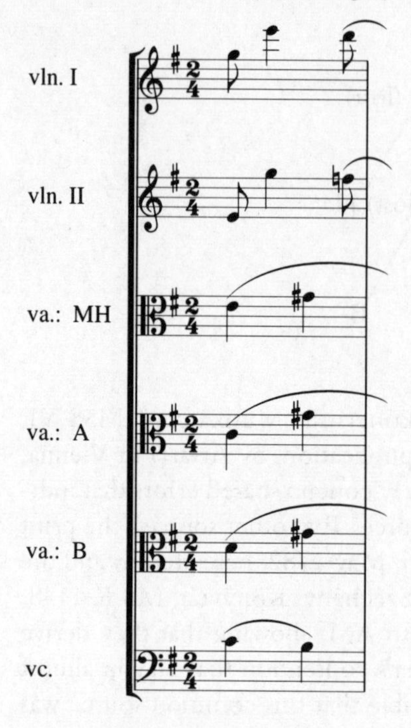

witnesses differ in their reading for the first note in the viola, bar 251 (see Example 4–6).[44] Feder and Gerlach print the reading of MH. It is most likely that Y transmitted the reading D, clearly an error because of the C major harmony. It was emended by conjecture for Artaria's print (although not with felicity because the part now leaps by augmented fifth C–G♯), and was copied, unremarked, into B.

In another passage, the editors accept the reading of BH over the agreement of AM, despite the fact that the latter are treated as the principal sources. In bar 79 of the Finale of Hob. III:38, AM give the note C as the pickup to bar 80 in the second violin, a clear error on harmonic grounds and on the basis of the parallel passage at bar 8 (see Example 4–7).[45] This reading, however, calls into question the estab-

[44] Feder and Gerlach, *Streichquartette "opus 20" und "opus 33": Kritischer Bericht*, p. 54. See also Haydn, *Streichquartette "opus 20" und "opus 33"*, ed. Feder and Gerlach, p. 110.

[45] Haydn, *Streichquartette "opus 20" und "opus 33"*, ed. Feder and Gerlach, pp. 128, 130; and Feder and Gerlach, *Streichquartette "opus 20" und "opus 33": Kritischer Bericht*, p. 58.

Example 4–7: Joseph Haydn, String Quartet, Hob. III:38, fourth movement

a. bars 79–80

b. bars 8–9

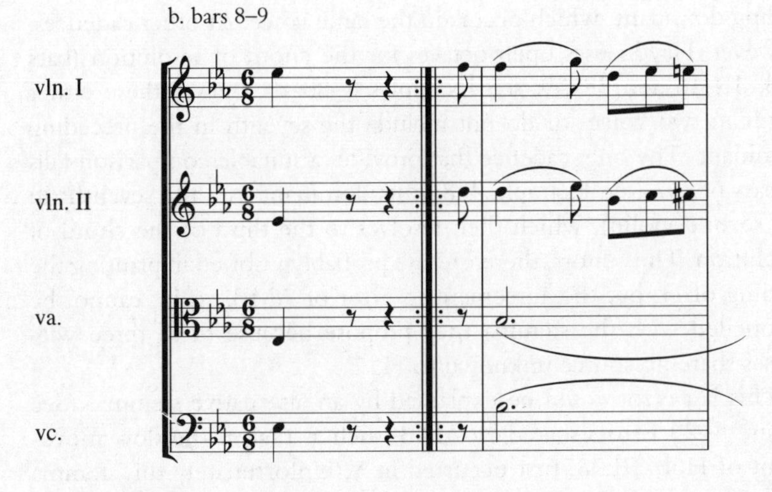

lished stemma. The disposition of the readings generates a limited number of explanations, most of which are unlikely. Witnesses AM could have erred independently, but there is no palaeographic evidence that would encourage independent error. Or the error was present in X, whence it entered A (through Y) and M; then BH might have emended conjecturally and independently. Such actions are clearly not impossible, but there does not seem to be evidence of other such conjectures in these two sources. Finally, AM might share a witness below Y. Agreements of AB in error against M argue against that conclusion. In short, Feder and Gerlach are correct in printing the shared reading of BH, but the agreement in error of AM cannot be explained satisfactorily by their stemma.

Elsewhere they ignore the stemma altogether. In the Largo of the same quartet, AMB agree in reading a full bar's rest for the second violin at bar 51, against H, which gives the note A (see Example 4–8a).[46] This cadence presents grave difficulties of interpretation because of the absence of parallel passages in the movement on the one hand, and the weight of the sources, including the two principal witnesses, AM, on the other. At first glance, the reading of H would seem reasonable and necessary because it supplies the third of the chord of resolution (F major, V) and it resolves the seventh of the preceding dominant, which occurs in the same voice. At other cadences, however, Haydn uses open octaves for the chord of resolution (bars 7–8, 15–16 and 38–39; see Examples 4–8b–d), but all these either occur in two voices or do not include the seventh in the preceding dominant. The only cadence that provides a suitable comparison falls at bars 66–67 (see Example 4–8e): its dominant uses the seventh (in the second violin), which then resolves to the third of the chord of resolution. The editors, therefore, are probably justified in printing the reading of H, but the agreement in error of AMB, again, cannot be reconciled with the stemma they propose because these three witnesses share no source unknown to H.

This last error could be explained by an alternative stemma. (See Figure 4–2.) Errors shared by AMB, such as that in the slow movement of Hob. III:38, first occurred in Y. Unfortunately this stemma does not account for the error shared by AM against BH in the Finale of the same quartet (see Example 4–7 above). This stemma also iden-

[46] Haydn, *Streichquartette "opus 20" und "opus 33"*, ed. Feder and Gerlach, p. 127; and Feder and Gerlach, *Streichquartette "opus 20" und "opus 33": Kritischer Bericht*, p. 57.

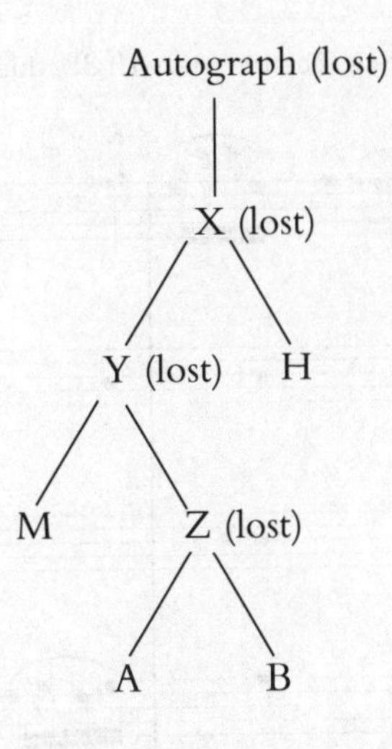

Figure 4–2

tifies H as virtually the best witness, as I discuss in Chapter 3 above, a status that conflicts with the accepted position of AM. The agreement of any of AMB with H guarantees the reading of X. For any reading of H to be challenged, all of AMB must disagree with it.

These difficulties with Feder and Gerlach's stemma do not impugn the method itself, but they raise questions about their application of it. A more important issue regarding the utility of filiation in this case is that of scribal initiative. We saw, above, that all idiosyncratic readings in the sources of Josquin's motet, *Domine, ne in furore*, are not necessarily removed through the reconstruction of the archetype. Is it appropriate here to incorporate readings of the archetype, X, into the final edition, or do the witnesses exhibit the same kind of scribal independence? In fact, virtually all the variants recorded in Feder and Gerlach's apparatus fall into two categories: scribal errors (as determined by stylistic analysis), or orthographic variants such as the position of dynamics and articulation marks.[47] None suggests the presence of scribal revision or reinterpretation. The reconstructed archetype, therefore, is likely to resemble Haydn's text much more closely than the reconstruction possible in the Josquin example, provided it is based on a sound stemma. Hence it constitutes a more reliable entity for the establishment of the final edited text, and permits the elimination of a number of readings on strictly numerical grounds.

[47] Feder and Gerlach, *Streichquartette "opus 20" und "opus 33": Kritischer Bericht*, pp. 53–68.

Example 4–8: Joseph Haydn, String Quartet, Hob. III:38, third movement

a. bars 50–51

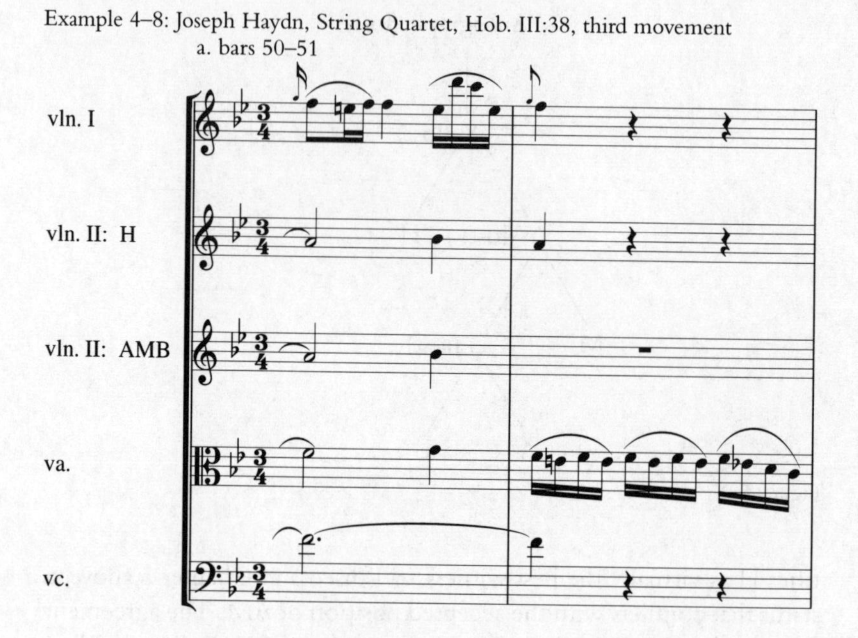

b. bars 7–8

c. bars 15–16

Eclecticism

Nevertheless, a stemma cannot solve all problems. Even where the edited text incorporates many readings from the reconstructed archetype, as in the example from Haydn, the editor must still decide between readings of equal stemmatic weight. And the more open the processes of transmission are to contamination from the oral, performing tradition and scribal independence, the more likely that the editor will rely on a single source as a "best text," using the stemma to illuminate the historical relationship between it and the other sources. We thus return to the position taken near the beginning of the discussion: every source is a special case. The editor considers each source, and perhaps each reading, on its own merits. The sources' historical circumstances and relative authority affect the weight given to each, and a stemma can assist in graphically depicting some of these relationships. Ultimately, however, it is the editor's responsibility to sift through the evidence and establish a text that best reflects the evidence of the sources.

For example, Hans Eppstein, who describes but does not print a stemma in his edition of the Bach Suites for Violoncello Solo BWV 1007–12 (as discussed in Chapter 3 above), prints readings from all four principal sources in his final edited text. At several places where three of the sources agree against the fourth, he selects the singular reading despite the implications of his stemmatic deductions.[48] In particular, he prefers the reading of B (Kellner's copy) over the agreement of ACD (Magdalena Bach's copy and the later copies associated with Westphal and Traeg) in some eleven passages, a preference that offers a measure of support for the bipartite stemma I suggest above in Chapter 3. Even more striking is the eclecticism exhibited by Alan Curtis in his edition of Monteverdi's *L'incoronazione di Poppea.* According equal weight to both manuscript scores, Curtis prints readings from both, "giving only those [variants] I felt were somehow 'usable' or at least 'curious'. Those just plain wrong have been omitted."[49]

Theoretical sources

Discussions of the work or repertory in theoretical sources form a final group of sources that deserve special consideration.[50] One issue of particular importance is to determine whether the theorist's comments are descriptive or prescriptive. Discussions in the former category can be very helpful in forming a conception of the critical reception of the piece. Prescriptive comments, however, can be misleading. A

[48] Eppstein, *Sechs Suiten für Violoncello solo: Kritischer Bericht*, p. 23.

[49] Monteverdi, *L'incoronazione di Poppea*, ed. Curtis, p. xb. The manuscripts are Venice, Biblioteca Nazionale Marciana, MS It. IV 439 (= 9963), and Naples, Conservatorio di Musica S Pietro a Majella, MS Rari 6.4.1. Curtis' treatment of these sources accords with Alessandra Chiarelli's stemmatic assessment, "*L'Incoronazione di Poppea* o *Il Nerone*."

[50] Feder, *Musikphilologie*, pp. 34–35.

Example 4–9: Gradual *Saluum fac seruum* beginning, Marchetto of Padua, *Lucidarium* 11.4.62

theorist might be judging a piece or repertory on the basis of some abstract standard, the knowledge and understanding of which can be valuable for apprehending the theorist's conception of musical practices in that work or repertory. But such prescriptive comments might give a false idea of the readings of the actual piece under discussion. Modal theory in plainsong provides an example.

Theorists attempted to classify plainsong melodies according to the eight ecclesiastical modes for two reasons. First, melodies, such as antiphons and the responsories in matins, functioned as refrains for verses that were sung to recitation formulae. Singers needed to know the modal identity of these melodies in order to select the correct formula for the verse. Second, the mode determined the placement of the melody within the gamut, and therefore fixed the position of tones and semitones within the melody. Not all plainsong melodies fit the system, however. One example is the Lenten Gradual *Saluum fac seruum*. The fourteenth-century theorist, Marchetto of Padua, discusses two possible versions of this melody, one beginning on B and ending on D, the usual final of mode 1, and the other beginning on F and ending on A, the cofinal of the same mode.[51] He expresses a preference for the latter on aesthetic grounds, alluding to other authorities who believe that it sounds better when it begins with two consecutive whole tones (see Example 4–9).[52]

As Example 4–9 shows, however, a graver difficulty may be the ascent through a diminished fifth, B–F, with which the version on B commences. Marchetto further notes that, when the melody ascends, the version on F requires F♯, a note that, technically, does not exist on

[51] Marchetto of Padua, *Lucidarium*, 11.4.59–72, ed. and trans. Herlinger, pp. 420–27.

[52] Example 4–9 is taken from Marchetto, *Lucidarium*, 11.4.62, ed. and trans. Herlinger, pp. 422–23. Herlinger construes the example from the surrounding discussion, even though no suitable example exists in the sources of the treatise; see *ibid.*, p. 423 note u.

the gamut. He therefore proposes that the other version (that beginning on B) be modified to begin on B♭, also a note not found on the gamut.[53] He finds that difficulty to be "less incommodious" than the F♯ necessary for the version beginning on F.[54] The problem with this discussion lies in Marchetto's attempt to make the melody fit modal theory. No extant medieval source preserves the melody in the form prescribed by Marchetto.[55] Moreover, the earliest surviving version with accurate pitch information, that in Montpellier, Bibliothèque de l'École de Médecine (hereafter Mo), MS H. 159, a version clearly unknown to Marchetto, begins on B and avoids all the problems that concerned Marchetto (see Example 4–10).[56] Faced with a melody that did not accord with his notion of the gamut, Marchetto modified the melody to accommodate the theory. His discussion still holds interest for its treatment of modal theory, but it does not contribute to any text-critical consideration of this plainsong.

The ongoing dialogue between composer and theorist can provide important evidence, especially when they are the same person, as in the case of Rameau, Schoenberg, Hindemith and Babbitt. Hindemith himself stated that the revision of *Das Marienleben* (which was not to appear until 1948) would constitute a "practical elucidation" of the principles enunciated in *The Craft of Musical Composition*.[57] The practices of composers continually reshape the thinking of theorists, but composers themselves do not necessarily remain immune to critical and intelligent discussions of musical form, style and idiom. On the matter of contrapuntal techniques, for example, Haydn, Mozart and Beethoven were all influenced by Johann Joseph Fux's *Gradus ad Parnassum*, as their careful studies of the text indicate.[58] Contemplation of this text and the com-

[53] Marchetto, *Lucidarium*, 11.4.65–71, ed. and trans. Herlinger, pp. 422–27.

[54] "Minus inconveniens"; Marchetto, *Lucidarium*, 11.4.65, ed. and trans. Herlinger, pp. 422–23.

[55] See the discussion in Herlinger, ed. and trans., *The Lucidarium*, p. 421 note s.

[56] Mo H. 159, fol. 82v, where it is written over an erasure; a second version of the melody for the refrain is cancelled. Transcribed in Hansen, *H 159 Montpellier*, no. 773, pp. 237–38.

[57] "Praktische Erläuterung"; Hindemith, *Unterweisung in Tonsatz: Theoretischer Teil*, p. 252. This passage is omitted from the English translation, *The Craft of Musical Composition*, I, *Theoretical Part*, trans. Mendel. See Neumeyer, *The Music of Paul Hindemith*, pp. 137–67.

[58] On Haydn, see Mann, "Haydn as Student"; and "Haydn's Elementarbuch." On Mozart, see Oldman, Heartz and Mann, "Zum vorliegenden Band," in *Thomas Attwoods Theorie- und Kompositionsstudien bei Mozart*, ed. Hertzmann, Oldman, Heartz and Mann, pp. VII–XVIII. On Beethoven, see Nottebohm, *Beethoveniana*, pp. 177–97 (revised version of "Beethoven's theoretische Studien," *Allgemeine Musikalische Zeitung*, ser. 2, 1 [1863], 685–91, 701–8, 717–22, 749–54, 770–75, 784–89, 810–14, 825–29, 839–43; and "Nachtrag au dem Artikel 'Beethoven's theoretische Studien'," *Allgemeine Musikalische Zeitung*, ser. 2, 2 [1864], 153–58,169–72). In general, see Mann, "Preface to this Edition," in Fux, *Gradus ad Parnassum*, ed. Mann, pp. XVIIb–XIX.

Example 4–10: Gradual *Saluum fac seruum* Mo H. 159, fol. 82v

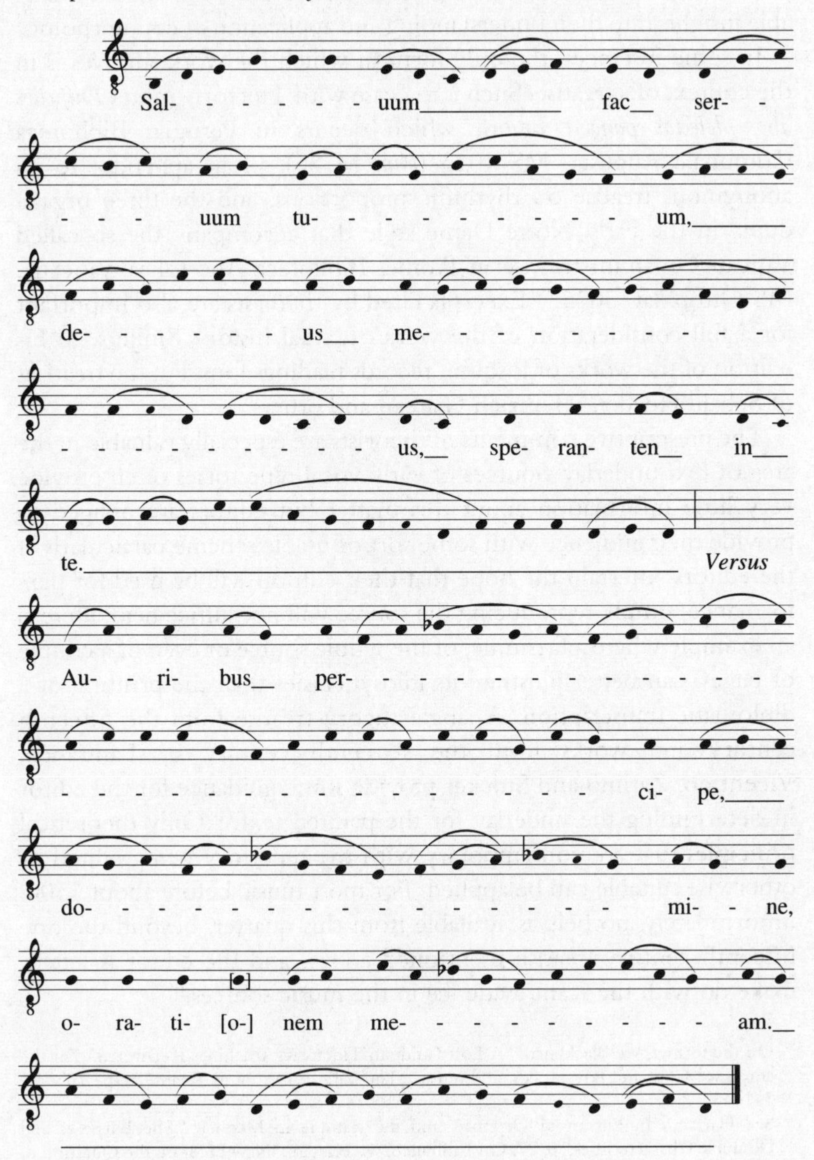

posers' reactions to it might well furnish editors of their works with valuable insights into their understanding and application of counterpoint.

In some instances, the only form in which the work survives is in the context of a treatise. Such is the case with Tinctoris' motet *Difficiles alios delectat pangere cantus*, which occurs in Perugia, Biblioteca Comunale Augusta, MS 1013 (*olim* M 36), as an appendix to an anonymous treatise on rhythmic proportions, and the three organa dupla in the early Notre Dame style that accompany the so-called Vatican Organum treatise in Rome, Biblioteca Apostolica Vaticana, MS Ottob. lat. 3025.[59] Excerpts cited by theorists are also important for a full consideration of the work's textual history. Smijers, in his edition of the works of Josquin, records readings found in the treatises of Sebald Heyden, Heinrich Glarean and others.

The prescriptive comments of theorists are especially valuable in the area of text underlay. Sources of early vocal repertories often provide very little information about this matter but editors are obliged to provide their audience with some sort of usable scheme particularly if the editors entertain the hope that their edition will be used for performance; simply reproducing the source will not suffice here. Here is an example where a facsimile, of the whole source or even of a couple of pages, can better illustrate its idiosyncrasies than the printing of a diplomatic transcription. A single theory treatise from the fifteenth century and works from the sixteenth century by Lanfranco, Vicentino, Zarlino and Stocker provide some guidance for the editor in determining the underlay for the printed text.[60] Only theoretical principles that are contemporary with the repertory being edited or otherwise suitable can be applied. For most music before about 1500, unfortunately, no help is available from this quarter, beyond the one fifteenth-century treatise mentioned above, and the editor is left to make do with the scant evidence in the music sources.[61]

[59] On the former, see Blackburn, "A Lost Guide to Tinctoris's Teachings Recovered." For the latter, see Godt and Rivera, eds. and trans., "The Vatican Organum Treatise," especially pp. 341–45.

[60] See Harrán, "In Pursuit of Origins"; and the critique in Mendel, "The Purposes and Desirable Characteristics," p. 27. On Lanfranco, see Harrán, "New Light on the Question of Text Underlay." Vicentino: Harrán, "Vicentino and His Rules of Text Underlay." Zarlino: Zarlino, *Le istitutioni harmoniche*, 4.32–33, pp. 339–41. Stocker: Lowinsky, "A Treatise on Text Underlay."

[61] See Reaney, "Text Underlay in Early Fifteenth-Century Musical Manuscripts"; Perkins, "Toward a Rational Approach to Text Placement"; H. M. Brown, "Words and Music in Early 16th-Century Chansons"; Baumann, "Silben- und Wortwiederholungen"; Harrán, "On the Question of Word–Tone Relations"; Bent, "Text Setting in Sacred Music of the Early 15th Century"; and Perz, "Zur Textunterlegungspraxis."

Editorial emendation

In the final stage of establishing the text, editors may find passages where none of the preserved readings is convincing. After defending that position they may then proceed to emend by conjecture.[62] Even though the likelihood of recovering the composer's original reading is slight, an emendation that arises from detailed knowledge of the composer's and the piece's style might well be an improvement over an engraving, typesetting or copying error. Two passages from J. S. Bach's *Brandenburg* Concerti illustrate the problem. In the first movement of the Third Concerto (BWV 1048), Bach writes parallel octaves between the second violin and the first viola (bar 122; see Example 4–11a), clearly an oversight as a second passage from the Fourth Concerto (BWV 1049) shows.[63]

In the Finale of the Fourth Concerto, the first flute and continuo proceed in parallel octaves (bar 162; see Example 4–12a). When the passage recurs in transposition (bar 166), Bach repeated the error, recognized and corrected it without returning to bar 162 and amending it there (see Example 4–12c-d).[64] Heinrich Besseler, the editor of these works for the Neue Bach-Ausgabe, sensibly alters bar 162 so that it conforms with Bach's corrected version of bar 166 (see Example 4–12b).[65] It is most likely that, had Bach noticed the similar problem in the first movement of the Third Concerto, he would have corrected it also. The octaves are not as exposed in this passage as in that from the Fourth Concerto, but, as Besseler notes while defending his emendation (see Example 4–11b), the composer adjusted the voice leading in the next bar of the Third Concerto to avoid similar octaves between the second violin and cellos and basses.[66] In fact, throughout the passage, bars 122–24, either the second or the third violin is in danger of moving in parallel octaves with a lower voice, and, in every case but the one emended by Besseler, Bach avoided the octaves by altering the figure in the upper voice. Besseler's reading does not necessarily correspond to what Bach would have written, but it at least

[62] Feder, *Musikphilologie*, p. 68.

[63] Besseler, *Sechs Brandenburgische Konzerte: Kritischer Bericht*, p. 84. The autograph is Berlin, Deutsche Staatsbibliothek, MS Am. B. 78.

[64] Besseler, *Sechs Brandenburgische Konzerte: Kritischer Bericht*, p. 99.

[65] Bach, *Sechs Brandenburgische Konzerte*, ed. Besseler, pp. 137–38.

[66] Besseler, *Sechs Brandenburgische Konzerte: Kritischer Bericht*, p. 85; cf. Bach, *Sechs Brandenburgische Konzerte*, ed. Besseler, p. 88.

Example 4–11: J. S. Bach, *Brandenburg* Concerto No. 3 BWV 1048, first movement, bar 122

Example 4–12: J. S. Bach, *Brandenburg* Concerto No. 4 BWV 1049, third movement, bars 162 and 166

provides a version that would have been stylistically acceptable to the composer.

On the other hand, the opposite extreme, the temptation to improve the composer, holds equal danger. Let the editor not be accused of printing the piece the composer would have written had he or she known as much as the editor. Nowhere is the editor's sensitivity to style and historical possibility more important than here. An extraordinary example in this regard is Jacques-Louis Monod's edition of *A Survivor from Warsaw*, Schoenberg's Op. 46.[67] In several places, Monod emends Schoenberg's text so that it accords with his

[67] Schoenberg, *A Survivor from Warsaw, Op., 46*, ed. Monod.

row analysis. He offers this justification. "Our purpose ... has been to publish a score that would not only reflect the composer's text but also attempt to solve the problems raised by any oversights contained therein."[68]

Composers sometimes make scribal errors while copying a score. For example, bar 22 employs the form of the row Monod labels as b, the first hexachord appearing in the woodwinds and two solo violas, the second in the horns. But the second trichord in the horns presents E♭ in place of E♮, which would be required by the row. The error was caught and corrected in time for the first edition, presumably by René Leibowitz, who prepared the score from which the print was engraved.[69] Leibowitz made another correction, this time in bar 34, and its reception by Monod and the editors of the Schoenberg edition shows the dangers of conjectural emendation. Beginning in bar 33, the lower strings and brass present the first hexachords of row forms A and b″, to which the upper strings, upper brass and woodwinds respond with the first hexachords of D and a (see Example 4–13a).[70]

The motive in the first and second violins and violas (bar 34), as given in Schoenberg's manuscript, does not accord with this form of the row, and outlines the uncharacteristic interval of an octave, D–D (see Example 4–13b for the competing readings and 4–13c for the score). Leibowitz' emendation of the first note in the figure, which appeared in the first edition, gives the correct pitches for the row presentation but in the wrong order. Monod restores Schoenberg's original first note and changes the last note to produce the correct pitches and order for the row. At the same time, he creates an exact motivic uniformity in the two row presentations, as now the upper strings play the same figure as the cellos and basses. This emendation forces Schoenberg's music into a rigidly prescriptive motivic and serial structure. Nevertheless, it is certainly more convincing than the solution proposed by Josef Rufer and Christian Martin Schmidt for the Schoenberg edition. They print the manuscript reading as an irregu-

[68] Schoenberg, *A Survivor from Warsaw*, ed. Monod, p. II. See also Neighbour, review of Arnold Schönberg, *Sämtliche Werke*, Abteilung V, Reihe A, Bd. 19: *Chorwerke II*, ed. Josef Rufer and Christian Martin Schmidt; *Die Jakobsleiter*, piano score, arr. Winfried Zillig; and *Weihnachtsmusik*, ed. Leonard Stein, p. 445.

[69] For the row analysis, see Schoenberg, *A Survivor from Warsaw*, ed. Monod, pp. II–III; and Schönberg, *Chorwerke II: Kritischer Bericht*, ed. Schmidt, p. 74. On this passage, see *ibid.*, p. 66; Schoenberg, *A Survivor from Warsaw* (New York, 1949), p. 5; and *idem*, *A Survivor from Warsaw*, ed. Monod, p. IV.

[70] See Schönberg, *Chorwerke II: Kritischer Bericht*, ed. Schmidt, pp. 66–67; and *idem*, *A Survivor from Warsaw*, ed. Monod, p. IV.

Example 4–13: Arnold Schoenberg, *A Survivor from Warsaw* Op. 46, bars 33–34

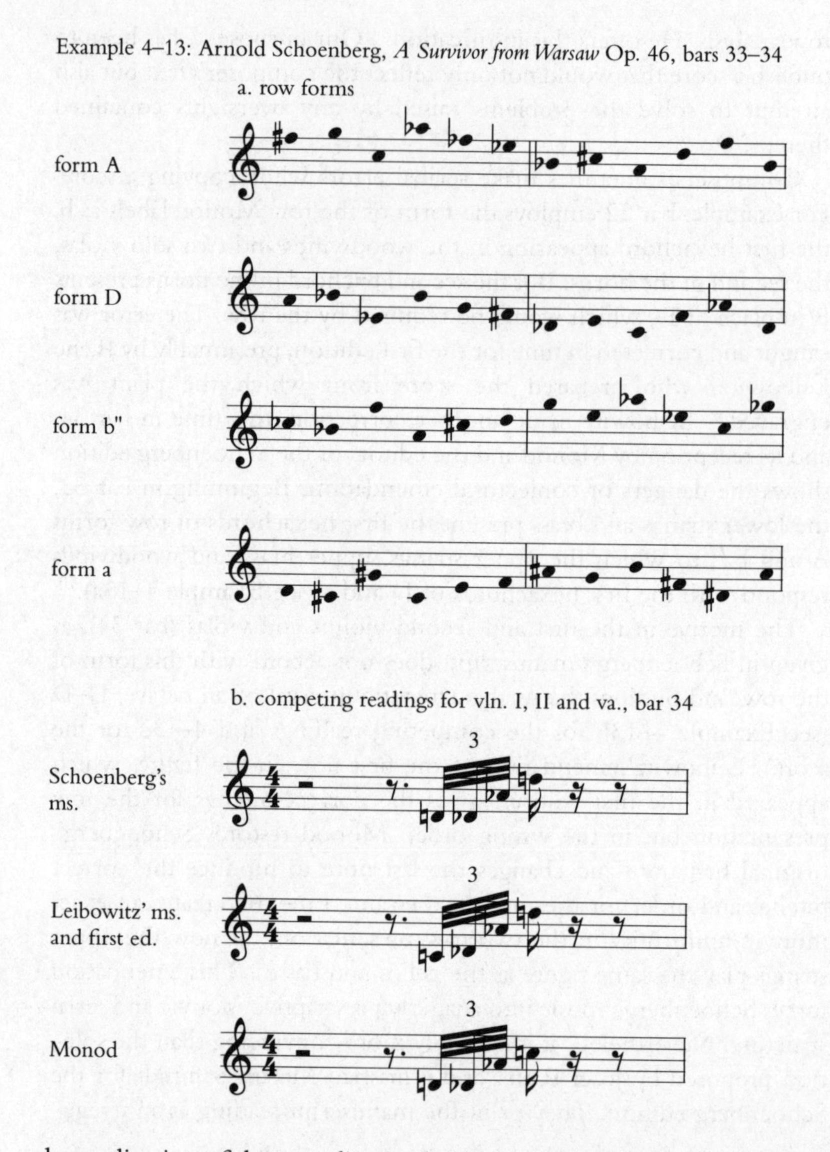

lar application of the row, disregarding the octave D–D that the motive outlines.

Elsewhere, however, Monod moves back in the compositional process and finds Schoenberg's rigour wanting. His sense of rectitude is evidenced by his revisions to bars 73–78, where the offending lines are doubled in several instruments.[71] In bar 73, for example, he

[71] See Schoenberg, *A Survivor from Warsaw*, ed. Monod, p. VI.

changes a note in the line doubled by the second clarinet, first bassoon and harp. It seems quite unlikely that Schoenberg made a simple scribal error in writing the score: it would have been necessary for him to make the same mistake several times in copying out the doubling voices. Monod, therefore, is recomposing to make the piece suit his aesthetic ideals regarding the application of serial techniques.

Editing the literary text in vocal music

In the case of vocal music, the concept of text includes the literary texts that form part of the piece. Consequently, editors of vocal genres should be prepared to present an accurate edition of the literary texts involved, conforming to the highest philological standards. Many editions of vocal music are marred by incorrect transcription, spelling, capitalization, punctuation and syllabification. To be fair, not all musicologists are equipped to undertake these tasks, and some series, Das Erbe Deutscher Musik, for example, state that their editions are not a suitable forum for philological work, *per se*.[72] Nevertheless, the literary text is as much a part of the work as the music, and so it must be edited with the same care. Editors should not hesitate to consult philologists or even enlist them for a cooperative edition to ensure the highest quality of the final product. The results achieved in recent editions of medieval secular monophony by E. J. Dobson and F. Ll. Harrison, and Samuel N. Rosenberg and Hans Tischler demonstrate the promise such collaboration holds.[73]

Criticism and editing

Throughout the foregoing discussion, the issue of the editor's critical acumen has re-echoed repeatedly. How is it developed and applied? Simply put, it is the judgement of any and all possible readings of a text in regard to their merit and value; and it is the nexus of the most complete knowledge of the text, its composer and their histories with the creative and imaginative faculties of the humanistic scholar.[74] Let editors be scientific in their methodology and humanistic in its

[72] "Das Erbe deutscher Music," pp. 25, 33–34.
[73] Dobson and Harrison, eds., *Medieval English Songs*; Rosenberg and Tischler, eds., *Chanter m'estuet*; and Rosenberg and Tischler, eds., *The Monophonic Songs in the Roman de Fauvel*.
[74] See the discussion of critical method in Feder, *Musikphilologie*, pp. 83–125.

Example 4–13: (continued)

Example 4–13: (continued)

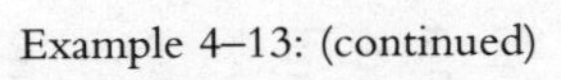

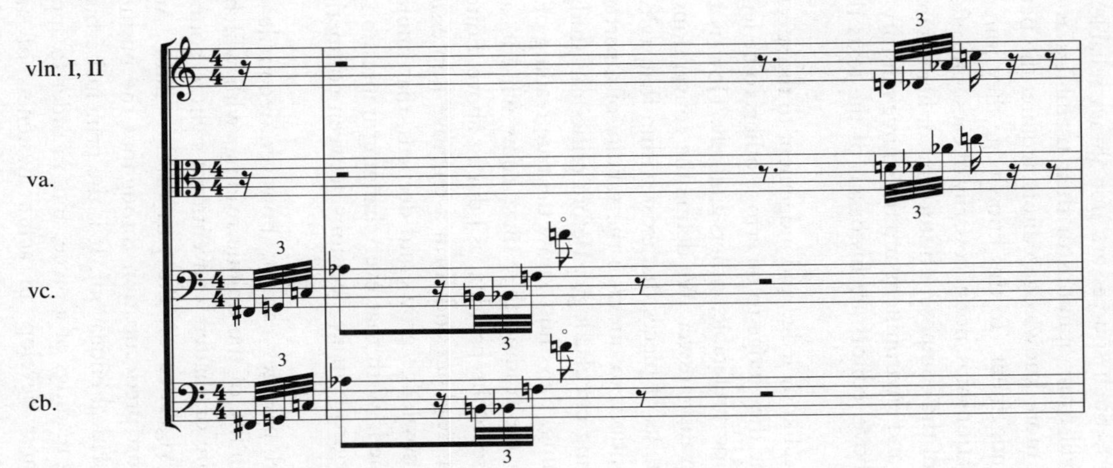

application. The editor begins with the acquisition of knowledge through the accessible documentary and musical sources. Guidance may be forthcoming in the form of secondary materials, of which editors avail themselves wherever possible in order to avoid unnecessary duplication of effort. Such sources are not always reliable, of course, and so editors will form opinions of their usefulness as the research progresses. The more knowledge editors acquire, the better informed will be their judgement. To this knowledge they join the synthetic ability to see relationships, not necessarily of cause and effect, between various aspects of the composer's history, his or her environment, the piece's history and environment and the source's history. As I discuss in Chapter 1 above, editors are historians of the texts they edit.

Editors apply this critical knowledge and judgement to the specific readings of the text. Some they judge to be errors, others to be legitimate variants, some to be preferable, others unlikely. How is this done? There is simply no easy answer. We define the conventions of a particular style by the texts of pieces that exist within that style. If we then use those conventions to question the validity of a particular reading, we are applying circular logic. Before critics can study a text to ascertain its meaning, they must know the true reading of it. Before they can establish the reading they must know what it says. Now there are ways to resolve this paradox, as I discuss above. Editors begin with uncontentious readings and form a tentative impression of style. As the critic's knowledge grows and deepens, that impression is continually modified. With that ever changing impression as a guide, the critic can begin to make decisions between competing readings.

The appeal to parallel passages cannot, however, reconcile all textual problems. The validity of the unique reading, with which a composer redefines a genre or shatters conventional stylistic boundaries, demands ceaseless vigilance on the part of the editor. And style is the critic's foremost preoccupation throughout the business of editing, or any other critical endeavour. It is the principal arbiter in judging the competing readings of a piece, and, in order to apply it as such, the critic must develop an acute awareness of and sensitivity to style and its constituent elements. Mere knowledge cannot suffice to produce this sensitivity. The critic must understand as well.

And that is the crux of editing. It is far from being a mechanical reconstruction of lost archetypes or the equally mechanical reproduction of surviving sources. It is the critical investigation of the text and its readings in order to establish the likelihood of their truth within the historical context of the piece. Whether that truth is attainable is a larger question to be pursued in Chapter 6 of this study.

5

The presentation of the text

This facet of editing has received more attention in musicological writing than any other. One explanation for the wealth of this tradition is the propensity of musicologists for a factual kind of editing that attempts to represent, in a concrete and specific way, the relationship between source and edited text. Accordingly a great deal of thought has gone into the mechanisms used to portray this relationship.[1] A second explanation is that different repertories require vastly different modes of presentation. The editors of a piece of plainsong and an opera by Richard Strauss, for example, each confront an entirely distinct set of problems. Accordingly editors have devoted considerable space to describing, discussing and defending the approaches their editions exhibit.[2] Therefore this chapter is not intended to offer a comprehensive treatment of the issue for three reasons.

First it would be impossible to cover every eventuality. Second there exist several distinguished studies that treat many of the possibilities. And third the concern of this book is more with the formulation of a generalized framework within which each editor will create a methodology for the task at hand, than with specific cases themselves. Consequently I present here some general comments, not in the hope that they will supersede the existing contributions, but in order to show that the critical approach, developed in the preceding chapters and earlier stages of the editorial process, can be applied equally to this last phase of the procedure; thereby I suggest to the prospective editor that a consistent, critical attitude can be exercised throughout the multitude of jobs that must be tackled in the course of producing an edition.

[1] See, e.g., Brown, "Editing," pp. 843b–47b; and Caldwell, *Editing Early Music*, pp. 13–113.
[2] See, e.g., the editorial policy statements collected in Dadelsen, ed., *Editionsrichtlinien*.

The first critical decision in this phase is what the needs of the potential audience are, and how best to address them. Georg Feder proposes no fewer than eight different types of edition that each address different requirements: facsimile, diplomatic print, corrected print in modern notation, critical edition, historico-critical edition, edition "for scholarship and practice," "Urtext edition," and the edition based on the history of the work's transmission.[3] To be sure, the distinguishing characteristics of the last five categories are not altogether transparent. A historico-critical edition, for example, differs from a critical edition in that it includes an explanatory commentary; in a critical edition, according to Feder, the apparatus constitutes a commentary on the printed text.[4]

As the following discussion shows, I find some of these distinctions of so little significance that many of the categories can safely be merged. I would, in turn, suggest that four types of editions should satisfy most needs: photographic facsimile, an edited print that replicates the original notation, critical edition and interpretative edition. Three of these categories serve specialized audiences, while the remaining type, the critical edition, will probably include most editions prepared under scholarly auspices, and as such receives most of the space in this chapter. I shall begin with the other three options, however, because each accomplishes something that the critical edition, consequently, need not attempt.

Facsimile editions

The photographic facsimile is well established as an important form of publication in musicology. Many of the major sources of Western music, including works of the present century, are already available, and more are sure to be produced.[5] The advantages of the procedure are obvious. All or most of the visual information presented in the source is retained and presented in the facsimile in a degree of detail that cannot possibly be reproduced by verbal description or printed replications of the original notation. Many nuances of the notation and, especially, the disposition of the notational symbols on the page relative to one another are thus clearly depicted

[3] Feder, *Musikphilologie*, pp. 135–57. [4] *Ibid.*, pp. 140–51, especially 147–48.

[5] For manuscripts, see Abravanel, "A Checklist of Music Manuscripts in Facsimile Edition"; and Coover, "Composite Music Manuscripts in Facsimile." For facsimiles of early prints, see Marco, *The Earliest Music Printers of Continental Europe*.

for the benefit of those who are unable to consult the original sources.

One of the first scholarly applications of this type of edition occurred in the field of plainsong. The early publications of the monks at Solesmes met with serious opposition from within the Catholic Church. Under the leadership of dom André Mocquereau, they sought to answer their critics by publishing photographic facsimiles of the most important chant manuscripts in the series Paléographie Musicale, which began publication in 1889.[6] Through the modern technology of photography, which seemed to transmit a higher truth than a printed transcription, Mocquereau hoped to prove the validity of the Solesmes editions. The eventual acceptance of these editions by the Vatican, starting with the *Graduale romanum* of 1908, was due, in no small part, to the evidence presented in the Paléographie Musicale.

Nevertheless, there are limitations. Photographs rarely reproduce all the details of the original document, and the variables of lighting, film speed and contrast, exposure, and processing ensure that two photographers will create two quite different photographic records of the same source. For example, the manuscript Chartres, Bibliothèque de la Ville, MS 520, which was destroyed during World War II, is now again available in David Hiley's facsimile edition, which depends on two microfilms produced before the war.[7] When Bryan Gillingham reproduced the twelfth-century Aquitanian *uersaria*, he screened each photograph on the computer with a programme that enhanced the contrast.[8] The results make the facsimiles easier to use in some cases than the manuscripts themselves. Along with the writing on the manuscript, however, any marks or shadows on the film become enhanced, too, and might appear to the user to be inscribed on the parchment. Consequently, no matter how clear the photographs are, they do not completely replace surviving sources. On the other hand, some manuscripts have deteriorated and become more difficult to read over time. Earlier photographs, however, might preserve a state of the source that is easier to read.[9]

[6] See Rousseau, *L'école grégorienne*, pp. 22–35; and Combe, *Histoire de la restauration*, pp. 125–77, 189–91, 205–7. See also Bergeron, "Representation, Reproduction, and the Revival of Gregorian Chant," pp. 106–57.

[7] Hiley, ed., *Missale Carnotense (Chartres Codex 520)*, see I, 6–7.

[8] Gillingham, ed., *Paris Bibliothèque Nationale, fonds latin 1139*; *Paris Bibliothèque Nationale, fonds latin 3719*; and *Paris B.N., fonds latin 3549 and London, B.L. Add. 36,881.*

[9] Such is the case with the autograph of J. S. Bach's Mass in B Minor, Berlin, Staatsbibliothek Preußischer Kulturbesitz, Mus. ms. Bach P 180; facsimile edition: *Messe in H-moll BWV 232*, ed. Dürr.

Other problems make facsimiles unsuitable for general use as editions. Manuscripts are often difficult to read by anyone but specialists because the handwriting is not easily legible. Faced with this barrier to comprehension, the editors of the Beethoven sketchbooks in the series published under the auspices of the Beethovenhaus in Bonn originally printed a full diplomatic transcription of the book alongside photographs of a few pages from the sketchbook.[10] This solution was found to be unsatisfactory by scholars who desired wider access to the books themselves. The editors eventually circumvented the obstacle by printing the full photographic facsimile together with the transcription, starting in 1968.[11] Manuscripts and prints of early music pose an additional complication in that aspects of the notation are unfamiliar. These very reasons make the publication of facsimiles an indispensable tool for the further enlightenment of the musically literate public, scholarly and otherwise. The same difficulties of comprehension make it certain that facsimiles will be used, in most cases, for reference and study rather than as performing materials. Of course the nature of graphic notation in much twentieth-century music, such as the works of George Crumb, makes the use of facsimile editions obligatory for those pieces.

The editor plays a limited role in preparing a facsimile edition, but some intervention can greatly improve the utility of the volume. In the first instance, of course, only the most important sources deserve this treatment, and so the choice of source for reproduction requires careful consideration. Some original sources are not properly paginated or foliated. The editor can provide a consistent system by printing the appropriate numbers in the margin above or below the photograph. Bryan Gillingham's facsimiles provide good examples. He supplies printed folio numbers in Paris, Bibliothèque Nationale, fonds latin, MS 1139, where the foliation is not always easy to read, and page numbers in the musical portion of Paris, Bibliothèque Nationale,

[10] Schmidt-Görg, ed., *Drei Skizzenbücher zur Missa solemnis*, I, *Ein Skizzenbuch aus den Jahren 1819/20*; Weise, ed., *Ein Skizzenbuch zur Chorfantasie*; Weise, ed., *Ein Skizzenbuch zur Pastoralsymphonie*. For an explanation of the policy, see Schmidt-Görg, "Vorwort," in *Drei Skizzenbücher zur Missa solemnis*, I, *Ein Skizzenbuch aus den Jahren 1819/20*, pp. 8–9.

[11] Schmidt-Görg, ed., *Ein Skizzenbuch zu den Diabelli-Variationen*, part 1, *Faksimile*; and Schmidt-Görg, ed., *Drei Skizzenbücher zur Missa solemnis*, I, *Ein Skizzenbuch aus den Jahren 1819/20*, part 2, *Faksimile*; II, *Ein Skizzenbuch zum Credo*, part 2, *Faksimile*; III, *Ein Skizzenbuch zum Benedictus und zum Agnus dei*, part 2, *Faksimile*. See Schmidt-Görg, "Vorwort," in *Ein Skizzenbuch zu den Diabelli-Variationen*, part 2, *Übertragung*, p. 7 (the same foreword also appears in the transcription volumes of *Drei Skizzenbücher zur Missa solemnis*, II and III).

fonds latin, MS 3549, and London, British Library, Additional MS 36881.[12] Then, a table of contents or, if the source contains a large number of items, an index facilitates consultation of the volume. The series Paléographie Musicale provides an exemplary model of indexing.[13]

Finally, an introduction can serve several purposes. There editors can clearly identify the source that is reproduced. If the subject of the facsimile is a print, they can specify exactly which copy was photographed. If more than one copy was used, they give the source for each page (most conveniently in tabular form). Manuscripts, of course, are cited in the usual way, by city, library and shelf number. Editors can also specify what reduction, if any, was used in the photographic reproduction, and, if the facsimile is black and white, comment on how colour is used in the original source. The introduction may also treat the historical circumstances of the source and the work or works it transmits, together with such biographical information about the composer or composers as is necessary. The degree of detail accords with the familiarity of the publication's audience with the composer, work and source. Famous composers do not require fresh biographies in this setting. The editor need only place the source and its content in their historical context. A clear photographic reproduction of the source, then, printed on good quality paper, and prefaced with a succinct introduction that makes the edition's audience comfortable with the material, is an invaluable resource for the continued study of its repertory.

Printed replicas of the original notation

The second type of specialized edition is the printed edition that replicates the original notation. This is not a diplomatic transcription, like those printed in the editions of the Beethoven sketchbooks, because those simply transfer Beethoven's manuscript sketches into legible printed form. The type I suggest here not only permits the same enhancement of legibility, but also allows editors the opportunity to revise and correct the text according to their critical investigations of the work and its sources. Therefore it is a critical edition. The actual

[12] Gillingham, ed., *Paris Bibliothèque Nationale, fonds latin 1139*; and *Paris B.N., fonds latin 3549 and London, B.L. Add. 36,881*.

[13] A contrary example is the facsimile of the autograph manuscript of the *Brandenburg* Concerti, Bach, *Brandenburgische Konzerte*, which contains neither pagination nor a table of contents.

procedure by which the text is established is a matter for the individual editor to decide, as discussed in Chapter 4 above. Because editions in this category constitute a form of facsimile (using printed fonts rather than photographs, as in the previous type), and because musical notation tends to be idiosyncratic from source to source, many editors will choose to base their edition on a single principal source, in the application of the "best-text" method. This practice is observed in the series published by Ogni Sorte Editions, whose exemplary contributions in this category of editions are discussed below.[14]

This category will consist, almost exclusively, of music written before about 1600. Among specialists in these repertories there continues to grow an interest in the original sources and their interpretation in performance. Part of this arises from the aspiration to authenticity, or at least its trappings, but more important, I believe, is the realization that transcriptions into modern notation simply cannot capture all the nuances of the original. In medieval Aquitanian notation, for example, it is impossible to represent ligation and liquescents adequately in modern notation. Yet they are most important in forming the character of the music and would undoubtedly affect performance. The performers who devote themselves to early music wish to confront the sources directly, and allow the notation to shape their interpretations.[15]

This approach is not altogether new. To a degree, it was used by the monks of Solesmes in their modern editions of plainsong, and other editions of medieval music from the first half of the twentieth century.[16] These editions, however, present a somewhat idealized form of the notation. The notation developed at Solesmes, in particular, incorporates many symbols that have nothing whatsoever to do with medieval notations, but instead correspond to their own ideas about the performance of plainsong. The type of edition proposed here more consciously (and conscientiously) imitates the notational style of the original. Such is the example set by Ogni Sorte Editions. Their publications include edited parts written in a replica of Petrucci's printed notation.[17] Critics might object that this practice, too, smacks

[14] Margaret Bent suggests a similar type of edition for early music, "Editing Music," p. 391b.

[15] This is the motivation for the publications of Ogni Sorte Editions, on which see below. See also Mendel, "The Purposes and Desirable Characteristics"; and Brett, "Text, Context, and the Early Music Editor."

[16] E.g., Misset and Aubry, eds., *Les proses d'Adam de Saint-Victor*; and Wagner, *Die Gesänge der Jakobsliturgie*.

[17] See the Foreword printed in each edition, e.g., Taruskin, ed., *Coment peult avoir joye/Wohlauf gut Gesell von hinnen*, facing p. 1.

of an idealized notation (the actual words of Richard Taruskin, the series' general editor, are "a somewhat standardized notation").[18] A spot check against available photographic facsimiles, some of which are printed in the editions themselves, revealed, however, that such differences as exist between source and edited text are purely calligraphic. That is, both texts transmit the same notational symbol, but that in the printed text appears in a more regular form. The difference is analogous to a change of font in a literary text.

It is certainly not easy to read these early notations and the suggested approach would surely alienate, at least initially, many prospective users of such an edition. The Ogni Sorte editions include "A Brief Guide to Fifteenth- and Sixteenth-Century Notation for Users of the Parts." The potential benefits, nevertheless, are significant. The performing nuances in the notation of early, non-measured music can be incorporated in the print. In mensural music, the editor need not impose the limitations of a modern rhythmic and metrical notational system that was never designed with the subtleties of perfect and imperfect values, coloration or proportions in mind. It is true that, if the music is presented in parts, as it is in the sources, the simultaneities between the voices of polyphony are not easily visible. Ogni Sorte Editions solve this problem by printing a score in modern notation along with the parts in early notation. This difficulty, however, might actually serve to focus more attention on the melodic aspects of the individual lines, arguably the most important aspect of these repertories, and less attention on relatively unimportant harmonic events.

Tablature also benefits from being reproduced in this way in view of the fact that details like fingerings and voicings can be communicated more directly. If the editor is unwilling to demand that the user be familiar with the original notational forms, a compromise would be to provide a simultaneous edition, with the modern transcription running parallel to the facsimile of the original notation, as John Boe and Alejandro Enrique Planchart have done in their edition of Beneventan tropes, as well as the monks of Solesmes in their more recent editions of plainsong.[19] The chief difficulty of this type of edition is its uneconomical format; another is getting anyone to look at the facsimile portion.

Because this type of edition is critical, editors will usually supply the

[18] In the series Foreword, see previous note.

[19] E.g., Boe, ed., *Beneventanum troporum corpus*, II, *Ordinary Chants and Tropes for the Mass*, part 1, *Kyrie eleison*, part 2, *Gloria in excelsis*; and *Graduale triplex*.

apparatus that accompanies more conventional types of critical editions. I discuss the nature of the apparatus in more detail below, where I suggest how these materials might be presented. The introduction, in addition to setting the historical context of the work, as it does in a facsimile edition, also includes a discussion of the procedure used to determine the text. When the edition is based on a single source, the editor usually indicates any differences between it and the final edited text. As I discuss below, the best place for such a list is not at the bottom of the page of musical text, but appended to the back of the edition, if not in a separate volume. The critical apparatus also contains readings from other sources that pertain to the establishment of the text. If the editor chooses to print an eclectic text, a fuller selection of readings is required. Some users of the edition would also benefit from a discussion of specific points of interest, either in the form of a commentary cued to individual passages, or more general treatments in the form of appendices. Below I discuss some of the possible topics and strategies of presentation.

Interpretative editions

The final type of specialized edition to be considered generates a certain amount of controversy: the interpretative edition. It was in response to such editions, which were thought to obscure the original notation and text of the composer with editorial performing indications, that the Königliche Akademie der Künste in Berlin began to issue *Urtext* editions in the last decade of the nineteenth century, as discussed in Chapter 1 above. More recently, however, proponents of the *Urtext* concept have conceded that editorial intervention is inevitable, and they allow the addition of performing marks, albeit limited to fingerings and bowings.[20] There will always be a demand for editions that record aspects of the performing style of important performers, and they play an extremely important role in the communicating of much great music to students and to the editor's peers and colleagues. Moreover these editions constitute repositories of information about the performance and interpretation of the work. Some scholars maintain that they transmit a kind of oral tradition of the style of performance: great performers study with great teachers, who pass on insights into the meaning of the work from previous generations.

[20] Bente, "Ermittlung und Vermittlung," p. 530.

In the past, it would seem that the chief problem with these editions lies not in the addition of editorial performing indications, but that the performer/editor expends little effort to ensure that the printed text is faithful to the testimony of the sources. And, occasionally, such an editor rewrites the piece to conform to his or her taste. Leonard Rose prints a version of Haydn's Cello Concerto in D major, Hob. VIIb:2, that differs substantively from the authentic sources.[21] For example, he alters the cello part without warning to his audience in the three bars leading up to the cadence at bar 64 of the opening movement, and then he cuts the next six bars. These alterations, however, stem from the arrangement of the Concerto made by François-Auguste Gevaert, who is only given credit for the piano reduction in Rose's edition.[22] Rose is somewhat more responsible in his edition of Chopin's *Introduction and Polonaise Brillante* Op. 3. He adopts the arrangement of Emanuel Feuermann, who appropriates passagework originally written for the piano into the cello part.[23] Rose clearly marks the music as an arrangement but, as in the Haydn Concerto, does not indicate in any way how it differs from the sources.

More performers today have academic training, and exhibit a greater interest in the source materials of the repertory they perform.[24] Ultimately, these circumstances are sure to be reflected in the editions they will prepare. It is to be hoped, moreover, that scholars will collaborate with performers in their editorial endeavours in order to create an edition that presents a text of the highest quality to which performers can add their interpretative marks. A great deal of the repertory that is most likely to appear in interpretative editions has already been published in reliable, scholarly, critical editions. In some cases, these might provide a suitable base text for the performer/editor's interpretative edition.[25] The possibility of such collaborative editions, between the publishers of scholarly and commercial editions, might make the undertaking of scholarly editions more feasible economically. And this consideration, in turn,

[21] Haydn, *Concerto in D major*, piano reduction by Gevaert, ed. Rose. The authentic sources are the autograph, Vienna, Österreichische Nationalbibliothek, MS ohne Signatur, and the print issued by Johann Anton André of Offenbach in approximately 1804; see Haydn, *Konzerte für Violoncello und Orchester*, ed. Gerlach, pp. 121a–23a.

[22] Haydn, *Concert in D dur*, arr. Gevaert.

[23] Chopin, *Polonaise Brillante Opus 3*, arr. Feuermann, ed. Rose. See, e.g., the cadenza at the end of the Introduction, bar 37. Cf. Chopin, *Complete Works*, XVI, *Chamber Music*, ed. Paderewski, Bronarski and Turczyński, pp. 15–30.

[24] Gülke, "Philologie und musikalische Praxis."

[25] Bente, "Ermittlung und Vermittlung," p. 531.

might affect the presentation of the musical text in the critical edition, as I discuss below.

To this point, a distinction is emerging between what performer/editors might change or add in an interpretative edition, and what they might not. Most will feel more comfortable giving advice in the matter of performing indications than with other textual matters, although that situation is changing, too, as noted in the previous paragraph. Would proponents of the copy-text method recognize this distinction as one between substantives and accidentals? In Chapter 4 above I discuss the applicability of these concepts to music and suggest that all aspects of notation are, in fact, substantive. When performer/editors take it upon themselves to supplement the performing indications provided by the composer, they do no more than express in writing the freedom most composers expect them to assume in performance.

By the addition of phrasing marks, for example, they change the substantive text of the piece, but in many repertories this type of alteration stands well within the bounds of the performer's discretion. The same understanding applies to the composition of a cadenza, the realization of a figured bass, or the ornamentation supplied by Geminiani to Corelli's Sonata Op. 5 no. 9, mentioned in Chapter 4 above. There is a limit, however, and it would seem to be overstepped in the examples cited above from the cello literature. Gevaert, Feuermann and Rose are certainly free to alter the text as they have, but this is not so much editing as arranging, and most users would appreciate being informed not only of the difference, but also where and how the text has been changed.

Some editors and publishers expend a great deal of energy on distinguishing the marks of the editor from those of the composer. If, however, editors make clear in their introduction the nature of the indications added, there is no need to make a graphic distinction. Janos Starker makes such a statement in the Foreword to his edition of the Bach Suites for Violoncello Solo. "This edition represents bowings and fingerings evolved through hundreds of performances and recordings noted as faithfully as it was possible. ... Perhaps the main benefit of this edition will be that if my recorded or performed versions of these Suites coincide with the player's taste, then the mechanical means described herein will be of help. In short I claim nothing else but the fact that most of the time this is the way I play these masterpieces."[26]

[26] Bach, *Six Suites for Unaccompanied Violoncello*, ed. Starker, inside front cover.

Many users will find it useful to know the source of the text on which the edition is based, and the editor might also refer the user to the appropriate critical and facsimile editions. There is normally no need to append a critical apparatus, which lies more properly in the province of the critical edition, unless the editor has made revisions to the text other than performing indications. In that case, a list, preferably at the end of the edition or in the introduction, will enlighten the user. Performers might also consider adding discussions of their interpretation either in appendices or a commentary.

Two famous examples of the latter approach are the edition of Beethoven's piano sonatas by Artur Schnabel and Alfred Cortot's editions of Chopin.[27] The visual presentation of this material requires some comment. In both cases, the editor printed an extensive commentary, dealing with all manner of subjects but principally matters of interpretation in performance, at the bottom of the page. At first, this layout seems jarring and unfeasible. In places, the prolixity of the commentary swells up to drive all but a system or two of music from the page.[28] Such an arrangement is familiar from scholarly editing in literature, where the critical notes and commentary often appear on the same page as the text, and occasionally threaten to overwhelm it.

The way in which editions of literature and music are used, however, differs significantly. Readers of a poem can read a line or two, perhaps a sentence or a stanza, and then refer to the notes and commentary for clarification. Or they can ignore the commentary altogether and simply read the poem. Some might even do the reverse, read the commentary and not the poem. Most users of an edition of music, however, would follow quite a different path: they would play from the score. In so doing, they would have no opportunity to consult the commentary under normal conditions, that is, when playing through a complete movement or piece. One does not usually play a couple of bars, and then pause to read the editor's comments. Moreover, page-turns constitute a significant obstacle for the pianist, and this arrangement greatly increases the number of them in any given movement.[29]

[27] Chopin, *24 préludes*; *Ballades*; and *Pièces diverses*, ed. Cortot. Beethoven, *32 Sonatas for the Pianoforte*, ed. Schnabel.

[28] See, e.g., Beethoven's Sonata Op. 111, ed. Schnabel, II, 821–62. A full page without commentary contains five systems; because of the commentary, two pages carry only two systems, pp. 832 and 852.

[29] The first movement of Op. 111, for example, requires eight page-turns, ed. Schnabel, II, 821–36. In contrast, Heinrich Schenker's edition, printed in the same format, needs four: Beethoven, *Sämtliche Klaviersonaten*, ed. Schenker, IV, 595–602.

Nevertheless, several factors show that this type of layout is not as inconvenient as it may appear at first. In modern performing conventions, no pianist would perform the works published in these editions from the written score; pianists normally memorize the music for recitals, and so the layout of these editions provides no impediment to normal performing situations. The utility of these editions in practice sessions, where piano music finds its heaviest use, is not without qualification. It is true that pianists might play a few bars, then read the commentary and attempt to apply it to the pertinent passage. Conversely, they might try the opposite: read the interpretative note and try out the passage. For the principal work of practising, however, playing over longer passages and complete sections or movements, the layout of these editions becomes extremely cumbersome because of the frequency of page-turns.

One might propose that a second edition, one with a more conventional layout, be employed for this phase, but that second edition might well present quite different readings of the musical text, in addition to the performing markings. The chief utility, then, of the editions by Schnabel and Cortot is for study, as opposed to practising, at the keyboard. They are not really practical for playing, even though they contain a great deal of useful information for the performer. As I discuss below, a much more suitable place for this type of commentary is at the end of the edition or perhaps in a separate volume. This arrangement, too, possesses advantages and disadvantages, and these are also treated below. In summary, my objection to Schnabel's and Cortot's editions, and others of the type, lies not in their content, but in their layout. The interpretative edition, as a class, can only enhance our understanding of the music. Moreover, although most such editions are the products of distinguished soloists, there is no reason why conductors, chamber musicians, or specialists in early and contemporary repertories could not offer editions of this type for the music they themselves perform.

Critical editions

The three classes of editions discussed hitherto appeal to specialized audiences who require particular types of information for their specific needs. It is quite possible for the same work to appear in editions that belong to more than one of the three categories, and so the editor who wishes to prepare a critical edition need not worry about replicating all the information contained in them. The audience of the critical edition is the general musically literate audience: performer, student, scholar, and the musically literate general public. The critical edition is, or ought to be, the primary printed or written vehicle by which music is communicated to its public.

Therefore, the purpose of a critical edition is quite simple: to transmit the text that best represents the historical evidence of the sources. That evidence is open to interpretation, and so two editors will, in all likelihood, produce two different editions of the same work. That is the nature of historical and humanistic research, and is not in the least to be regretted. Editors may also differ as to their preferred mode of presentation. The suggestions that follow, therefore, are not intended to form a definitive system, but rather offer the solutions that I find appealing among the available alternatives. In particular I recommend that the reader consult the discussions presented by John Caldwell in his *Editing Early Music*, from which I cite especially pertinent passages below.

The first priority for such an edition is clarity in the presentation of information to the user. The editor communicates many different types of information to the user, including pitch, rhythm, metre, instrumentation, tempo, dynamics, articulation, and even greater particulars like bowing, pedalling, registration, breathing, or, in vocal music, literary text. It is the responsibility of the editor to present these disparate elements in such a way that the user can immediately comprehend and coordinate them. A musical score or part is an extremely complex piece of visual communication. The solution is not to reduce that complexity but to enable the user to grasp it efficiently.

One of the first issues to confront the editor, then, is when to retain notational elements used in the original sources, where those differ from modern conventional usage. The choice will depend on a balance between two factors: fidelity to the substance of the music and ease of comprehension by the user. The dual option of the photographic facsimile or the edited printed replica makes it unnecessary to retain archaic notational features from the original source that will render the music difficult for the modern user to understand. Either type of specialized edition can do an efficient job of communicating the idiosyncrasies of a particular source. On the other hand, there will, in the foreseeable future, continue to be a market for modernized editions of early music, which need not be held as a misrepresentation of the original notation if the editor gives a clear exposition of the principles of the modernization.

Another preliminary issue is the layout of the page. I suggest that, in the main body of the edition, those pages on which the text of the piece is presented, only the text be printed. Scholars might prefer to see a full apparatus and even commentary on the same page as the text, but two considerations make this procedure unfeasible. First, as noted above in regard to the editions of Cortot and Schnabel, it renders the edition awkward to use for performers as anything but a document to study, especially because of the increased number of page-turns it necessitates. Second, a clean text, without notes and commentary, can serve as the basis for commercial editions reprinted photographically from the pages of the critical edition. G. Thomas Tanselle makes this suggestion concerning the texts of novels.[30] He notes that not all readers require the full scholarly apparatus, but all appreciate a carefully edited text. Therefore commercial publishers may be more willing to use the text of scholarly editions, which at least transmit texts based on scholarly investigation, if they can simply photo-reproduce it.

Among music publishers, Bärenreiter is issuing study scores that reproduce the texts of their critical editions, those of Bach and Mozart, for example.[31] The musical public is thus able to purchase the scholarly text in a reduced format without the scholarly apparatus at a lower price. Editors of the Bärenreiter scores furnish a brief introduction based on the fuller treatment found in the critical edition, and refer users to its critical apparatus. The possibility of increased sales in the smaller format may make scholarly editions a more attractive (or perhaps less unattractive) economic undertaking for publishers. Furthermore, the text of a critical edition could also perform the same function for an interpretative edition, in photo-reproduction with the performing indications superimposed, as suggested above. Practical considerations may intervene, as when the phrasing marks and dynamics in the critical edition conflict with the preferences of the performer/editor. Here, we can only hope that the scholarly text will still become the basis of the interpretative edition, even though it must be reset.

Banished from the bottom of the page, the scholarly apparatus can

[30] Tanselle, "Some Principles for Editorial Apparatus."

[31] Vötterle, "Die Stunde der Gesamtausgabe," pp. 290–91.

only appear, then, in the introduction or appendices, which in turn either precede or follow the edited text of the work, or occupy a separate volume. There are advantages and disadvantages to all arrangements of this material. If they appear anywhere other than the bottom of the page, they are easier to ignore, as Philip Brett observes. Nevertheless, as Brett also notes, that fact, sad though it may be, is no reason not to continue publishing such materials.[32] In fact, it provides all the more motivation to present them efficiently and attractively. Some members of the audience will never consult the scholarly apparatus, but more, including some who need to, will if the information is presented clearly in an easily comprehensible format. Below I discuss some of the ways in which this goal might be accomplished.

Perhaps the most controversial type of arrangement is the publication of a separate volume containing the critical apparatus and commentary. Two objections are usually raised to this type of presentation. First, some critical reports simply never get published, and second, two separate volumes, even if they would be equivalent in size to the same material packaged in a single volume, will inevitably be more costly. The latter aspect can also be considered an advantage, however. The volume containing the text alone will probably be cheaper than a single volume that includes the text and scholarly apparatus. Therefore some members of the audience who might balk at purchasing the entire package (whether in one volume or two) will have the option of purchasing just the text (or just the commentary, for that matter!).

The first objection, meanwhile, is empty. Any editors who allow their editions to appear without the critical material run the risk of seeing their work dismissed as uncritical and unsubstantiated. And just because some editors in the past have transgressed in this regard, there is no reason to discourage other editors from adopting this course of action, especially because it offers one advantage that no other presentation can match: the user can consult text and commentary simultaneously while the text retains a format that is usable in performance. (One can always consult both when the commentary is printed at the bottom of the page, but that arrangement threatens the utility of the text, as discussed above.) I believe that this advantage is so significant that it should remain a viable option.

[32] Brett, "Text, Context, and the Early Music Editor," pp. 97–98. See also Mendel, "The Purposes and Desirable Characteristics," pp. 22–23; and Feder, *Musikphilologie*, pp. 145–46, who regrets the inconvenience of a separate volume for the critical report, and advocates the use of footnotes.

The musical text

Our discussion begins with the presentation of the musical text itself.[33] The first page of the work carries, at the top, the work's full title, as determined by the editor's consultation of the sources, with the composer's name, if known (speculative attributions are identified as such), his or her dates (even if the composer is well known), the date (and place of composition, if it appears in the source material) of the work insofar as it can be established, and the name of the editor. Copyright data can be placed at the bottom of the page. Much or all of this material will also appear on the title page or its verso, yet it is a convenience to the user to have this information at his or her disposal adjacent to the text, and, in an age when photocopying daily erodes the composer's, editor's and publisher's opportunities for royalties, this material might constitute some discomfort, if not a deterrent, to those who would infringe copyright.

The usual mode of presentation is score notation. The only exception would be, of course, solo works for performing media whose music normally occupies a single staff, voice or wind instruments, for example. In producing a score, the editor has the option either to follow the modern conventions in the order of the parts, or to accept that given in the sources; those from the seventeenth and eighteenth centuries often differ from modern practice.[34] The question to be answered here is whether fidelity to the text is more important than the apprehension of the reader. In this case, however, it would seem that, because the modern convention of scoring is well established, the communication of the arrangement of the original source can be accomplished more efficiently and effectively by a facsimile. A photograph of the first page of the source, then, could be placed for this purpose in the introduction.

In most cases, therefore, the modern conventions regarding the order of the parts will be used: woodwinds, brass, percussion including pianoforte and harp, and strings, from top to bottom of the page. In a concerto, the solo instrument or instruments normally appear between the percussion and the strings, although different formats are necessary in Baroque concerti, where the placement of the solo instruments might more properly reflect their positions in the normal

[33] On score preparation in general, see Roemer, *The Art of Music Copying*; Heussenstamm, *The Norton Manual of Music Notation*; and Mender, *Music Manuscript Preparation*.

[34] Caldwell, *Editing Early Music*, pp. 80–86.

orchestral score, for practical reasons. A good example is J. S. Bach's *Brandenburg* Concerto No. 5 (BWV 1050), where the cembalo obbligato, now part of the continuo, now a soloist, is perhaps best placed at the bottom of the score, as the composer did in the autograph.[35]

When voices are used with orchestra, the convention in earlier music up to the mid-nineteenth century is to place them between the viola and violoncello parts; more recent composers locate them between percussion and strings. Modern practice normally follows contemporary sources where they provide unambiguous evidence about the placement of the voices. In other cases, a solution that is both consistent with contemporary practice and clear to the user seems preferable. In chamber music, the score follows normal orchestral usage, with two exceptions: the pianoforte, when used, is placed at the bottom of the score, and, when French horn forms part of a woodwind ensemble, it normally is placed above the bassoon. Again, preferences of the composer, as documented in contemporary sources, will likely supersede editorial convention.

In most cases, the first system of a piece is complete regardless of whether all parts have music in that first system, and each line of the score is fully identified, including transposition, especially if, subsequently, the "pocket-score" format, wherein parts that rest for a given system are not printed in that system, is used. If the orchestration for subsequent movements changes, particularly if parts are added, the editor can also print complete the first system of the pertinent movements. Editors, especially of works that involve large performing forces, might find this approach so uneconomical as to jeopardize the feasibility of the edition, and so they might want to adopt the "pocket-score" format throughout, first system included. In that case a full list of the performing forces, printed on the page facing the first page of the score and perhaps including an indication of those instruments or vocal parts that participate in only some of the piece's movements, would be most helpful and convenient for the user.

Notation

When editors come to choose the actual musical symbols to be used in their edition, the first issue they will address is whether they will incorporate the notational elements used in the original sources in

[35] Berlin, Deutsche Staatsbibliothek, MS Am. B. 78.

cases where modern conventional usage differs. Let us begin with the question of clefs. To note a part at the same pitch level in a different clef does not change the substance of the part. Composers used C-clefs well into the nineteenth century to designate the various vocal ranges (for example, C-clef on the bottom line, so-called soprano clef, for soprano voice). A reality of modern music-making is that most musicians are comfortable reading only three clefs: modern treble, bass, and transposing treble clef (reading an octave lower than noted). And so editors who print Beethoven's Ninth Symphony with C-clefs for soprano, alto and tenor voice parts are not serving their audience well. Those who need to know the distribution of the original clefs can be so informed in the editor's introduction. Therefore modern treble and bass clefs will provide the greatest utility for vocal parts, including, of course, the transposing treble clef for tenor, always printed with the numeral 8 immediately below it to distinguish it from the non-transposing treble clef.

Of course, various instruments still use the C-clef in modern convention, notably viola and bass-clef instruments for passages in the high register. Where an instrument conventionally uses two or more clefs, the edition will normally present the clef changes that occur in the sources. If different sources transmit clef changes in different places, the editor can either select a single source whose clef changes make the text as easy as possible to read, or establish a system that accomplishes the same thing. In vocal parts, where there is sometimes a choice of clef available, a useful rule of thumb is to choose the one that permits the fewest leger lines. The treble clef, transposing treble clef for tenor and bass clef normally cover all possibilities. Temporary octave displacements to avoid leger lines are not normally necessary. Players of instruments that explore the extreme ranges (e.g., flute and violin) are prepared to read well above the staff. Sometimes, of course, the sources indicate that it is obligatory to note the music in this way, and in some passages the displacement from noted pitch is optional, as happens occasionally in a repeat. Of course the usual octave transpositions (for piccolo or contrabass) are preserved.

Other instruments conventionally transpose, as well, and their treatment is more complex. Composers up to about 1900 usually wrote score and parts for transposing instruments (the French horn, for example) at reading, as opposed to sounding, pitch, and professional performers are equipped to transpose those parts when the sounding pitch of modern instruments differs from that of the instruments for which the parts were written. Valves have replaced crooks on the French horn, and the professional player of the modern horn pitched in F is prepared to transpose any and all parts written for natural horn, as are trumpet- and clarinet-players for their respective parts. There is no need, then, to manipulate those parts for the benefit of their modern professional users. Editors who see as their intended audience amateur or student players might feel obliged to seek another solution, and perhaps transpose the parts for the equivalent modern instrument.

After 1900, however, with the concept of key becoming ever more remote, composers began objecting to the convention of transposing instruments and some, such as Schoenberg, wrote their scores at sounding pitch, although they specify in those scores the use of instruments that conventionally transpose. Many publishers have adopted the compromise of printing the score at sounding pitch and transposing the pertinent parts. Because of the complexity of many of these parts, the added burden of transposition at sight would only serve to make the music less accessible to its users. And so the convention of providing the players with transposed parts is a useful option that editors of twentieth-century music might consider adopting.

In the use of key signatures, the editor normally follows the lead of the sources. Signatures from the so-called common-practice period bear implications of key and therefore tonality that much music from periods both before and after does not warrant. Editors, then, modernize or regularize with caution. Some early music uses partial signatures where different parts carry different signatures, and occasionally one encounters eighteenth-century works equipped with what appears to be one sign too few in the signature. In my experience, however, the addition of an editorial signature can simplify the presentation considerably. A troped version of the so-called Gloria A or Prima occurs in the eleventh-century apostolic Mass for the feast of Saint Martial compiled by Adémar de Chabannes.[36] This melody contains many passages in which the notes F and B are linked directly, either by leap or by conjunct motion, and most observers would prescribe the application of B♭.[37] To avoid cluttering the score with a large number of editorial accidentals, I added a signature of one flat,

[36] Bosse, *Untersuchung einstimmiger mittelalterlicher Melodien zum "Gloria in excelsis deo"*, no. 39, pp. 95–96.

[37] E.g., Guido of Arezzo (Adémar's exact contemporary), *Micrologus*, 8.10–13, ed. Smits van Waesberghe, pp. 124–25, despite his obvious discomfort with the note; see Pesce, *The Affinities and Medieval Transposition*, pp. 20–21.

complemented by a full discussion of the manuscript and theoretical evidence bearing on the issue. This solution has the advantage of leaving the score relatively free for the edition's users to mark in their preferred accidentals.

The treatment of accidentals is quite a different matter. It is usually not possible to convey every nuance of the sources unequivocally where their conventions differ from modern ones: a facsimile can communicate them much more efficiently. Instead the user needs a clear convention that indicates which notes are chromatically inflected in the source, and which ones the editor feels should be so inflected in practice but are not in the source. The first question is the duration of the accidental, and there are two choices. Where barlines are used in the edition, the accidental remains in effect for the duration of the bar unless cancelled, in the modern convention, regardless of the source's usage. If barlines do not appear, the accidental only affects the note it precedes and those immediately repeated at the same pitch. This system has the advantage of being simple and efficient, and does not clutter the score with fussy accidentals.

The second question is where to place the accidental. Accidentals that appear in the source are usually printed on the staff with the notes they affect, in the conventional manner. In early vocal music, it has now long been conventional to place those introduced on editorial authority above the staff, directly above the note affected, and there is no reason to alter that custom. Such accidentals usually apply only to the note above which they appear and immediately succeeding notes on the same pitch, irrespective of whether barlines are used. They need not be cancelled. *Musica ficta* is obviously the largest single source of such accidentals, and editors of early music will likely familiarize themselves with as many of the available sources, both primary and secondary, as possible. Some editors might prefer not to indicate accidentals generated by *ficta*, but that course seems more suitable for an edition that replicates the original notation and for the specialist audience of such editions. Non-specialist users, an important segment of the audience for a critical edition, will need some guidance in the application of *ficta*.

Editorial accidentals in later music (after *c.* 1600) and in instrumental music, particularly where chordal textures are possible, require different treatment. In most cases, the composers indicate accidentals through a more specific notation (tablature in instrumental music, for example) that does not depend on the conventional application of *ficta*.

Therefore, most editorial accidentals clarify potentially ambiguous readings or suggest corrections for scribal errors and omissions. A preferable place for such accidentals, then, is on the staff. Whether they should be visually distinguished from other accidentals is a question to be addressed more properly when the whole issue of editorial marks is raised.[38]

Any case where there is the slightest chance of ambiguity calls for editorial resolution: for instance when a note appears an octave away from a note that is altered by an accidental, or when there is any possibility that an accidental might not be cancelled by the barline. These accidentals might not be needed, strictly speaking, especially in the second case where the accidental is either cancelled by the barline or must be renewed. Nevertheless if they can facilitate the reading of the text, particularly in the dissonant idiomata of the twentieth century, they should be included. I call them "courtesy" accidentals.

Modern time signatures imply a great deal about the metrical structure of a piece that is not warranted in much early music. Hence a modern time signature is normally used only when the music is organized in the pattern of regular accents that the signature indicates. Of course much twentieth-century music uses time signatures to indicate a regular pattern of irregular accents (as in Bartók's complex signatures), or frequently changing time signatures to indicate irregular accents (as in Bartók and Stravinsky); or, when combined with metronome markings, to indicate more complex relationships (as in Elliott Carter's metrical modulation). For music before *c.* 1750, however, the practice given in contemporary sources usually provides the best guidance.

Pieces in mensural notation that are transcribed with modern rhythmic values present a more complicated problem. A reduction in note values, always indicated by the editor, often aids in the comprehension of the music, as I discuss below. The editor also gives the mensuration sign, of course, but it is unnecessary or even misleading to print a modern time signature. Modern notation denotes perfect and imperfect values by means of, respectively, dotted and undotted notes, and the implications of metrical pulse that a signature carries is foreign to much of this music. Some of these difficulties are revealed in the current edition of Dunstable, in which the compound

[38] Cf. Caldwell, *Editing Early Music*, pp. 29–33, who advocates four levels of accidentals, a system I find too complex for immediate comprehension in reading and performing.

signature $\frac{3}{4}\frac{6}{8}$ occurs frequently, usually with the mensuration sign **O**, in an attempt to indicate the shifting metre.[39]

Metrical issues also affect the use of barlines in mensural music. Many editions, particularly those in the series Corpus Mensurabilis Musicae, print *Mensurstriche*. These are short barlines placed between the staves of a single system, but not on them, usually at the end of each breve, whether perfect or imperfect. This practice avoids the use of ties, as notes can be given their full rhythmic value, even when they extend beyond the tempus. It also promotes the smooth rhythmic flow of the music without the disruption of regular periodic accents that are promoted by modern time signatures and barlines throughout the staves. At the same time, the *Mensurstrich* gives the scholar or performer enhanced visual orientation for the orderly rhythmic, as opposed to metrical, progression of the parts together.[40]

A minor difficulty with this type of rhythmic notation is the coordination of the end of a line and the end of the durational value. It is useless to attempt to end each system at a point where all voices end their respective notes together; inevitably some voices hold their notes over to the next system. For such voices, the easiest solution is to select a durational value that completes the line, and tie it over to the value at the beginning of the next system that completes the duration of the note. This solution provides a clear visual presentation of the durational values and the rhythmic relationships between the voices. The alternative, to print the full durational value as the last note of the line, and then to leave blank space at the beginning of the next line to correspond to the leftover value of the note, is visually disruptive and hard to follow.

Sources from the sixteenth century in score notation, however, frequently use barlines drawn through the system at the end of each breve or equivalent.[41] Many modern editors feel that the audience for mensural music is now sophisticated enough to understand that the note after a barline does not deserve an accent, and so, supported by the source evidence, they print conventional barlines. A particularly good

[39] Bukofzer, ed., *The Works of John Dunstable*, p. xvii; see, e.g., *Aue regina celorum, aue decus*, *ibid.*, pp. 62–64.

[40] Cf. the criticisms of *Mensurstrich* in Lowinsky, "Early Scores in Manuscript," pp. 156b–169; Mendel, "The Purposes and Desirable Characteristics," pp. 17–20; and Caldwell, *Editing Early Music*, p. 49. See also the contributions of Arthur Mendel (p. 729 and n. 6), Myroslaw Antonowycz (p. 731) and René Lenaerts (p. 733) to the Symposium "Problems in Editing the Music of Josquin des Prez."

[41] Lowinsky, "On the Use of Scores"; and "Early Scores in Manuscript."

compromise appears in the Ogni Sorte Editions, where the score, in modern notation, uses barlines, and the parts, written in a replica of mensural notation, do not. Certainly barlines facilitate the immediate comprehension of the rhythm and especially the rhythmic relationships between voices. And perhaps *Mensurstriche* represent a compromise between the unbarred presentation of parts in original notation and the needs of modern score notation. Nevertheless, I find the *Mensurstrich* a creative solution to the performing problem of avoiding metrical stress in non-metrical music. A case can be made for either mode of presentation, and the choice will depend on editorial preference as well as the editors' assessment of the needs of their audience.

In score presentation notes that occur simultaneously are of course printed in exact vertical alignment. In passages where a relatively narrow range of rhythmic values is employed, spacing that is proportional to those rhythmic values facilitates reading by both performers and scholars. Thus four eighth notes take the space of two quarter notes or eight sixteenth notes. Of course this spacing is uneconomical and in some circumstances, where a wide range of rhythmic values occurs, it simply cannot be used. For example, when a bar that consists of a single whole note follows one that contains sixteen sixteenth notes, one would not apportion the same amount of space to both bars. Nevertheless the proportional arrangement can, when used for appropriate passages, be a highly desirable feature, in my view.

The literary text, in vocal music, is aligned with the music. As I mentioned in the previous chapter, text underlay is a contentious issue in many repertories of early music, and editors should be prepared to defend their decisions on the basis of contemporary theoretical sources and the attendant secondary scholarship. These decisions, strictly speaking, belong to the stage described in the previous chapter, but they will obviously affect the way in which the text is presented. Once the underlay has been determined, how should the literary text be printed? When a single note sets the syllable, most printers centre the syllable under the note. In melismata, however, or where two or more tied notes set the syllable, the first letter of the syllable is conventionally aligned with the first note of the setting.

A hyphen is placed between all syllables of a word, and, in a melismatic texture or where two or more tied notes are used, several hyphens spaced out will indicate the prolongation of an internal syllable through its musical duration. If the final syllable of a word is set to a melisma or sustained with tied notes, the usual symbol of prolongation is a solid base line (or ground-level line) extending to the last notational symbol that pertains to the syllable, and any punctuation is placed between the syllable and the line. To avoid the misapprehension of this line as an additional line of the staff, the text is printed far enough below the staff that the distance between the lowest line of the staff and the base line is visibly larger than that between adjacent lines of the staff. Because of the presence of text in vocal music, dynamics and other expressive signs are placed above the staff rather than below it, where they occur in instrumental music.

The treatment of beams and slurs in vocal music is a matter that will require some sensitivity on the part of the editor. The usual convention in music prior to 1900 is to use unbeamed notes for texted passages, and many singers prefer it because it graphically shows the relationship between text and music. A melisma, then, is doubly noted by the use of beamed notes and a slur. Since 1900, however, a growing number of composers have adopted the practice of beaming notes wherever possible irrespective of the presence of text, presumably for greater ease in reading the rhythm, which, of course, is sometimes very complex. Texted and untexted beamed notes are distinguished, respectively, by the presence of the text and by slurs.

To complicate matters further, some twentieth-century composers place a slur above a texted passage to indicate phrasing; others connect two notes that set different syllables with a slur to stipulate a portamento between the notes. In most other uses of beamed notes and slurs, the convention followed by the composer is clear from the existing source materials, but occasionally composers are inconsistent and sometimes editors will have strong feelings about which method will permit a clearer presentation of the text for the edition's user. Each alternative provides greater clarity in one aspect of the presentation while sacrificing some in another, and editors will seek the solution that best suits the problem at hand.

Beaming in early instrumental music also deserves some thought. Grouping in later repertories usually accords with metrical divisions: groups of two eighth notes in $\frac{3}{4}$, and groups of three in $\frac{6}{8}$. In non-metrical music, however, these groupings carry no meaning but may mislead the user into attributing metrical significance to beamed groups in a manner analogous to the barline. Again, one solution, to beam in the modern manner, grouping notes according to perfect or imperfect division at the level of tempus or prolation, provides a clearer visual indication of the rhythm. The other, not to beam at all, or to beam irrespective of tempus or prolation, is more difficult to read but may avoid implying a misleading metrical shape.

The marking of editorial interventions in the text

The discussion has hitherto not considered how editorial contributions should be treated in the presentation of the text, with the exception of editorial accidentals in early vocal music. The editor's critical investigation of the sources very often reveals problems with the text that the editor will want to rectify in a critical edition, as discussed in Chapter 4 above. Should these editorial interventions be distinguished visually in the final printed text? When they are distinguished, the user has the advantage of comprehending, at a glance, what notational signs are added by the editor. The disadvantages, however, are twofold: first, no uniform system exists to make these distinctions; and second, whatever system is used, it can disrupt the visual flow of the music and distract the user, particularly in performance.

In response to the first problem, Georg Feder reports on the more complex systems used in philology, where editorial additions or conjectures are marked by angle brackets, and deletions by square brackets.[42] First, it is misleading, in a musical text, to print material that should be deleted. A performer needs to know what to play, not what is in the source but should not be played, according to the editor. The place for that information is the critical apparatus. Therefore, square brackets have no real application, with their traditional philological sense, in musical texts.

Second and more important, the relative meanings of square and angle brackets are also disorientating. When quoting in standard scholarly writing, authors mark editorial additions with square brackets. This usage is familiar to all authors and readers. In scholarly editing, however, the meaning of the square bracket is exactly the opposite, and the angle bracket carries the force usually assigned to the square bracket in quotations. The current edition of Haydn, for example, employs a modified version of the philological system with three different brackets each carrying a different significance.[43] Moreover, these signs usually repeat information already recorded in the critical report. Hence, I suggest that this complex (and, I believe, potentially

[42] Feder, *Musikphilologie*, pp. 141–42; see also Caldwell, *Editing Early Music*, p. 103.
[43] "Joseph Haydn. Werke," pp. 83–86; and Feder, "Gedanken über den kritischen Apparat."

confusing) system be abandoned in favour of the convention of scholarly quotation, which was adopted in a slightly altered form by the NMA.[44]

My own preference, however, is not to mark editorial contributions at all, a policy endorsed by the NMA in cases where the text does not depend on "authentic" sources.[45] Instead, all interventions by the editor are clearly entered in the critical report.[46] The musical text is relieved of a certain amount of clutter, to facilitate reading and comprehension. The disadvantage, of course, is that the edition's users may not look in the critical report to verify the source of readings. The only solution to that problem is to present the critical reports as efficiently and attractively as possible, a point I already made and to which I shall return below.

Another difficulty is that some members of the audience will take the suppression of editorial signs as an attempt to present the editor's text as the composer's. The text of any critical edition, however, is the editor's text. Responsible scholars make every effort to determine, on a critical and historical basis, what the composer's text is, but that determination is irrevocably intertwined with interpretation, the editor's interpretation. So long as editors inform their audience of their policies and procedures, and apply their system of notification consistently, they cannot seriously be accused of misleading the user. A further advantage of suppressing editorial markings is that the resulting clean page of musical text is all the more suitable for photoreproduction in other types of editions, either study scores in smaller format or as the base text for an interpretative edition.

Early music

The edition of early music does, however, require the addition of some editorial signs and the special treatment of some notational features. Often the score of such music is constructed from the separate voices, recorded either in partbooks or in motet-style, wherein all voices are written separately as monophony on a single page or opening. When creating a score, the editor decides on the order in which the voices are to be presented. The most useful rule of thumb is to observe the range of each voice and place them on the score with

[44] "Wolfgang Amadeus Mozart. Neue Ausgabe sämtlicher Werke," pp. 114–15.

[45] "Neue Mozart-Ausgabe," p. 63.

[46] Wallnig, "'Produkt im Kopf'," p. 541, expresses a preference for this mode of presentation.

the highest at the top and lowest at the bottom. Sometimes two or more voices operate in the same range and here some arbitrary means must be adopted to determine their place in the score: by the name given in the part (contratenor usually appears above tenor), by the pitch of the first or last note of the piece, or by the behaviour of the voices at cadence points. Names of the parts given in the source can usually be retained, although archaic terms require explanation in the introduction or commentary.[47]

Another difficulty the editor of early music faces is whether to reduce the rhythmic values, and if so, by how much. There are many conflicting conventions in this matter, to the extent that it is possible to say that no consensus exists among the most recent editors of these repertories.[48] The problem is twofold. First the graphological form of the notes in these early notations is often remote from the modern notes taken to be their equivalents, the semibreve and the modern whole note, for example. Second, insofar as these notes are graphological equivalents, when literal transcriptions are used, they seem, to the modern user, to consist of inordinately long values. The time signature $\frac{3}{1}$ is hardly familiar to the modern musician, but it results from the literal transcription of a piece by Machaut marked with the mensural symbol **O**.

The problem, then, is to choose a reduction that provides the edition's audience with rhythmic values placed in a familiar context and that communicates the approximate tempo of the piece. Now determining that tempo can be a tricky business for much early music, but the editor normally picks a reduction that gives the fundamental tactus a reasonable value, that is, one beat to the half, quarter or eighth note, according to the character of the music. The criteria on which that choice is made include sensitivity to the palaeography of the source and the rhythmic style of the piece. Here, instead of being dogmatic about the reduction necessary for a particular chronological period or repertory, the editor accommodates the idiosyncrasies of individual styles, all in order to communicate the text of the piece to the edition's user with the utmost clarity. The reduction, once it has been selected, is clearly designated at the top of the score.

A helpful supplement to this indication of the reduction is the preliminary staff, a device used by many modern editors.[49] This is printed at the left margin preceding, in each voice, the modern clef with

[47] Caldwell, *Editing Early Music*, pp. 52–53. [48] *Ibid.*, pp. 13–27, 45–50. [49] *Ibid.*, p. 10.

which the edited text of the piece begins, and on it are printed the clef, key signature, mensuration sign and first few notes for each voice as found in the source. Among the many benefits of this practice is the opportunity to compare the graphic symbols of the first few notes in source and modern edition and so make clear to the reader their relationship as well as the reduction of note values. Furthermore it renders the displacement of the original clefs and other notational devices immediately comprehensible to the edition's user, and so can communicate some of the information about the source that might be transmitted by a facsimile. And there will be instances where it is not economically feasible to reproduce a facsimile for these purposes, in a large collection of medieval or Renaissance songs, for example: a sample page or two will illustrate the source's idiosyncrasies, but the exact displacement of clefs, and mensuration signs for each song is best left to the preliminary staff.

Analogous to the question of reduction, but more complex, is the treatment of proportion. Here it is important not merely to choose the correct modern rhythmic values but especially to suggest the relationship between the notes that precede the proportion and those affected by it. Contemporary theorists are not unanimous on the interpretation and significance of proportions, and the complexity of the issue calls for the editor to address the solutions chosen for the edition in detail.[50] Nevertheless most users will appreciate some guidance in the text itself as to how to interpret the signs, and here the various conventions allow for some ambiguity. The usual course is to use the following type of equation.

♩ = ♪

The difficulty is deciding which value applies to the preceding, and which to the succeeding passage. An unambiguous system would be to supplement the equals sign with arrows that show to which passage each value pertains.

♩ ← = → ♪

This set of symbols would occur just before the first note affected by the proportion and make clear to the user the ongoing rhythmic shape of the piece.

[50] For a discussion of proportion signs and their significance, see Berger, *Mensuration and Proportion Signs*.

Finally, three types of brackets are usually added by the editor to designate various notational nuances of early music: ligatures, *coniunc-turae* and coloration.[51] Because these palaeographic signs bear directly on matters of rhythm and text underlay, it is important to mark them clearly. Each uses a different type of horizontal square bracket. The first is designated by a continuous bracket, the second by a broken bracket and the third by a framing bracket with no line between. Where the music is unmeasured, as in plainsong and early polyphony, the ligature may be designated by a slur rather than a bracket because, in these repertories, it is without rhythmic significance.

Liquescents also require special treatment. Many early notational symbols imply additional notes and at the same time suggest performing nuances. The notes that can be inferred from these symbols, the *plica*, for example, are conventionally printed, in unmeasured music, smaller than the main notes, and slurred to the note to which they are appended; if this note is ligated, a second slur joins all of the notes of the ligature including that implied by the liquescent. In measured music the slur is retained but, for ease of reading, the note is printed at the same size as the rest of the text but with an oblique slash through its stem; if the liquescent is part of a ligature, the note inferred from it is included under the bracket of ligation. Naturally these guidelines cannot hope to cover all of the eventualities that will arise in the editing of early music, and the demands of the specific repertory under consideration will guide the editor.

Apparatus, commentary, appendices

We now turn to the content and presentation of the critical apparatus. There are two possible positions for the apparatus: at the bottom of the page, as is customary in literature, or after the printed text, preferably in a separate volume. Above, I expressed a preference for the latter arrangement on several grounds. It preserves a clean page, minimizes page-turns, and allows the edition to function in photo-reproduction as the base text for other editions. This presentation also allows the editor more room to present a fuller selection of variants without having to worry about the apparatus swelling up to dominate the visual impact of the page if it were printed in the bottom margin of the principal text. Here the editor places all substantive variants.

[51] Caldwell, *Editing Early Music*, pp. 35, 38–39, 103–4.

These will primarily concern matters of pitch, including accidentals, but may also concern larger issues such as key or time signatures, as well as performing indications like articulation, dynamics and other expression marks.

First and foremost, editors indicate in the apparatus any substantive changes they have made through conjectural emendation by giving the sources' reading or readings they felt to be corrupt and in need of emendation. Second, where the sources disagree in giving readings of nearly equal merit (readings from our second category above, reasonable competing readings) from which one has been selected for the text, the source of that reading is indicated in the apparatus with the other reading or readings of nearly equal merit and their sources. If a source contains so many appealing but rejected variants that it threatens to dominate the apparatus, the editor might seriously consider editing it separately.

There is no need to reproduce, in the apparatus, all of the notational nuances found in a particular source. Some scholars insist that the user be able to reconstruct a source from the apparatus, and this exercise is profitable up to a point. Many variants, of musical orthography, for example, are much more efficiently, and, in some instances, economically communicated by a facsimile. Consequently, I feel that it is a waste of energy and resources to fill up the apparatus with trivial readings. The primary purpose of the apparatus is to report those readings that affected the editor's deliberations on the final reading chosen for the printed text. A good compromise, I believe, is presented in the Neue Schubert-Ausgabe. At the end of each volume, a critical, and rather full, selection of the most important variant readings is given. This is satisfactory for most users of the edition. The full critical report, meanwhile, has been placed on deposit at several major libraries where it is available to specialists who need access to a complete record of the sources and their readings.[52]

Each entry in the apparatus begins with a clear, unambiguous reference to the place in the text, usually by naming the part concerned and the pertinent bar number or numbers. In unmeasured vocal music, the literary text can function as a lemma. Then the source, using sigla given in the introduction's discussion of the sources, is identified and the variant is given. Here I strongly suggest that musical notation, con-

[52] "Neue Schubert-Ausgabe," pp. 80–81. See also Bent, "Editing Music," pp. 390b–91a, who criticizes some of the monumental editions for their undigested critical reports.

sistent with the conventions adopted for the edition, be used. In my experience nothing is less comprehensible than a string of alphanumeric characters to indicate a musical variant.[53] On the other hand, the user will immediately grasp the significance of a variant given in musical notation. Unfortunately, this method of presentation is not particularly economical in terms of space, and so provides another reason not to include every notational variant in the apparatus. I would unequivocally advocate a shorter, critically selected list that may well see more general use because of an attractive layout in musical notation, over a fuller list of variants presented in a less easily comprehended format and therefore consulted by only the most dedicated.

Perhaps the most important part of the edition is the critical commentary, a section often not present in music editions, and, when it does appear, it often resembles an apparatus, including little more than an account of the variant readings. The preparation of an edition entails a host of decisions made on the basis of the editor's critical perception of the work and its text. In many cases, the reasoning behind these decisions is not entirely self-evident from a simple listing of variants, no matter how detailed or complete that list is. Members of every constituency in the edition's audience, scholars, performers and the musically literate public, will appreciate a detailed discussion of the issues and interpretative thinking that led to those decisions.

The commentary, therefore, is the place for editors to explain their course of action as it pertains to specific readings and passages. No subject is off limits. Editors might discuss the choice of readings or emendations they have made together with specific points of interpretation as they arise in the text. Again, for the convenience of the user, this commentary could be printed in a separate volume for simultaneous consultation. More general issues, like performance practice, *musica ficta*, ornamentation, articulation, tempi and metronome marks, pedalling, bowing, breathing, and dynamics, can be addressed in separate appendices, which also might accompany the above-mentioned commentary in a separate volume. These discussions might not be as exhaustive as independent studies of these questions, and they can direct the edition's user to such independent studies as exist. Nevertheless they provide valuable guidance to the edition's user.

[53] E.g., the Textual Commentary in the Byrd Edition (London, 1973–). See also the discussion in Caldwell, *Editing Early Music*, pp. 8–10, who regrets that economics makes the use of algebraic formulations for the apparatus necessary. Feder, *Musikphilologie*, p. 146, recommends the use of musical notation.

Let us now take each of these parts of the edition in turn, perhaps in the order in which they will appear in the edition. Other alternatives in the order of presentation are certainly viable, according to the demands of the repertory and the editor's approach and preference, but the one given here will serve as a useful example. In the introduction, the editor establishes the historical context of the piece or repertory under consideration. Detailed historical discussion might be deferred to independent studies, but any user of the edition can benefit from a paragraph or two on the place of the piece within its composer's output, its genre or its era. Next comes the description of the sources, probably in some form like that suggested below in Appendix C, and a discussion of their classification and use. The inclusion of a sample page or two in facsimile can be very useful in orientating the user to the sources. Thence the editor can introduce a general account of the editorial method employed in the edition. Here editors might present the point of view and the approach they have adopted. A statement about what this edition contributes to the state of knowledge about the piece and its relationship to previous editions could find a place in the introduction as well.

Immediately following the text proper of the piece appear those sections, movements, arias, etc., that are optional or replacements for other sections of the text. Their position in the text is clearly marked, both in the text proper and at the beginning of their own presentation. A full discussion of when it is appropriate to use them is more properly deferred to an appendix. Normally the material presented here comprises relatively complete sections, like complete movements, or is at least well defined, such as the optional ending of Stravinsky's *Petrushka* for concert presentation. Smaller-scale variants are best placed in the apparatus, while larger collections of such variants, such as Paul Hindemith's revision of *Das Marienleben*, deserve an independent edition.

Next, optimally in a separate volume, come the critical apparatus, the explanatory commentary, and the appendices that deal with individual aspects of the text. The editor might wish to include, at the end, a bibliography; it is very likely, however, that bibliographic citations in the commentary or in footnotes to the introduction and appendices will suffice for the more detailed references. Nevertheless, a list of the most important published material on the piece or repertory could prove very useful for the edition's user, especially if the editor provides a brief discussion of the merits of each item. An index to the introduction, commentary and appendices can greatly simplify and expedite the use of the edition.

Performing materials

The editor's job is not done yet, however. Most instrumental ensemble pieces will require the extraction of parts. It is conventional for some ensembles to play from the score, pianoforte duo, or solo singer accompanied by pianoforte, for example, and much modern chamber music cannot practically be performed from parts because of the complexity of the relationships between voices. Nevertheless, for most music this task is obligatory, and will require some care in its execution. Much of the work is, of course, purely mechanical, but there are a couple of issues that deserve comment. First is the matter of page-turns. Most musicians have to turn their own pages and so the music must be arranged on the page so that some opportunity is given for the page-turn. If the editor cannot contrive to end the recto page with the ending of a movement or number, the next best solution is to end it with a bar's rest or more, or to begin a verso page with a rest. It is not adequate to cover up a careless page ending with *V. S.* (*volti subito*, "turn quickly") and leave the players to their own devices.

Rests of many bars are usually broken up so that rehearsal letters or numbers can be included; otherwise the player must always count from his or her last entry, a tedious chore indeed for percussion or brass players in the traditional repertory. The judicious use of cues, especially at the end of a long rest, can be of great benefit to the orchestral or chamber player, and can expedite rehearsals. Finally, if a player is silent for an entire movement or number, the editor simply marks the part *tacet* ("it is silent"), and need not then write out the rests.

A more delicate task is the preparation of a keyboard reduction for vocal works with orchestra, or concerti. Again, with a great deal of modern music, this is simply not a practical undertaking, although a short score, instead of a proper keyboard reduction, is more useful to the player than no reduction at all. This is the imaginative solution used in the published version of Henri Dutilleux' concerto for violoncello and orchestra entitled *"Tout un monde lointain ..."*;[54] here the reduction can be used in rehearsal with a pianist to provide cues for the soloist without trying to replicate the orchestral texture.

[54] Dutilleux, *"Tout un monde lointain ... ."*

In the traditional repertory, and in at least some twentieth-century music, it is both possible and desirable to provide a keyboard reduction, both for rehearsal and, in cases where economic factors dictate it, performance. In preparing such a reduction, the editor needs to exhibit a light touch, for the fundamental decisions to be made involve knowing what to leave out in order to make the reduction playable. Some decisions will be easy enough: all octave doublings need not be included. Others, however, will require a great deal of sensitivity as the editor must capture the essence of the orchestral part without incorporating all its details. In fact the editor recomposes the piece in effect, a challenging and formidable task, to say the least, taxing the editor's knowledge and awareness of the composer's style to the fullest.

Electronic format

Up to this point I have discussed the presentation of the text in the traditional form as a score printed in book form, using modern notation. This format generates a certain amount of claustrophobia because the demands of performing permit only the musical text to occupy the page. Other material that should be available for simultaneous consultation is moved to the back of the volume or perhaps a separate volume, where it is altogether too easy to ignore. If, however, the editor employs a machine-readable medium, this material can be available for immediate recall to the screen. The edition itself need be no different in substance or arrangement, but in place of the printed page, the much more flexible colour video screen is substituted. Some video screens cause significant eye-strain, and one of the constraints on the development of electronic formats for editions of music is the need for a monitor that is more comfortable to use. Moreover, I know of no software package that will do all of the tasks mentioned below, but programmes with similar capabilities are under development for literature and I am sure that the situation in music will soon be rectified.

The principal requirement for such a programme, aside from crystal-clear graphics, is the capability to open several windows simultaneously at the whim of the user. Any portion of the edition could, of course, fill the entire screen, but if the screen can be divided into windows, several portions of the edition could be consulted at once. I give several possibilities here, although the list should not be considered to be complete.

(1) Two versions of the same piece from different sources.
(2) The score with a complete critical apparatus including those readings that I originally suggested be included in a critical appendix.
(3) The score with critical commentary.
(4) The same portion of the score in both windows with editorial articulation, dynamics and other expressive marks in one window.

All of these involve only two windows, and, of course, there is no reason why that number could not be increased.

These suggestions primarily concern the scholar. Even more promising I think, are the benefits that could be derived by the performer particularly in ensembles. If the performer reads from a monitor, page-turns are no longer necessary. Either a foot switch can be arranged by which the player can give the command for the next page, or, better still, the programme can be organized to scroll in real time, perhaps according to a pre-set metronome mark or to the beat given by the conductor with an electronic baton that, via electronic interface, controls the tempo of the music. Other visual indications can be included in the programme in real time to assist in orientating the performer in passages employing complex rhythm. These indications could perhaps replace the click tracks used by some recent composers, and certainly they would have a pedagogical application. Performers could switch the screen, during rests, to show the whole score or that for a portion of the ensemble. Timpani players would certainly rejoice in this feature and cues need never be entered again. The screen could also be set to show several of the lines from a score, should that arrangement make it easier to follow the piece, say during exchanges or dialogues between instruments.

Conductors could themselves enter markings, like bowings, dynamics and articulations, or, perhaps with greater efficiency, an assistant beside the podium could do so, marking every part simultaneously and uniformly. Such marks could appear in a colour that would distinguish them from the text of the edition proper (and hence the need for a colour monitor). The programme might have the capacity to delete all such marks and restore the original text of the edition at a single command. In other words it should not be possible to delete or alter any portion of the original text, although various markings can be superimposed on it. Sets of markings could also be written into a file so that they could instantly be recalled and imposed on a score or parts. These features would greatly expedite rehearsals. This medium would be ideal for the interpretative edition: the markings could be written into a separate file that could then be added to the text of the piece. A cellist could approach the Suites of J. S. Bach with the expression marks of Starker, Fournier and Ma available for consultation at the push of a button.

In the interests of greater clarity for the user, whether performer or scholar, and greater flexibility, I believe that the electronic presentation of editions of music holds great promise. The expense of equipping a library or an orchestra with the required machines is sure to be great, and the problem of immediate obsolescence equally discouraging. Of course, an essential feature of the hardware that needs to be developed for this application is downward compatibility: that is, new equipment must be able to read and operate all existing software and data. Despite the hurdles that have yet to be cleared in this area, I am certain that developing technologies will only make the presentation of and access to the type of material presented in an edition of music more flexible and efficient.

6

Conclusion: the posture of the editor

Throughout the preceding discussion, I define the task of editorship as a purely interpretative undertaking. As the work of editing proceeds, editors develop a critical attitude towards the subject of their edition based on an intimate knowledge of the piece, its style and its historical context. Here I address the issue of what place that attitude might take in the final product and what its value is for the user.

The need for the adoption of a critical attitude in editing stems from the fact that, in humanistic studies, there is no such thing as objectivity. In every stage of editing, including transcription, there will arise many questions for which there are no clear-cut right or wrong answers: ambiguities between parallel passages such as exposition and recapitulation, even distribution of reasonable competing readings between sources, text underlay, conflicting key signatures, and so on. Editors who attempt to maintain a cool attitude of objectivity through this maze can follow one of two paths: they can merely present all the ambiguous evidence and let the user decide (sheer dereliction of duty), or they could attempt to resolve with finality every such question (a course that may lead to the misrepresentation of evidence that is genuinely ambiguous, or does not permit a definitive interpretation). A much more reasonable approach, I feel, is to adopt a critical attitude towards the piece, composer or repertory, based on the kind of intimate study necessary for the preparation of an edition in any event, clearly expressed to the user and, most important, consistently applied.

The adoption of the first course of action described above constitutes dereliction of duty because such an edition affords the user little real help in untangling some of the complex issues involved in understanding a piece of music, whether for the purpose of editing, performing or scholarly appraisal. Many of the most famous and highly regarded editions of music fall into this category because their editors felt it more important to present all of the source evidence than to digest it in any way for the user. Moreover these are often mistakenly considered to be critical editions, because, although the final text might be reached by the application of critical thought, the steps taken to those conclusions are not clear from the critical apparatus. Certainly the works of the greatest masters, Shakespeare in literature and J. S. Bach in music, for example, are deserving of an edition in which all the readings of the principal sources are given (perhaps best termed an omnibus edition), although facsimiles of the most important sources might render the user even greater service. Users confronted with this type of edition do have the opportunity to decide for themselves on many of the ambiguous issues. To arrive at these judgements, however, they must replicate many of the steps that the editor has already completed.

A truly critical edition is one in which the editor assembles the source material in the same way it is collected for an omnibus edition. Then, however, the editor's critical faculty is exercised on this material in order to determine what is to be printed, either as the text of the edition, or the evidence on which it is based. The users of such an opinionated, or critical, edition are not prevented from drawing their own conclusions. In the introduction and appendices the editor of a critical edition can present all the data that would be found in a conservative or omnibus edition, and so the users' capability of formulating their own judgements is not in the least impaired. On the contrary I would hope that the kind of critical commentary I advocate would in fact challenge and stimulate users to arrive at their own conclusions.

Critical editions should generate critical users. The advantage a critical edition offers its users is guidance from a scholar who has devoted a considerable amount of time, energy and imagination to the problems of the piece and whose opinion is therefore worth considering. This is not to say that users need not do any thinking for themselves, nor that they must agree with the editor in every particular. But a critical attitude should stimulate a critical response, of which one possible manifestation is a competing edition. Many of these ambiguous issues can never be resolved definitively, either because source materials have perished or because ambiguities were present from the original compositional conception of the work. Therefore no edition is definitive, and, perhaps more important, the truth is simply not ascertainable.

The editor should not capitulate, however, in the face of such an apparently hopeless situation. A hypothesis, an educated guess, drawing on intensive and extensive study of the work and its historical context, and presented to the user as speculation, is much more valuable than a simple acknowledgement that the truth cannot be known, no matter how valid that acknowledgement is. The greatest works of music, as of literature, have attracted and will continue to attract the attentions of editors whose approach varies considerably, and so it is inevitable that several editions of a given piece might exist, each different in many aspects. If such is the case, invariably the truth will fall somewhere in between the competing editions, and the student of the work is better served by consulting all editions or as many as is practicable. In this way the users themselves can draw conclusions about the whereabouts of that truth.

Hitherto I have discussed the edition as if it were a tool only for professionals, whether scholars or performers. Critical editions of the type I advocate could largely replace descriptive writings as an introduction to the repertories for students in a historical context. It seems preferable to make the music itself available to students so that they can immediately begin making critical evaluations of it. Again I take an analogy from literature, where students generally begin by reading the literature itself, and only at a more advanced stage tackle secondary materials. Music students too often begin with the great monuments of textbook literature instead of the music itself, and this practice inhibits critical inquiry. Therefore editions that can stand on their own and offer an introduction to a composer or repertory, to the historical and cultural setting, will enable the student to address the music and its problems of meaning in a direct way. Some such editions are available (e.g., the Norton Critical Scores), but they do not seem to have yet displaced the descriptive historical textbook as the point of departure for the historical study of music.

The critical attitude of the editor can be useful in providing a point of entry to the piece or repertory for a widely varied audience. It can bridge the gap between less experienced users and the repertories, especially in the case of obscure genres and eras. Professional scholars and performers should respond critically to the attitude of the editor. All users should be provided with the equipment to enter into an informed dialogue with the composer, piece or repertory, and should be challenged and stimulated to undertake such a dialogue. The act of editing is in itself an act of criticism, of evaluation of those matters that cannot be resolved definitively, and it should in turn permit, even promote (not to say provoke) further acts of criticism.

7

Epilogue

(1) An edition of the music copied in the hand of Adémar de Chabannes (989–1034)

A prominent theme throughout this discussion concerns the development, by each editor, of specific methodology for specific editorial projects. Here I present an outline of the approach I adopted for an edition of early eleventh-century monophony and offer a critique of two recent editions by other scholars, each of whom has developed a distinctive critical method for dealing with music that presents individual problems. These editions all represent special cases in every phase of their production, like all editions. Like all editions, a number of contrasting approaches could have been chosen with equal success, although each would have resulted in a quite different edition, presenting the material in a different way for varying audiences. The choices I made, for example, are not definitive, but the best alternatives, in my judgement, for the various conditions under which the edition was created. My intention here is to show what factors influenced those choices, and how the form of the edition developed as successive stages of production were met.

Adémar de Chabannes is a well-known literary figure from early eleventh-century Aquitaine. A monk at the Abbey of Saint Cybard in Angoulême, he was active as a historian, homilist and polemicist.[1] His family was also well connected in the ecclesiastical hierarchy of the city of Limoges, where he pursued his advanced education at the Abbey of Saint Martial under the tutelage of his uncle, Roger de Chabannes,

[1] On Adémar's biography, see Landes, "The Making of a Medieval Historian." For further bibliography, see Grier, "*Ecce sanctum*," p. 28 n. 2.

who eventually became the Abbey's cantor.[2] As part of these studies, Adémar achieved professional competence as a musician, skilled in the technology of musical notation, and intimately familiar with the liturgical repertories practised at Saint Martial. The evidence for these conclusions rests in three surviving music manuscripts copied in Adémar's hand that once formed part of the monastic library at Saint Martial.[3] These show that Adémar is the earliest named music scribe, and the earliest known composer to leave music in autograph. The bulk of the music preserved in his hand constitutes a new liturgy in support of the fraudulent claims for the apostolic status of Martial, patron of the Abbey that bears his name in Limoges.

An edition of this music was commissioned to form part of Adémar's Collected Works to be published in the series Corpus Christianorum Continuatio Mediaeualis (Turnhout, Brepols). The placement of the edition in this distinguished series was a significant factor in many of the decisions that needed to be made about the overall conception of the edition and its eventual presentation. Corpus Christianorum Continuatio Mediaeualis publishes Latin texts from the central and later Middle Ages, and appeals primarily to medievalists engaged in research on philosophy, theology and ecclesiastical history. Texts are printed in Latin, without translation, and commentary is normally restricted to a critical apparatus, which lists variant readings, and a secondary apparatus, with references to sources, like the Bible and patristic writings, cited or quoted in the work. Introductions are sometimes quite extensive, and principally treat the manuscript sources and their interrelationships.

Moreover, because this edition was to form part of Adémar's Collected Works, it had to address the concerns of readers who were drawn to Adémar through an interest in his other writings, and only became aware of his musical activities incidentally. I felt it necessary, therefore, to discuss in some detail the historical context in which Adémar pursued these activities, and how they relate to his other writings. Finally, my edition is the first music to be published in the series, and therefore, because my audience would include medievalists who are not musicologists, I made every effort to make the edition access-

[2] On Roger, see Grier, "Roger de Chabannes."

[3] The three manuscripts are Pa 909, 1121 and 1978. Delisle, "Notice," pp. 350–53, identified his hand in Pa 1121 and 1978. The appearance of Adémar's hand in Pa 909 was first unequivocally noted by Hooreman, "Saint-Martial de Limoges," pp. 16–30. See also Emerson, "Two Newly Identified Offices," pp. 33–35; Grier, "*Ecce sanctum*," pp. 35–40; and Grier, "Editing Adémar de Chabannes' Liturgy," pp. 18–23.

ible to as wide an audience as possible without sacrificing the importance of the music in its overall impact. This last point is of some consequence because the edition presents a good deal of music not available elsewhere in print, and I therefore also directed it to an audience of specialists within musicology. This combination of circumstances naturally resulted in some compromises that were not necessarily the ideal solution for one or the other constituency, but it seemed best to strive for accessibility in most areas.

The sources: Pa 909

Our principal source for Adémar's musical activities is Pa 909. It, together with Pa 1121, forms part of the celebrated group of Aquitanian troper-prosers. These manuscripts are organized in libelli in which pieces of the same liturgical classifications are grouped together.[4] Pa 909 originated in the scriptorium of Saint Martial as a commission for the neighbouring Abbey of Saint Martin.[5] The production of the libellus of Proper tropes, with which the codex begins, was interrupted at a late stage, after several later libelli had been completed and assigned signatures within the larger structure of the manuscript.[6] The reason for the interruption was that Adémar took over the project in order to insert his newly composed apostolic liturgy for the feast of Saint Martial, along with other related materials (see Table 7–1). Most of Adémar's additions form part of the apostolic liturgy for Martial himself, or of liturgies for his companions, Austriclinian, Justinian and Valery. The sequentiary (fols. 110r–125v, completed on fols. 198r and 205r–v) is a significant exception to this pattern. Although it contains an important group of sequentiae for the feast of Saint Martial (introduced by a rubric that explicitly acknowledges his apostolicity), the motivation for its inclusion is rather to be sought in Adémar's passion for the genre. A second

[4] Crocker, "The Repertoire of Proses," I, 190–95, 246–58; Chailley, "Les anciens tropaires," pp. 169–71, 174–77; Chailley, *L'école*, pp. 81–83, 88–92; Husmann, *Tropen- und Sequenzenhandschriften*, pp. 118–19, 130–31; and Evans, *The Early Trope Repertory*, pp. 48–49. On the libellus structure of this type of manuscript in general, see Huglo, "Les *Libelli* de tropes"; and Huglo, *Les livres de chant liturgique*, pp. 64–75.

[5] Chailley, "Les anciens tropaires," p. 174; *L'école*, p. 90; and Grier, "*Ecce sanctum*," pp. 68–69.

[6] Chailley, "Les anciens tropaires," p. 175, and *L'école*, p. 89; Gaborit-Chopin, *La décoration*, p. 183; Evans, *The Early Trope Repertory*, pp. 32–33; and Grier, "*Ecce sanctum*," p. 35. On the manuscript's structure, see Crocker "The Repertoire of Proses," I, 248–58; Chailley, "Les anciens tropaires," pp. 174–77, and *L'école*, pp. 88–92; Husmann, *Tropen- und Sequenzenhandschriften*, p. 119; and Grier, "Editing Adémar de Chabannes' Liturgy," pp. 19–23.

Table 7–1 Adémar de Chabannes' Additions to Pa 909

Folios	Inventory
41r–48v	Proper tropes (fols. 42r–46v Troped Mass for Saint Martial)
59r–61v	Proper tropes
61v–62r	Alleluias for Saint Martial
62v–77v	Office and miscellaneous liturgical items for Saint Martial
79r–85v	Offices for Saints Valery and Austriclinian
110r–125v	Sequentiae (fols. 118r–119v Sequentiae for Saint Martial)
177v–178r	Alleluias for Saint Martial
198r	Sequentia
198r–201v	Prosae for Saint Martial
202r–205r	Versus de Sancto Marciale LXXta IIo
205r–v	Sequentia
251r	Processional antiphon for Saint Martial
254r–257v	Tonary: additions by Adémar

sequentiary in Adémar's hand also occurs in Pa 1121, and so further reflects that enthusiasm.

The Introit of the Mass and several items of the Office include verses that are sung to melodic formulae, as discussed in Chapter 4 above. Adémar does not normally indicate the formula, or tone, to be used, and for this information, the tonary in Pa 909 (fols. 251r–257v) became an invaluable source. This section of the manuscript belongs to the first layer, and so, although Adémar did not compile or inscribe the text, he did write in the musical notation; moreover he made several changes to the literary text of the tonary, from which I deduce that he went over its contents with some care when he entered the music. Therefore I conclude that the tonary represents Adémar's own knowledge of these melodic formulae and their application, and I used it as the primary source for the verse tones that require them.

Pa 1978

The flyleaves at the back of Pa 1978 consist of a bifolium with both music and text in Adémar's hand (fols. 102r–103v). The contents are portions of an Office for Saint Cybard (the patron of his home Abbey in Angoulême), and of what seems to be an Office for the octave of Saint Martial. The matutinal responsories of the latter are written in full, but the antiphons are cued *ut supra*. Adémar thereby refers to a complete set of antiphons written above, probably in the Office for the feast itself, in a portion of the manuscript that does not survive. This is exactly the arrangement of materials in the episcopal Offices for the feast and the octave of Saint Martial in Pa 1085, an antiphoner written before the Dedication of the new Abbey church at Saint Martial on 18 November 1028.[7] The folios that constitute the flyleaves in Pa 1978 are not consecutive, and therefore came from a gathering of at least two bifolia.

Pa 1121

The libelli of tropes, both Proper and Ordinary, in Pa 1121 were written at Saint Martial before the Dedication of 1028, as no mention of that ceremony occurs among them. Their *terminus ante quem non* is probably the death, in 1025, of the cantor Roger de Chabannes: Pa 1121 is most likely the creation of the new cantor who succeeded Roger at Saint Martial. Adémar's signature occurs three times in the sequentiary of Pa 1121 (fols. 58r–72v), including the colophon in which he identifies himself as the scribe who wrote the musical notation in the book (*notauit*; fol. 72v).[8] He also wrote the limited amount of literary text that occurs in the sequentiary. The sequentiary is an independent libellus, added by Adémar after the libelli of tropes were completed, and written after the sequentiary in Pa 909. These two libelli are the only complete collections of items for the cycle of the liturgical year copied by Adémar, and, aside from many similarities in structure and repertory, they demonstrate a particular interest, on Adémar's part, in the untexted or partially texted sequence.

Adémar organized the sequentiary around two cycles for the liturgical year: the first (fols. 58r–70r) largely duplicates in content and order the sequentiary in Pa 909; the second (fols. 70r–72v) contains no sequences shared with Pa 909, and so I take it to be an appendix that Adémar added to his original collection. Each is incomplete. The last two sequences in the appendix (on fol. 72v) are assigned to the feast of John the Baptist (24 June), and so indicate that the appendix covers about half the liturgical year. The libellus begins, on fol. 58r, with the sequence for the second Sunday of Advent, and is missing its first folio, which would have contained a series of pieces for the first Sunday of Advent.[9] This

[7] Feast of Saint Martial, Pa 1085, fols. 76v–77r; octave, fols. 77v–78r.

[8] The colophon has been printed in full several times; the most recent correct transcription is in Escudier, "Des notations musicales," p. 36 n. 3.

[9] Crocker, "The Repertoire of Proses," I, 192; and Husmann, *Tropen- und Sequenzenhandschriften*, p. 130. But cf. Huglo, "Codicologie et musicologie," pp. 78–79, and "On the Origins," p. 14 and n. 15 (note on p. 18), who states that the single leaf fol. 64r–v belongs to the following gathering (fols. 65r–72v) and not the preceding.

sequentiary, therefore, constitutes a "second edition" by Adémar, expanded by the inclusion of the appendix.

Codex Pa 909, then, was clearly Adémar's principal manuscript. It contains, in autograph, the liturgy for Saint Martial in its fullest form as conceived by Adémar. Pa 1978 seems to transmit a revision of the Office liturgy. In particular some responsorial verses from Matins are not found in Pa 909; in the edition, these were incorporated in a separate section immediately after the edition of the apostolic Office in Pa 909. The sequentiary in Pa 1121, on the other hand, is a "second edition," and contains some revisions to his first version in Pa 909. Because the sequentiary in Pa 909 contributes to the apostolic profile of the codex, it was taken as the principal source for this repertory, although its text was compared in every instance with Pa 1121, and corrected from it where necessary. The unica in Pa 1121 were added to the edited sequentiary as an appendix, in the same way they are added to its sequentiary.

Other sources

Despite this wealth of autograph sources, it was necessary to become familiarized with the historical, liturgical and musical context within which Adémar produced these witnesses. Therefore I consulted the surviving liturgical books from Saint Martial in order to determine what materials were at his disposal while he was working on Pa 909, what use he made of them, and how his codices influenced subsequent books produced at Saint Martial. Sources for the Mass are well known. Codices Pa 1120 (fols. 46r–51v) and 1121 (fols. 28v–32r) contain troped episcopal Masses for the feast of Saint Martial that predate Adémar's apostolic liturgy, and Pa 1119 (fols. 54v-61v) transmits a version of the apostolic Mass that is a direct copy of Adémar's Pa 909. These witnesses served as a check on the material in Pa 909, and suggested several corrections and clarifications of Adémar's readings.

Two manuscripts attest to the celebration of the Divine Office in Limoges during the early eleventh century. Pa 1085 is an abbreviated antiphoner written at Saint Martial before AD 1028, as noted above. It contains an episcopal Office for the feast of Saint Martial. The same Office occurs in Pa 1253, a breviary, which transmits the texts of the Office in full. Later Office sources from Saint Martial date to the period following the purchase and forcible occupation of the monastery by Cluniac monks in 1062–63, and those sources consequently accord with the Cluniac liturgy.[10] Nevertheless the antiphoner Pa 1088 constitutes the only available resource associated with Saint Martial for certain chants, and from it I drew *Ciues apostolorum*, a responsory for Matins of the feast of Saint Martial that Adémar indicates by cue only in Pa 909 (fol. 68r).

The liturgy of both Mass and Office includes spoken texts, and, although there is no evidence that Adémar composed or adapted texts in these categories for his apostolic liturgy, they would certainly have formed part of its celebration. Therefore I sought, among the available sources of these texts from Saint Martial, those which were closest in date to Adémar's lifetime. For the Office, Pa 1253, which was probably known to Adémar, provided the lections. No Mass lectionary or official sacramentary survives from the early eleventh century, but three sources do permit us to form a good idea of the identity and texts of the spoken items for the Mass. Codex Pa 821 is a sacramentary from the eleventh century that was associated with Saint Martial, but did not enter the Abbey's library until 1210, when it was purchased by the librarian, Bernard Itier, as a note on fol. 142v records. Another sacramentary, Pa 822, was used for the liturgy at Saint Martial. It dates from after the Cluniac takeover and resembles Pa 821 in many details. I used these two sources for the spoken prayers in the Mass. The Mass lections are found in Pa 890, a thirteenth- or fourteenth-century lectionary.

These sources were supplemented with the other surviving music manuscripts from tenth-, eleventh- and twelfth-century Aquitaine. My goal in consulting these witnesses was not to establish an original or definitive Aquitanian reading for any of these chants, but to heighten my awareness of the traditions and contexts within which this music was circulated in Aquitaine during this period. In particular, I attempted to locate the various sources from which Adémar might have learned specific pieces. For example, many of the sequentiae found in Pa 1121 but not in Pa 909 are transmitted in Pa 1118 and 1084, both of which originated in southern Aquitaine around AD 1000. It seems likely, then, that Adémar gained access either to one of these codices, or to a sequentiary that carried a similar repertory,

[10] On the Cluniac takeover, see Grier, "A New Voice in the Monastery," pp. 1068–69 and n. 74. The sources are Pa 743, an eleventh-century breviary, and Pa 1088, a thirteenth- or fourteenth-century antiphoner. On their Cluniac affiliation, see Hesbert, *Corpus antiphonalium officii*, V, 407–44, especially 411, 424–25, 429–33, 443.

sometime between the compilation of Pa 909 in AD 1029 and the copying of the sequentiary in Pa 1121. Therefore the sequentiaries in Pa 1118 and 1084 form part of the musical context in which Adémar worked.

Transcription

The transcription of Adémar's music hand posed only one significant problem, and that was to choose a pitch on which to begin. His heighting is uniformly accurate, and he is quite careful to provide a *custos* at the end of each line, sometimes in the form of the letter *e*, designating *equaliter*, or the same pitch. He uses other *litterae significatiuae* only to confirm large jumps that are accurately heighted; these are *alt* or the letter *l* (*altius* or *leuate*, higher) and *io* (*iusum*, low).[11] Therefore the relative pitch within a given melody is secure. The absence of a clef, however, throws the overall position of each melody within the gamut into uncertainty. Many of the melodies appear in sources with secure absolute pitch information, or, in the case of the tropes, are associated with a melody that is known from such a source, the most important of which is, naturally, Montpellier, Bibliothèque de l'École de Médecine (hereafter Mo), MS H. 159 because its date is so close to Adémar's lifetime.[12] Adémar's versions were compared with those in Mo H. 159 to determine the starting note. If the chant in question was a trope, its host chant was located in Mo H. 159 to determine its starting note, and then I worked backwards from the first note of the host chant to the beginning of the trope.

Adémar equipped many of the chants in Pa 1978 and 909 with an indication of their mode by placing roman numerals at the opening of each melody. This system, incidentally, is also to be found in Pa 1085, although the roman numerals are a later addition.[13] Again, the principle involved working backwards, this time from the last note of the piece, which I took to be the usual final of the mode indicated by the roman numeral, to the first note of the melody. This method does not allow for the possibility of transposition by a fifth to the cofinal, but there was no way of telling when, or indeed whether, Adémar intended any chant to be so transposed.

[11] For further bibliography, see Grier, "Roger de Chabannes," pp. 66–67.

[12] Reproduced in facsimile in *Antiphonarium tonale missarum, XIe siècle, Codex H. 159 de la Bibliothèque de l'École de Médecine de Montpellier*; and transcribed in Hansen, *H 159 Montpellier*.

[13] Huglo, *Les tonaires*, p. 111.

By one or the other of these two methods, all but a handful of the chants could be transcribed with certainty. For the remainder, I relied on the all too uncertain method of modal analysis. For example, the lengthy processional antiphon *Aue pastor* (Pa 909 fols. 73v–74v) is, to the best of my knowledge, without concordance. Its melody bears many of the characteristics of mode 2, particularly in the way in which it treats the tonal region below the final. Melodies in mode 8, however, share many of the same characteristics, and the chant could be transcribed equally well in that mode. There are some exposed leaps from the subfinal up a fourth, which, in mode 8, would result in a leap of a tritone, F–B; this problem could be avoided, though, by the application of B♭. If B♭ is consistently applied to a transcription in mode 8, the intervallic structure of the melody is exactly the same as a transcription in mode 2 without B♭. With some trepidation, then, I transcribed *Aue pastor* to end on D, in mode 2, but hastened to add a note explaining the uncertainty of the situation. This is precisely the kind of problem that is best handled by a detailed editorial comment. No definitive solution is possible, but the edition's user has enough information to evaluate the editor's choice and decide whether the evidence justified it.

The establishment of the text

As evidence from the sources accumulated, it became clear that a reconstruction of the apostolic liturgy, as Adémar would have recognized it, would be feasible. Consequently, Pa 909 became the principal source for that portion of the edition, including the sequentiary, which, as noted above, contributes to the rhetoric about the apostolicity, and editorial decisions commenced from its text. Wherever possible, it was compared with contemporary Aquitanian versions of the melodies to check the validity of the melodic tradition recorded by Adémar. It is well documented that chants in this tradition, particularly tropes, are subject to some substantive variation in the course of transmission.[14] When Adémar's versions vary from other contemporary sources, it is essential to determine whether they do so in ways that accord with the perceived notions of this melodic tradition.

Here, of course, a critical evaluation of style is the only criterion by

[14] See the seminal studies of Treitler, "Oral, Written, and Literate Process"; "Transmission and the Study of Music History"; "Observations on the Transmission of some Aquitanian Tropes"; and "The 'Unwritten' and 'Written Transmission'."

which one can judge these readings. Above all I attempted to preserve a conservative, if critical, attitude, in that I required overwhelming evidence to convince me that a variant in Adémar's version was in fact a copying error. I was motivated less by a reverence for Adémar's accuracy in copying than by a respect for the level of legitimate, substantive variation that could occur in the transmission of this repertory. It seemed preferable to retain an idiosyncratic reading that could not be proven incorrect, than to homogenize the text according to the weight of the recorded Aquitanian tradition. In Chapter 3 above, I discuss the kind of evidence I demanded in order to accept a particular reading as erroneous. Adémar copied the last few notes of a Gloria trope, and the subsequent cue to the Gloria melody, a second too low. The reading of Pa 1119 alerted me to the problem. When I compared all other Aquitanian versions of the Gloria melody, they were found to agree with the cue in Pa 1119. Consequently I corrected the edited text to accord with Pa 1119. What makes this reading in Pa 909 an error, rather than a substantive variant, is the combination of the unanimity of the Aquitanian tradition in the Gloria melody with the fact that the melody in Pa 909 is not varied in shape: Adémar simply erred in the heighting.

Similar problems occur in the sequentiary, although here we have two sources in Adémar's hand to consult, Pa 909 and 1121. Where the two sequentiaries differ, the main text of the edition could accommodate only one reading, obviously. To decide between the two, the testimony of other Aquitanian sequentiaries was summoned, but that too presented some problems. Heighting in the sequentiaries of Pa 1084 and 1118 is better than in the tropers and prosers found in those codices, but still not precise enough to be certain about specific intervals. A group of later sequentiaries (in Pa 1133, 1134, 1135, 1136 and 1137) exhibit varying degrees of reliance on Adémar's sequentiaries, and so their evidence cannot be considered independent. There remain only the sequentiaries in Pa 887, which is roughly contemporary with Adémar, and Pa 1871, copied in southern Aquitaine, possibly in Moissac, in the second half of the eleventh century, that provide accurate heighting and an independent tradition. On the basis of their readings, it would seem that Adémar rectified a good number of copying errors in Pa 909 when he made his "second edition" in Pa 1121. A critical examination of the nature of the evidence offered by these witnesses was obligatory to determine which preserved independent and reliable readings.

At an early stage in the project, I decided that all pieces would be presented complete, irrespective of the form in which Adémar gives them. Factors affecting this decision are discussed below in the section on the presentation of the edition. Here it suffices to say that this policy led directly to the most perplexing problem of the whole editorial process, namely, the completion of pieces given only in part by Adémar, as the following example illustrates. Immediately after the Introit tropes in the Mass for Saint Martial, Adémar gives the laconic rubric *AD GLORIAM*. The item that follows, *Rex apostolorum deus*, uses the familiar melody of *Regnum tuum solidum*, which is itself a trope element. It contains a lengthy melisma on the first syllable of *permanebit* that is generally set syllabically with added text in the form of a prosula.[15] *Regnum tuum* prosulae occur in sources from Saint Martial as parts of several different Gloria tropes: *Laus tibi domine* (*Regnum per te Christe*), *Omnipotens altissime (Sceptrum tuum benigne)* and *Laus tibi summe Deus* (*Sceptrum Deus aeterne*). Others occur in a group following the latter complex.[16] I take these to be alternatives to be inserted into the trope *Laus tibi summe deus*, in some cases for specific feasts (e.g., Dedication, *Regnum lumen aeterne*; Marian feast, *Salue Maria uirgo*; Peter and Paul, *Regnum apostolorum princeps*), as the rubrics in Pa 909 show (fols. 97r–98r).[17] The problem here is to determine to which trope Adémar's *Regnum tuum* prosula in the apostolic Mass for Saint Martial belongs. Its melody exactly matches that of *Sceptrum gloria sanctorum*, the introductory trope of the *Regnum tuum* prosula that forms part of *Laus tibi summe deus*. Therefore I give *Rex apostolorum deus* as part of that Gloria trope. The libellus of Ordinary tropes in Pa 909 gives a version of *Laus tibi summe Deus* (fols. 94v–95v), with music written in Adémar's hand. This version, then, was incorporated into the complete edited text.

All *Regnum tuum* prosulae are associated with tropes that are combined with so-called Gloria A or Prima (Bosse melody no. 39),[18] and so that melody forms the base liturgical text of the piece. Unfortunately, it was much more difficult to find an appropriate version of this melody. An untroped version of the chant precedes the Gloria tropes associated with it in Pa 1120 (fol. 82r–v) and 1119 (fol.

[15] Gautier, *Histoire de la poésie liturgique*, pp. 269–78; Dreves, Blume and Bannister, eds., *Analecta hymnica,* XLVII, 282–84; Rönnau, *Die Tropen*, pp. 179–87; Rönnau, "Regnum tuum solidum"; and Evans, *The Early Trope Repertory*, pp. 264, 269.

[16] See the inventories of Pa 1240, 1120, 1121, 909 and 1119 in Rönnau, *Die Tropen*, pp. 20–25.

[17] Given in Rönnau's inventory, *Die Tropen*, p. 23.

[18] Bosse, *Untersuchung einstimmiger mittelalterlicher Melodien zum "Gloria in excelsis deo"*, pp. 95–96.

90r–v). It is reasonable to deduce that it would have occupied a similar position in Pa 1121 and 909, and in the latter would have been equipped with music in Adémar's hand. The gatherings in each codex that would have contained the melody have not survived, however, and so I was forced to rely on the other two witnesses. The heighting of the notation in Pa 1120 does not transmit accurate relative pitch information, with the result that the only transcribable source left to me was Pa 1119. Its version, then, was used as the base text for the edition even though there were various problems with the accuracy of its heighting that needed to be resolved by reference to other Aquitanian sources for the melody.

This situation typifies my approach throughout the production of this edition: to make every effort to reconstruct the music as Adémar would have recognized it. Where that goal was demonstrably unattainable, the witness closest to Adémar, in time, place or both, was used as the base text. At the same time, this attitude did not prevent the application of critical scrutiny to Adémar's own texts, and several corrections were advanced on the basis of evidence from the larger Aquitanian tradition. My conclusion in such cases was that, had Adémar noticed the errors he was committing, he would have corrected them himself. It should be emphasized that this is my conclusion, based on the testimony of the sources, not a proven or provable fact.

And therein lies the difference between this type of edition and one that seeks to reproduce the composer's final intentions. I shall never know what Adémar's intentions were, but I can sift through the historical evidence of the sources, including those written in his own hand, to form my own conception of the music he composed and copied. And that conception is embodied in the edition. The goal of presenting the music most important to Adémar and of returning, as far as possible, to the versions known to Adémar, was in keeping with the aims of the Collected Edition in which this edition was to appear: to present all the texts that formed a part of Adémar's varied and prodigious output so that we might have a better understanding of this complex and passionate individual.

The presentation of the edition

The very nature of Adémar's output guarantees that medievalists from many different disciplines will be drawn to his work, a situation only reinforced by the appearance of the edition in the series Corpus Christianorum Continuatio Mediaeualis. These circumstances encouraged me to attempt to make this edition as accessible as possible to the non-specialist, while preserving its usefulness for the musicologist who would study Adémar's music or the performer who would sing it. First, the literary text of all items was printed twice: once in its normal place, underneath the music, and a second time separately. I located this second presentation after the music so that the music would not seem secondary in importance. The second concession to a non-specialist audience was the composition of a detailed commentary. Many of the editorial decisions required the investigation of technical matters in such areas as liturgy, palaeography, prosody and grammar, as well as purely musical issues. Therefore I felt it best to explain these issues as fully as possible. The commentary also included data about concordant sources, printed editions and the most important variants.

Third, as noted above, all items were printed in full, as they would have been sung in the eleventh century, as far as my sources would permit. Medieval music manuscripts are normally abbreviated by the omission of music and text available in another source or section of the same source. In the copying of tropes for the Introit of the Mass, for example, each phrase of the Introit, the host chant, is indicated only by a cue that usually consists of the first couple of words of the phrase; sometimes these appear without music. The full text of the Introit, text and music, is given in a gradual, together with all the other Proper chants of the Mass.

I elected to gather the various parts of each piece from the sources closest to Adémar in time and place and print them together as a single entity. It seemed inappropriate to leave non-specialists to their own devices for the expansion of the cues; instead of simply citing an appropriate source and letting them correlate it to the printed version as Adémar presented it, I felt it was easier for them to see the entire piece on the page together. For tropes, especially, there is some discussion in the scholarly world about the way they relate to their host chant;[19] it seemed preferable, then, to print the entire piece, tropes and host chant, together to permit further scholarly inquiry.

A fourth consideration was determined also by the issue of accessibility, but not only for non-specialists, and that was the decision to

[19] See Evans, *The Early Trope Repertory*, pp. 55–118; and Dennery, *Le chant postgrégorien*, pp. 112–19.

print the music with transposing treble clef; that is, treble clef sounding an octave lower than written. Some of the repertory in the edition was already published elsewhere, and in most cases was printed with this clef, and so I decided to use it also to facilitate comparison between editions.[20] It eliminates most leger lines, and the treble clef (transposing or otherwise) is most familiar to musically literate non-specialists. A similar line of reasoning led me to adopt modern notational devices for the music. Eleventh-century Aquitanian notation consists, for the most part, of *puncta*, and so the translation to modern, stemless noteheads retained at least some of the character of the original.

The resolution of the relatively few ligatures, mostly *clives*, into their constituent notes presented no problems. The treatment of liquescence was more delicate, but again the limited number of signs used by Adémar allowed me to adapt modern notational signs to indicate their occurrence. The loss of fidelity to the original, slight as it may be here, was compensated, in my mind, by the increased accessibility of the musical text to those non-specialists with a degree of musical literacy. Specialists would, in any case, refer back to the manuscripts directly for points of clarification, and the publishers were most generous in permitting the reproduction of facsimiles from the manuscripts to illustrate the edition and show the exact relationship between original notation and my adaptation of modern symbols.

The layout, contents and placement of the two critical apparatus required some consideration. The literary text is printed separately from the music with text, as noted above, and its apparatus appears here, printed at the bottom of the page in the normal manner. Because I wished to keep the pages of the music portion of the edition as uncluttered as possible, I printed its apparatus separately, and then placed it between the edition of the literary text and the commentary, which dealt with both musical and literary issues. This position was a compromise, as it moved the music apparatus away from the edited text to which it pertains, but it allowed the two sections of edited material (music and text, and text alone) to be adjacent. Then the music apparatus is closer to the commentary, in which some of the variant readings are discussed.

The matter of content was also a compromise. This edition does not

[20] Evans, *The Early Trope Repertory*, pp. 129–273; Weiß, ed., *Introitus-tropen*, I, *Das Repertoire der südfranzösischen Tropare*; Schlager, ed., *Alleluia-Melodien*, I, *bis 1100*.

purport to establish definitively the full Aquitanian tradition of this music, and so a complete listing of all variants was not suitable. It did seem useful, however, to cite in full all variants found in witnesses to which Adémar had access (Pa 1085 and 1253 for the Office, Pa 1120 and 1121 for the Mass) or that were copied from Adémar's manuscripts (i.e., Pa 1119 for the troped Mass). These manuscripts attest to the milieu in which Adémar worked, and they illustrate his methods in compiling and editing this material. A more selective group of variants was included from the other witnesses consulted in order to demonstrate, in broader terms, how Adémar's versions of these chants fit into the larger Aquitanian musical tradition. The more important of these variants, whether from codices close to Adémar's milieu or not, are discussed in the commentary, and these are marked in the music apparatus with an asterisk, to alert the user to that fact.

The commentary itself contains a wide variety of materials. As noted above, it gives full references to concordances in the Aquitanian sources and to printed editions. It also presents discussions of all points of interest that occurred to me in the course of making the edition. Many of these explain criteria, methods and procedures used to solve various editorial problems. Others address issues of history, liturgy, lexicography and transmission that seemed to me pertinent to an understanding of the meaning and context of the piece. And some discuss readings of interest for the history of the text. I present, for example, extensive discussions of the criteria that determined my choice of sources for the Gloria with trope *Rex apostolorum deus*; that discussion is summarized above. The exact application of the Psalm tone for mode 1 to the verses of the troped Introit also required thorough consideration in a note. As a final example, I cite two readings in the literary texts of the Introit tropes. Both exhibit aural confusion in their orthography: several witnesses give *iessit* for *gessit*, and in another trope *esternis* for *externis*.[21] These corruptions indicate, I believe, that the erroneous witnesses derived these items from the oral tradition, in which the aural confusion could arise. These examples give an idea of the range of material covered in the commentary. Notes are keyed to the edited text by lemma.

To all of this was prefaced the Introduction, in which I discuss the sources and their relationships, and the editorial procedures adopted

[21] The first reading occurs in the trope *Marcialis dominum*; the second in *Sedibus externis*. Three witnesses contain both corruptions: Pa 1120, 1084a and 1084c; Pa 1121 also transmits the corruption *iessit* in *Marcialis dominum*.

for the project, in much the same terms, in fact, as the discussion in this epilogue. Neither a biographical sketch of Adémar nor a discussion of his other works was necessary, of course, because the edition forms part of the Collected Works of Adémar. The treatment of the sources did lead to a summary of Adémar's musical activities, which then complemented the Introductions to the other volumes in the series.

This edition represents only one of many possible ways to present this material. It does not attempt to solve all problems with the music, and undoubtedly some critics will say that it creates some new ones. Perhaps that is a result of all scholarship. A key aspect of the edition, however, is the attempt to explain the critical reasoning that contributed to every editorial decision. These explanations were not motivated by a need to justify the edition and its procedures. Rather they are presented in order to afford the user the opportunity to assess the basis of the edition itself, to enable the edition's audience to weigh the evidence and its critical evaluation on their own terms, with the ultimate goal of determining the edition's usefulness and reliability. My intention was to foster new critical dialogues between the audience for the edition and the music presented in it. And if the edition helps to place Adémar's musical activities in the overall context of his output, and if the music is now more accessible to those who would study and perform it, the edition has done its job.

(2) Wolfgang Amadeus Mozart, *Symphony in C Major No. 36 K. 425 'Linz'*, ed. Cliff Eisen (London, 1992)

With the recent completion of the Neue Mozart-Ausgabe, the musically literate public can safely suppose that the texts of Mozart's works are now based on a firm scholarly foundation. As I remark in Chapter 1 above, however, new documents and new interpretations of familiar evidence continue to come forward, and already the NMA faces challenges. Nevertheless, any new edition of a work by Mozart must inevitably be measured against the pertinent text in the NMA. The NMA is widely available in its original form, and Bärenreiter, its publisher, has increased its market penetration through two complementary strategies aimed at opposite ends of the scale. For specialists who expect to spend a great deal of time with Mozart's works, Bärenreiter offers the complete set of editions in paperback. They have also issued study scores of individual works in a reduced size aimed at scholars or musicians who wish to add a few works of Mozart's to their collection. These marketing schemes are supported, of course, by the considerable scholarly prestige that surrounds the whole enterprise.

For a new edition to have any audience at all, therefore, it must establish that it presents a more reliable or authoritative text than does the NMA. That prospective audience would include scholars, performers (particularly conductors) and musically literate music lovers, all with distinctive requirements in an edition. They should expect a clear and succinct statement of the differences between the new offering and its competitor in the NMA, and they should be able to locate the principal variations in the text quickly and efficiently. The CD collector who follows a favourite recording with the score, the conductor who is considering the adoption of the edition for performance, and the scholar who might base stylistic and analytic observations on the text all need to know what makes this edition unique and worthy of consultation.

The *Linz* Symphony presents a unique opportunity for an edition to compete with the NMA version because, for this symphony alone among Mozart's mature contributions to the genre, no autograph survives. All new editions since World War II depend on two sets of manuscript parts, as mentioned in Chapter 3 above, one in Donaueschingen and the other in Salzburg. Cliff Eisen, who produced the current edition, stresses the importance of the Salzburg parts (Eisen's siglum Sm) for his text, noting that Friedrich Schnapp, the editor of the work for the NMA, used them for his 1971 edition, but relied principally on the Donaueschingen parts (DO).[1] Eisen further states that not all the differences between the sets of parts can be attributed to copying error; some might well represent the composer's revisions of the work. Where the parts differ, Eisen follows Sm and prints readings from DO in footnotes.

From these statements, I infer that, because Schnapp based his edition on DO, the principal differences between the editions will appear in Eisen's footnotes. This is not the case. First, Eisen prints only twelve footnotes, which caused me to wonder why Eisen and Peters (his publisher) had undertaken the edition if only twelve readings were changed from the NMA text. Of these twelve, fully half concern the bassoon parts in the Finale, which may have a simple explanation in performance conditions, as I discuss below. Among the other six, three deal with scoring, one with slurs, and the remaining two with one substantive variant that requires comment below. Eisen's Critical Commentary (pp. 65–70, but unnumbered) sheds no more light on differences between the editions because readings from the NMA are not reported there. On the contrary, a spot check reveals that Schnapp incorporated some readings from Sm into his text, further clouding the distinction between the two editions.

It is only when one turns to Eisen's article on the Symphony in the *Journal of the Royal Music Association* that one learns exactly why his edition is not only justified but necessary.[2] There he shows convincingly that many of the readings in Schnapp's edition come from neither DO nor Sm, and it is the retention of these readings in the NMA that requires a response in the form of a superseding edition, a response that Eisen here provides.[3] One claim that he makes is not fully defensible. Eisen implies that Schnapp's source for these readings is the AMA, but of the seven examples Eisen discusses, the two Collected Editions agree in only four.[4] Eisen also gives a most helpful table of

[1] Eisen, "Preface," in Mozart, *Symphony in C Major No. 36*, ed. Eisen, p. 3 (hereafter page numbers given in the text refer to this edition). Mozart, *Sinfonie in C ("Linzer Sinfonie") KV 425*, ed. Schnapp, pp. 3–62; this edition is reprinted with a slightly revised Preface (1986), and subsequent references are to this reprint.

[2] Eisen, "New Light." [3] *Ibid.*, pp. 88–92.

[4] In Eisen's first three examples, the AMA and NMA disagree, "New Light," pp. 86–89; these passages concern the first movement, bars 24–26, 97–99 and 128–29. For the AMA edition, see Mozart, *Symphonien*, pp. 37–80.

readings in which DO and Sm differ, indicating therein which reading Schnapp adopted.[5] To be fair, some of these readings do occur in the footnotes to Eisen's edition and the rest in his Critical Commentary, but nowhere are they grouped, as they are in Table 2 of his article, to show graphically the relationship between the two editions (Schnapp's and Eisen's) and the two principal sources.

Again, in fairness, Eisen refers the reader to the article in his Preface, and, one assumes in modesty, does not repeat the material published there. This is simply not adequate for a significant constituency among the prospective audience for this edition. Scholars may well have the time, inclination and energy to chase down bibliographic footnotes, but an editor simply cannot expect other members of the audience to share that proclivity (and there is no shame in not sharing it!). What Eisen's edition needs, therefore, is a cogent and concise summary of the arguments presented in his article; Table 2, showing important readings from DO and Sm, might also be welcomed. Some repetition would be involved, of course, but the edition's user (and purchaser) has every right to expect that the edition can explain itself. As it stands, the user has no way of knowing that many readings in the NMA are not authorized by either principal source, and that Eisen's edition identifies and rectifies the problem.

Eisen, in his article and the Preface to the edition, raises the possibility that Mozart revised the Symphony between its initial performances in 1783–84 and the sale of the Donaueschingen parts in 1786.[6] His chief evidence for revision is a variant in the second violin part of the slow movement, about which he says that both readings are "equally plausible" (bars 11 and 76; see Example 7–1).[7] I do not believe that the reading of Sm, which Eisen prints in his edition, is plausible, however. It introduces an unresolved dissonance (B♭) into the context of a chord that is already dissonant (I^6_4), but, more important, it attracts attention away from the much more pungent dissonance that follows on the last beat of the bar, where the first oboe, horn and violin have A against B♭, the seventh of the dominant chord, in the second violin. Eisen's adoption of this reading requires more discussion than he provides in either the article or his Critical Commentary.

If the reading from Sm is not authentic, Eisen's argument about compositional revision loses a good deal of its substance. Most of the

5 Eisen, "New Light," Table 2, p. 92, and discussion 92–93.
6 On the sale of the parts, see Schnapp, "Neue Mozart-Funde."
7 Eisen, "New Light," pp. 92–94; quotation 93.

Example 7–1: W. A. Mozart, Symphony No. 36, K. 425, second movement, bar 11

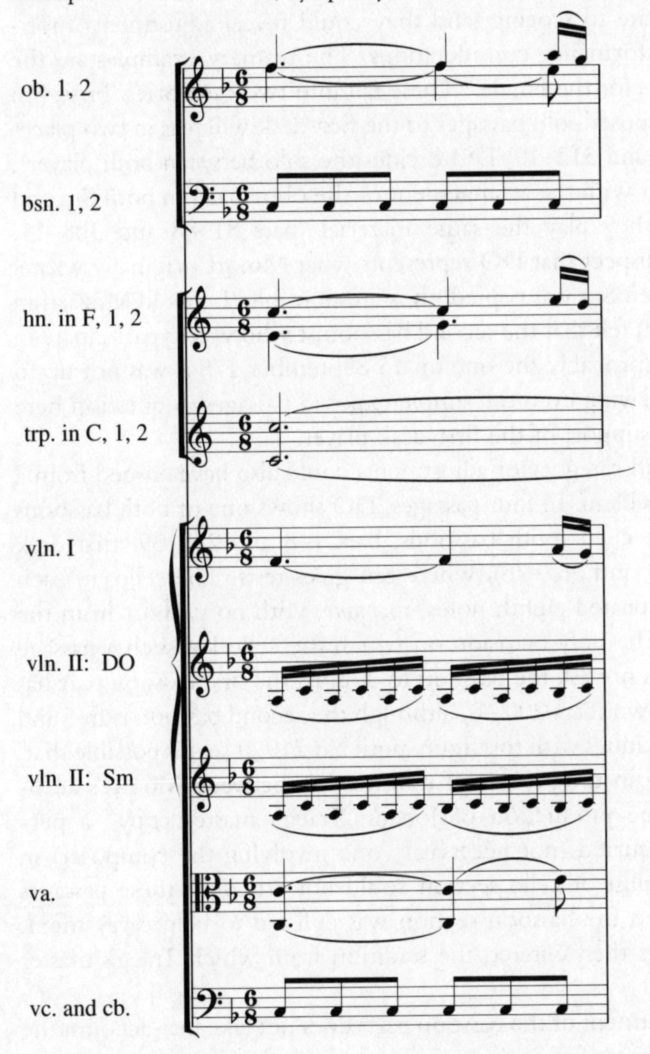

remaining readings that might have arisen from Mozart's second thoughts relate to scoring, and they could reveal adjustments motivated by performance considerations. The primary examples are the bassoon parts for the Finale.[8] These fall into two categories. First, Sm assigns all exposed solo passages to the first desk whereas in two places (bars 73–80 and 312–19) DO divides the solo between both players, in agreement with the arrangement of the oboe parts in both Sm and DO when they play the same material (bars 81–88 and 308–11, 320–23). I suspect that DO represents what Mozart originally wrote, but that, when Sm was copied, those responsible (Leopold Mozart, in all likelihood) felt that the second bassoonist who was to participate in the concert (probably the one on 15 September 1784) was not up to the task of playing even the simple exposed passages in question here without the support of the first-desk player.

The second category of adjustments could also have ensued from a personnel problem. In four passages, DO shows one or both bassoons doubling the cello (both bassoons, bars 1–8 and 232–39; first desk only, 132–41 and 367–76), where Sm gives rests. The cello, in each case, plays repeated eighth notes, in *piano*, with no support from the contrabass. The only occasion on which the cello has such a passage and DO does not ask the bassoon to double, the first bassoon part has a solo of its own (bars 200–4), although the second bassoon is free and the cello continues with this figure until bar 219. It seems possible that, at some time in the process of transmission between Mozart's autograph and the production of Johann Traeg's master copy,[9] a performance occurred (not necessarily one involving the composer) in which the cellist or cello section could not articulate these passages cleanly, and so the bassoon section was enlisted to help carry them. The markings then entered the tradition from which Traeg's master descended.

Eisen's treatment of the bassoon parts does not take into account the fact that both sets of parts were created for performance, and that musicians in every age adjust the music before them to accommodate the exigencies of performance. The modifications have the air of an impromptu solution to a problem that may have been foreseen (in Sm)

[8] The alterations in DO are described but not critically discussed in Schnapp, "Vorwort," in Mozart, *Sinfonie in C ("Linzer Sinfonie") KV 425*, ed. Schnapp, p. Va.

[9] Traeg, a Viennese music dealer, probably supplied the parts that Mozart sold to the court at Donaueschingen. Eisen, "New Light," pp. 82–83, 86–89, shows that his master copy was, at best, a copy of the autograph and not the autograph itself; see also the discussion in Chapter 3 above.

or arose in rehearsal (in DO). Eisen acknowledges only two sources for readings, compositional *fiat* (expanded to include revision) and scribal error, but this structure may not accord with the practical realities of performance.

Eisen's edition, then, supersedes Schnapp's contribution to the NMA, although the reader would appreciate being informed of that fact and the reasons for it somewhere in the edition itself, instead of having to ferret it out of an article in a scholarly journal, hardly the everyday reading of a large segment of the intended audience. Moreover most readers would be grateful for fuller discussions of some of Eisen's editorial decisions. Many musicians want to know not just the outcome of the decision but the procedure that went into reaching it. The place for such discussions is the Critical Commentary, which, in this edition, is really a critical report or apparatus because only four readings receive discursive comment. Many of the readings Eisen adopts are defensible but not so entirely self-evident as to require no discussion.

Finally, the existence of the Critical Commentary, even in its current form as an apparatus, is a notable virtue of the edition. Not only does it inform the user of Eisen's edition about the source evidence on which it is founded, but it also allows us to see to what degree Schnapp has conflated Sm and DO in the NMA, a task hitherto not possible in the absence of the critical report for that edition, which, to the best of my knowledge, remains unpublished at this writing, over twenty years after the appearance of the edition itself.

(3) Giuseppe Verdi, *Don Carlos*, 2 vols., ed. Ursula Günther (Milan, 1980)

Opera presents the editor with particular difficulties. First, source materials are often related to specific performances, whose historical circumstances, therefore, affect the nature and evaluation of the source evidence. And second, perhaps more than any other musical genre, opera undergoes a very public process of socialization. Once the score is created, opera companies, producers, directors, conductors and singers all have some say in the final shape of the work in performance. These contributions are frequently reflected in the source material, and so one of the principal tasks of the editor is to sort through these materials to determine the various states of the work, how they came into existence, and what forces and motivations were responsible for each. Opera depends on the collaboration of many specialists for its production, and the editor who would disregard their participation and seek, instead, the composer's text alone, not only denies the fundamentally social nature of the genre but also runs the risk of producing an ahistorical edition.

Many of these problems beset *Don Carlos*, Verdi's opera for the Universal Exposition of 1867 in Paris. Before 1969, most published scores in circulation transmitted versions of four and five acts that represented, respectively, the productions of Milan in 1883 (first performance 10 January 1884) and of Modena in 1886. Since then, the discovery of passages cut from the original Paris production but still present in the performing materials for that production now permits the reconstruction of the work's pre-production states.[1] The current edition assembles all the music Verdi composed for the opera over a period of some twenty years, including some, the early cuts from the original production, that has never been performed or published. Because of the importance of the material, and the complexity of preparing a comprehensive critical edition, Günther and the publishers, Ricordi, opted to issue a piano-vocal score first. Ricordi has also prepared performing materials that are based on this edition and are available on a rental basis, but the critical edition of the full orchestral score awaits publication in the Collected Edition under the auspices of Ricordi and the University of Chicago Press.

[1] Günther, "La genèse de *Don Carlos*"; *eadem*, "Vorwort," in Verdi, *Don Carlos*, ed. Günther, I, pp. V–XXXIII (hereafter page numbers given in the text refer to this edition); and Porter, review of Verdi, *Don Carlos*, ed. Günther.

Günther discerns seven discrete versions of the opera, on the basis of her investigations of the work's musical and documentary sources. They record their own sort of drama. Verdi struggled to reconcile his grand conception of this opera with, on the one hand, the needs and tolerance of his audience, and, on the other, his own instincts for dramatic economy. The first cuts, made during rehearsal for the première in Paris, were required by the direction of the Opéra because of the opera's length, but subsequent alterations were made as Verdi himself came to grips with the scale and demands of the work. Günther carefully documents these processes in the Foreword to the edition, tracing the composer's changing view of the opera through his correspondence. This edition, then, makes two significant contributions to the state of our knowledge about *Don Carlos*: first, it presents the music of these seven versions, especially the previously unpublished passages, and second, Günther gives a sensitive account of Verdi's role in the revisions.

Two aspects of this material and Günther's presentation of it give pause. First, she takes great care to distinguish no fewer than four distinct versions associated with the Paris première: the original version of 1866; the version of the trial performance, 24 February 1867; and those for the first two performances, 11 and 13 March (I, pp. X–XX). These document the public socialization of the work, as it developed from the composer's original plan to a production that accommodated the circumstances under which it was performed. In contrast, the other three versions, for Naples 1872, Milan 1883 and Modena 1886, are treated in monolithic fashion: in each case, Verdi produced a single set of revisions that apparently went through rehearsal without a single rewrite or alteration (I, pp. XX–XXI).

These may well be the facts, or the evidence necessary to reconstruct these phases of the later productions may be lacking or unavailable. And in any event, the Paris production, as the original, certainly deserves the careful documentation and discussion Günther presents. Nevertheless I find the picture unconvincing. Moreover the subsequent performance history of *Don Carlos* holds some importance because a central issue in understanding this work concerns Verdi's motivations for the later revisions. If Verdi was so convinced, for example, that the original, uncut version of 1866 best represented his conception of the work, why was so little of it restored in the five-act version of 1886?[2] Modern producers, directors and conductors of

[2] Only the first act as it was performed on 11 and 13 March 1867; see Günther, "Vorwort," I, pp. XX–XXI.

opera who are interested in mounting a production of *Don Carlos* need to know what adaptations were necessary for the subsequent productions as well as for the première.

The second worrisome point in Günther's presentation will concern the same constituency. We hear only Verdi's side of the story regarding the tribulations he underwent in revising the opera for the four principal productions. Our only source for the feelings, wishes and needs of the various directorships involved is Verdi's account in his letters, and he is clearly not a friendly witness. Again, modern directors will share the same concerns with their counterparts of a century ago, and might find the motivations for the direction's actions in this matter interesting. It is certainly not unusual or unfair for an editor to want to make the composer's case as clearly and convincingly as possible, but a balanced account, weighing the evidence on both sides, would lead to a firmer understanding of the work's history.

Because this edition presents a great deal of unfamiliar material, it serves several audiences, each of which brings special requirements to it: scholars, performers and artistic directors. The first issue that strikes all prospective users of the edition is the manner in which the differing versions are presented. Directors, conductors and singers, and their audiences, will determine the shape of the work in contemporary performance according to their tastes, needs and economic solvency. Therefore they need to comprehend the various discrete versions so that they can make informed decisions about what to perform and what to dismiss. Moreover, the piano-vocal score format indicates that the edition is also aimed at singers, pianists and conductors, who will use it in coaching and rehearsing. Singers, of course, perform from memory, and opera is rarely performed from the piano reduction, except in concert presentation, when the pianist is assisted by a page-turner. The fine details of layout, then, carry secondary importance. In a score of this size (two volumes totalling 669 pages of music) and complexity, however, it is obligatory that everyone be able to locate a particular passage rapidly and efficiently.

The tools that Günther and Ricordi provide for these challenges meet with mixed success. One difficulty is created by the solution for presenting alternate versions of the same passages, a feature that will require further comment below. They are printed consecutively in chronological order of composition. Therefore, when navigating between versions, one needs to know where a passage that belongs to one version ends and its replacement in a subsequent version begins, and so it is obligatory to be informed of the inclusive page numbers for each section. Günther, in fact, employs this strategy when she first introduces and discusses each version in the Foreword, giving the inclusive page numbers of all the sections that constitute each version (I, pp. X–XXI). This is by far the most efficient means of orientating oneself to the parts of the edition and these listings should have been printed in tabular form.

Two tables are subsequently presented, but they do not match the earlier listings in precision. The first comprises a table of contents for the five-act and the four-act version of Paris 1867 and Milan 1883, respectively (I, pp. XXXVIII–XXXIX). This is of virtually no use. It repeats information presented earlier in the Foreword and later in the second table (on which I comment below); it ignores the other five versions; it does not specify which of the four Paris versions it presents;[3] and it does not give inclusive page numbers, a deficiency that seriously undermines any benefit for the reader. The second table does include full pagination, but it, too, suffers from undue compression (I, pp. XL–XLIII).

Here Günther presents a synoptic, comparative table of contents in three columns that represent (1) the Paris versions of 1866–67 and the Naples version of 1872, (2) the Milan version of 1883, and (3) the Modena version of 1886. The last two are clear enough, and complement the listing given for them earlier in the Foreword, but the first column, by combining the four original Paris versions with the Naples revision, is virtually unintelligible. It is true that relatively few alterations distinguish the successive versions in this group, but little effort would have been required to duplicate the listings in the Foreword in exchange for a significant improvement in clarity. It is all the more puzzling that Günther would have made the first column so complicated in view of her advocacy for the original, pre-production version of the opera (I, p. XXX). Those who would reconstruct that version from this second table will find it a daunting task, and inevitably turn back to the discussion and listing in the Foreword.

The chief difficulty is the manner in which the five versions are distinguished. Passages that were cut from the original Paris version or added to the Naples production are designated by the sigla Günther gives them in the Foreword. But, in addition to recognizing them, the reader must also know which sections belong to which version. For

[3] It gives the content of the first performance, 11 March 1867; see Günther, "Vorwort," I, pp. XX.

example, passages designated P.d, e, f, g and h were cut before the trial performance of 27 February 1867 (Günther's second version), and two sections were added: the ballet in Act III (II, 311–46) and a replacement for P.f (II, 495–97). It is true that the table indicates how to proceed in order to reconstruct versions with or without the cuts, but no hint is given regarding to which versions the ballet in Act III belongs. The reader must return to the Foreword for this information (I, pp. X–XX), just as I did to write this passage. Moreover Günther assigns no sigla for the cuts that occurred after the opening performance, 11 March 1867. Therefore it is impossible to know, by consulting the table alone, that three passages were cut from the end of Act IV (II, 547–52, 564–74, 580–84) for the performance of 13 March (Günther's fourth version; I, p. XX). In short, the reader must have digested the entire Foreword in order to make sense of the first column of this table.

When we come to the score itself, we find that following a particular version through is, for the most part, a reasonably simple matter. In most instances, Günther places a footnote at the end of a section that indicates to which page to turn for which version. This is a simple and efficient method. Some startling and frustrating inconsistencies remain, however. Günther assumes that the reader has memorized the sections designated by sigla, and in which versions they belong. As we follow the third and fourth Paris versions, the Naples or the Modena version, for example, we successfully reach the end of p. 105 without incident. But no footnote there warns us that on the next page begins P.b, which is cut from all these versions. Even if we remember the cut, Günther gives us no indication where it ends, and thus where our four versions resume. We must page through to p. 111 where we find, too late to be helpful, a note indicating that this music continues from p. 105.

The Modena version, however, does not resume here; it skips to p. 132, and this fact is communicated in the most oblique fashion. A note on p. 105 states that, in RM,[4] the last bar of the page is omitted and the passage continues at bar 4 of p. 132. Now, RM is the principal source for the Modena version, as Günther indicates (I, p. XXI), and so the note has the tantamount force of stating that the Modena version itself omits all the music between pp. 106 and 132. Nevertheless, the wording could be clearer. Moreover the Modena

[4] Günther's siglum for the printed score of 1886, which contains the revisions for the Modena production; see "Vorwort," I, p. XLIV.

version, from p. 132 to the end of the opera, is identical to the Milan version, except for the numbering of the acts (Modena has five and Milan four acts; therefore Acts I-IV in the latter become II-V in the former), and so Günther abruptly ceases mentioning it in the footnotes. But she only communicates the exact relationship between the versions in her second table (I, pp. XL–XLIII), again relying on the reader's retention of details from the Foreword to use the score efficiently. Were the score less complicated, she would be justified in this expectation. It requires a certain effort to find one's way in this edition, and these difficulties will only prevent its acceptance.

The solution is simple. Print a table in the same format as Günther's second table (I, pp. XL–XLIII), but expanded to seven columns to accommodate all the versions, and give consistent directions in the footnotes for all versions. Günther expended a significant amount of energy in identifying these seven versions in the source materials, and it is regrettable that it is so difficult to trace them in the score. It would seem that, at a certain point, she decided that there were really only two versions: the original five-act version performed in Paris and Naples, and the four-act version for Milan, which was then converted into a five-act version for Modena by the addition of the first act from the Paris production. This analysis explains the structure of the two tables at the end of the Foreword (I, pp. XXXVIII–XLIII), which thus subvert the subtle distinctions she makes earlier.

A further point about the layout is mentioned above, and that is the arrangement of alternate versions of the same passages. Günther and Ricordi elected to treat all continuous passages of music as discrete sections. In cases where some music is changed in the course of such a section, the entire section is repeated. This is certainly a lavish solution, but it materially contributes to the bulk, expense and, in some respects, the awkwardness of using the edition. The duet between Philippe and Rodrigue that closes the second act in all versions occurs in four forms as outlined in Table 7–2. There is no question that the last version needs to be printed in full, as it shares only its first two pages with the other versions. The same conclusion may be reached concerning the Naples version. Some two-thirds of it is new. Still, one could print the current pp. 263–76 immediately after p. 231, and place a note at the bottom of p. 213 directing performers of the Naples version to continue on the appropriate page.

More extreme is the case of the two Paris versions, the second of which contains a single page, p. 248 (which replaces pp. 222–25,

Table 7–2 Verdi, Don Carlos, *Act II:*
Four Versions of the Duet between Philippe and Rodrigue

Version	Günther Edition	Identical Pages
Paris 1866–67 (versions 1 and 2)	I, 206–31	
Paris 1867 (versions 3 and 4)	I, 232–54	232–47 = 206–21 249–54 = 226–31
Naples 1872	I, 255–76	255–62 = 206–13 = 232–39
Milan 1883 and Modena 1886	I, 277–94	277–78 = 206–7 = 232–33 = 255–56

passage P.c), that differs from the first. Here the solution is even simpler. The editor could print the current pp. 206–25, 248 and 226–31, with footnotes at the bottom of pp. 221 and 225 to indicate which cuts to take for each version. If the Naples version were also incorporated, the order would be the current pp. 206–25, 248, 226–31 and 263–76, with notes on pp. 213, 221 and 225. The principle remains exactly the same as that used by Günther throughout: print alternate versions in chronological order of composition, and direct the reader where to skip in order to follow a particular version of the work. By introducing this plan at the level of the complete page, the duplication of pages is reduced with, one would hope, a corresponding reduction in cost and inconvenience.

Finally, this edition holds considerable importance for scholars because it introduces a great deal of music previously unpublished. Therefore it is inexcusable that the sources on which the edition is based are not adequately identified. These are listed with their sigla at the end of the Foreword (I, p. XLIV). It is possible that autograph materials in the archives of Ricordi (AN and AR, the autograph revisions for the Naples and Milan productions, respectively) may not carry a shelf number, but those in the Bibliothèque Nationale and the Bibliothèque-Musée de l'Opéra in Paris do, and they should have been reported, especially because they are the principal sources for the previously unpublished music.[5] Source AP is Verdi's autograph, in three volumes, prepared for the première, and CO is a copy of it,

[5] For the record, they are AP = Paris, Bibliothèque Nationale, Mus. Rés. MSS 1072–74 (see Günther, " La genèse de *Don Carlos*," p. 19 n. 12); and CO = Paris Bibliothèque-Musée de l'Opéra, A 619, I–IV (discussed but not identified by Günther, *ibid.*, p. 44; for the identification, see Rosen, "Le quattro stesure," plates between pp. 368 and 369).

in four volumes, made for the conductor of the first performances in Paris.

In short, the value of this important edition is seriously undermined by the difficulty in gaining full and efficient access to its greatest virtue: the complete music for the four principal productions that occurred during the composer's lifetime. A relatively minor problem in the mechanics of the presentation obscures the great accomplishment of its editor and could provide a significant deterrent in the widespread acceptance of this edition and the very important material it contains.

Appendix A

The sources: location

The location of sources largely involves bibliographic searching, and the principal resources are discussed here.[1] Every bibliographic tool is out of date the moment it is published, as I mentioned in Chapter 2 above, and so the editor is constantly searching for means of obtaining new data, and updating old. Some strategies are outlined here. Logical starting points are existing editions and thematic catalogues.

Anna Harriet Heyer, *Historical Sets, Collected Editions, and Monuments of Music: A Guide to Their Contents*, 3rd edn., 2 vols. (Chicago, 1980). D-K 1722.

Barry S. Brook, *Thematic Catalogues in Music: An Annotated Bibliography*, RILM Retrospectives, 1 (Hillsdale, NY, 1972). D-K 3035.

Hermann Wettstein, *Bibliographie musikalischer thematischer Werkverzeichnisse* (Laaber, 1978). D-K 744.

Studies of the composer, repertory or piece, such as the pertinent articles in the principal encyclopaediae, may give references to the relevant sources.

Friedrich Blume, ed., *Die Musik in Geschichte und Gegenwart*, 17 vols. (Kassel and Basel, 1949–86). D-K 46.

Stanley Sadie, ed., *The New Grove Dictionary of Music and Musicians*, 20 vols. (London, 1980). D-K 48.

Other national dictionaries and encyclopaediae of music provide detailed coverage of the composers and repertories of their respective countries.[2] Many of these studies and articles do not give comprehensive bibliographic information for all sources, but they often offer prospective editors a notion of the range and type of source material they can expect to consult in the course of producing the edition.

The most comprehensive catalogue of sources is the series published as Répertoire International des Sources Musicales (RISM). A monumental undertaking, it is indispensable for music before 1800, and some of the volumes, like Heinrich Husmann's on medieval trope manuscripts, are important original contributions to scholarship in

[1] The standard reference work for music bibliography is Duckles and Keller, *Music Reference and Research Materials*. It includes most of the works cited here, and I give the entry number, prefixed with the siglum D-K, at the end of each citation.

[2] See the list in Duckles and Keller, *ibid.*, nos. 1–235, pp. 1–45.

their own right. Nevertheless, in many areas, the coverage is inconsistent and incomplete, and virtually all data need to be confirmed. It is organized in several series and sub-series, among which several deal with writings about music. Series A catalogues music attributable to a single composer, while Series B treats collections of music. The series that concern music sources proper are listed here.

Series A/1: Karlheinz Schlager and Otto E. Albrecht, eds., *Einzeldrucke vor 1800*, 9 vols., RISM, A/1, 1–9 (Kassel, 1971–81). D-K 1817.

Ilse and Jürgen Kindermann, eds., *Einzeldrucke vor 1800: Addenda et corrigenda*, 2 vols. to date, RISM, A/1, 11–12 (Kassel, 1986–92). D-K 1818. These eleven (to date) volumes comprise a catalogue of prints that contain individual pieces of music, organized alphabetically by composer, with appendices in vol. 9 that list editions in which the composer is identified by initial and anonymous prints.

Series A/2: *Musikhandschriften 1600–1800: Datenbank-Index*, 2 microfiches and 16-pp. pamphlet, RISM, A/2 (Kassel, 1986). D-K 1823. An index of pieces contained in manuscripts held by European libraries, organized alphabetically by composer.

Series B/1: François Lesure, *Recueils imprimés, XVIe–XVIIe siècles*, RISM, B/1, 1 (Munich–Duisburg, 1960). D-K 1824. A catalogue of printed collections of music, organized chronologically.

Series B/2: François Lesure, *Recueils imprimés, XVIIIe siècle*, RISM, B/2 (Munich–Duisburg, 1964). D-K 1825. A catalogue of printed collections of music, organized alphabetically by title.

Series B/4: Gilbert Reaney, *Manuscripts of Polyphonic Music, 11th–Early 14th Century*, RISM, B/4, 1 (Munich–Duisburg, 1966). D-K 1822.

idem, *Manuscripts of Polyphonic Music (c. 1320–1400)*, RISM, B/4, 2 (Munich–Duisburg, 1969). D-K 1821.

Andrew Wathey, *Manuscripts of Polyphonic Music, Supplement 1 to RISM B IV, 1–2: The British Isles, 1100–1400*, RISM, B/4, 1–2, Suppl. 1 (Munich, 1993).

Kurt von Fischer and Max Lütolf, *Handschriften mit mehrstimmiger Musik des 14., 15. und 16. Jahrhunderts*, 2 vols., RISM, B/4, 3–4 (Munich–Duisburg, 1972). D-K 1819.

Nanie Bridgman, *Manuscrits de musique polyphonique, XVe et XVIe siècles: Italie*, RISM, B/4, 5 (Munich, 1991). Catalogues of manuscript sources, organized by their location, alphabetically by country, city and library.

Series B/5: Heinrich Husmann, *Tropen- und Sequenzenhandschriften*, RISM, B/5, 1 (Munich–Duisburg, 1964). D-K 1826. Same organization as volumes in B/4.

Series B/7: Wolfgang Boetticher, *Handschriftlich überlieferte Lauten- und Gitarrentabulaturen des 15. bis 18. Jahrhunderts*, RISM, B/7 (Munich, 1978). D-K 1820. Same organization as volumes in B/4.

Series B/8: Konrad Ameln, Markus Jenny and Walther Lipphardt, *Das deutsche Kirchenlied: Verzeichnis der Drucke von den Anfängen bis 1800*, 2 vols., RISM, B/8, 1–2 (Kassel, 1975–80). D-K 1876. A catalogue of printed sources for German hymns, organized chronologically.

Series B/9: Israel Adler and Lea Shalem, *Hebrew Notated Manuscript Sources up to circa 1840: A Descriptive and Thematic Catalogue with a Checklist of Printed Sources*, 2 vols., RISM, B/9, 1 (Munich, 1989). Same organization as volumes in B/4.

The search for printed and manuscript materials separates at this point. Manuscripts are, of course, unique artifacts, and are located by the library in which they repose. Prints, on the other hand, can exist in multiple (although, as discussed in Chapter 2 above, not necessarily identical) copies. RISM provides a starting point for music printed before 1800, but for music published since then, and to supplement the RISM listings, the researcher turns to the printed catalogues of the major research libraries, some of which possess significant holdings of printed music. The principal resources are listed here.[3]

Boston Public Library, *Dictionary Catalog of the Music Collection of the Boston Public Library*, 20 vols. (Boston, 1972). D-K 1968.

(London) British Library, Department of Printed Books, *The Catalogue of Printed Music in the British Library to 1980*, 62 vols., ed. Laureen Baillie and Robert Balchin (London, 1981–87). D-K 2166.

(Munich) Bayerische Staatsbibliothek, *Katalog der Musikdrucke*, 17 vols. (Munich, 1988–90).

New York Public Library, Music Division, *Dictionary Catalog of the Music Collection, New York Public Library*, 2nd edn., 44 vols. (Boston, 1982). D-K 2276.

Other libraries may have more specialized holdings, particularly the copyright libraries of the countries where the music was published. Not all copyright libraries have issued separate catalogues of their music holdings, and so the search must extend to the general printed catalogues, such as the *National Union Catalog*, which lists the holdings in North American libraries of books printed before 1956. Since 1953, a separate *National Union Catalog* for musical materials has appeared.

National Union Catalog: Music and Phonorecords, 11 vols. (Ann Arbor, 1958–73). D-K 1243. Quinquennial cumulations of the catalogue of the Library of Congress, covering accessions for the years 1953–72. Replaced by the following item.

National Union Catalog: Music, Books on Music, and Sound Recordings (Washington, 1973–). D-K 1244. Semi-annual issues, with annual cumulations. Also quinquennial cumulations (Totowa, NJ).

Many of these resources are accessible through computer networks, principally, in North America, OCLC and the Research Libraries Information Network (RLIN).[4] Between them, they cover most of the important collections in North America; some European libraries are listed in OCLC, as well.

The search for manuscript sources poses special challenges. Unlike printed materials, manuscripts are identified by their shelfmarks, which usually convey no information about their content. Moreover, many library catalogues of manuscripts do not provide adequate descriptions of their music holdings, as discussed in Chapter 2 above, and are poorly indexed. Some assistance is available in the form of RISM Series A/2 and the volumes of Series B that are concerned with manuscripts, as well as existing editions and thematic catalogues, as noted above. For early music, two dictionary articles provide useful overviews of the available sources.

[3] See also the list in Duckles and Keller, *ibid.*, nos. 1888–2524, pp. 335–446, which also includes catalogues of manuscript materials.

[4] See Duckles and Keller, *ibid.*, nos. 1223, 1226, pp. 220, 221, respectively.

Stanley Boorman, *et al.*, "Sources, MS," (and related articles) in *New Grove*, XVII, 590a–753b.

Harold E. Samuel, "Sources (pre-1500)," in *The New Harvard Dictionary of Music*, ed. Don Michael Randel (Cambridge, MA, 1986), pp. 773b–78a. D-K 399.

Manuscript sources of plainsong and Renaissance music are the subject of specialized and detailed catalogues.

Les Moines de Solesmes, *Le graduel romain: Édition critique*, II, *Les sources* (Solesmes, 1957).

Census-Catalogue of Manuscript Sources of Polyphonic Music 1400–1550, 5 vols. Renaissance Manuscript Studies, 1 (Neuhausen–Stuttgart, 1979–88).

Some libraries have issued separate catalogues of their manuscript holdings of music.[5] For most, however, the editor must consult the library's general manuscript catalogues, and these, of course, vary considerably in quality, consistency and comprehensiveness.

Paul Oskar Kristeller and Sigrid Krämer, *Latin Manuscript Books before 1600: A List of the Printed Catalogues and Unpublished Inventories of Extant Collections*, 4th edn. Monumenta Germaniae Historica, Hilfsmittel, 13 (Munich, 1993).

The title of this book should not discourage editors of later music from consulting it. It lists the manuscript catalogues of most libraries, and many of those institutions, such as the British Library, contain more recent manuscript materials that are described in these catalogues. The catalogues themselves must be used with caution, as discussed above and in Chapter 2. For researchers who are seeking previously unidentified sources, the catalogues provide a starting point from which to obtain some indication of the nature of each library's holdings. Once a library has been identified as a likely location for a particular source, the editor will probably need to make direct contact, through correspondence with the library or by consulting the source itself, either in microfilm or in person, in order to identify it positively.

Three important resources in North America hold large microfilm collections that are of great importance for medievalists. The Hill Monastic Manuscript Library, in Collegeville, Minnesota, is in the process of filming the complete holdings of European monasteries.[6]

J. Evan Kreider, "Austrian Graduals, Antiphoners, and Noted Missals on Microfilm in the Hill Monastic Manuscript Library at St. John's Abbey and University," *Notes: Journal of the Music Library Association*, 36 (1979–80), 849–63. D-K 1796.

idem, "A Checklist of Spanish Chant Sources at the Hill Monastic Manuscript Library, St. John's Abbey and University," *Notes: Journal of the Music Library Association*, 40 (1983–84), 7–29. D-K 1795.

In addition, the Medieval Institute at the University of Notre Dame holds a complete microfilm collection of Western manuscripts in the Biblioteca Ambrosiana of Milan,[7]

[5] See the list in Duckles and Keller, *ibid.*, nos. 1888–2524, pp. 335–446, which also includes catalogues of printed materials.

[6] On the collection in general, see Jeffery, "Music Manuscripts on Microfilm." D-K 2007.

[7] To the best of my knowledge, no catalogue of the musical materials in the collection exists; see *Inventory of Western Manuscripts in the Biblioteca Ambrosiana.*

and the Pius XII Memorial Library of St Louis University includes in its holdings microfilms of a very substantial number of manuscripts in the Biblioteca Apostolica Vaticana, Rome.[8]

Finally, new research that includes references to previously unknown sources, or more detailed description and discussion of familiar ones for the repertory under consideration, continues to appear. Tireless perusal of the *Music Index*, *Dissertation Abstracts* and *RILM* (Répertoire International de Littérature Musicale) *Abstracts*, all of which are now available in machine-readable form, will direct the researcher to new studies soon after their appearance. Editors of vocal music might find references to additional sources in editions and studies of the literary texts. In the case of early music, once the sources of the text have been identified, the semi-annual bibliography published in *Scriptorium*, which is indexed by city, library and manuscript shelf number, is indispensable.

[8] In general, see Krohn, "Music in the Vatican Film Library"; checklists of microfilm holdings are published in *Manuscripta*, the journal published under the auspices of the library.

Appendix B

The sources: inspection

Before proceeding to a technical discussion of the stage of inspection, it is perhaps useful to introduce some of the technical aspects and terminology of these endeavours. Two specialized disciplines concerning the study of books as physical artifacts have developed: codicology, usually applied to the study of manuscript books, especially in the medieval and early modern period; and bibliography, the study of printed books. Each has developed specialized vocabularies, and in many cases music borrows from them concepts and terms, although since World War II music bibliography has begun to blossom as a discipline in its own right. Fuller treatments of these issues are listed here.

Codicology:

A. Dain, *Les manuscrits*, 3rd edn., Collection d'Études Anciennes (Paris, 1975).

Léon Gilissen, *Prolégomènes à la codicologie: Recherches sur la construction des cahiers et la mise en page des manuscrits médiévaux*, Publications de Scriptorium, 7 (Gand, 1977).

Jacques Lemaire, *Introduction à la codicologie*, Université Catholique de Louvain, Publications de l'Institut d'Études Médiévales, Textes, Études, Congrès, 9 (Louvain-la-Neuve, 1989).

Music bibliography:

D. W. Krummel and Stanley Sadie, eds., *Music Printing and Publishing*, The Norton/Grove Handbooks in Music (New York and London, 1990).

D. W. Krummel, *The Literature of Music Bibliography: An Account of the Writings on the History of Music Printing & Publishing*, Fallen Leaf Reference Books in Music, 21 (Berkeley, CA, 1992).

Let us begin with the terminology for the source itself. The word manuscript means anything written by hand, and it is best used in this general sense. Thus it can be used to refer to handwritten additions to a printed text: "corrections are added in manuscript." It can be replaced, where there is certainty, by the term autograph, either as a noun or an adjective, to denote the hand of the composer. Some critics retain the term holograph as a synonym for autograph, but the principal application of the former expression is in the area of diplomatics, where it is employed to describe wills and other legal documents. Autograph is the standard term in a literary or creative context. An apograph, in bibliographic usage, is a manuscript not written in the hand of the author, but by another under his or her direct supervision, by an amanuensis.

These artifacts often appear in the form of a codex (plural, codices), which means a bound book (as opposed to a scroll, the usual form of the book in antiquity, which the Romans called *uolumen*) and is used primarily by scholars of the medieval and Renaissance periods to refer to manuscript books. This is a useful refinement of the term manuscript, provided that the object matches the definition. The general practice of scholars studying periods since the Renaissance is to use the nouns manuscript to denote any source written by hand, and book for a printed source. These distinctions are quite clear and should be retained, although of course further refinements such as score or parts can be applied in a musical context where appropriate.

From the source as a whole we move to its constituent parts. The writing surface, up to about AD 1400, is usually parchment, and thereafter paper. Parchment is animal skin, treated and scraped to create a usable writing surface. No matter how much it has been scraped, however, it retains a hair side and a flesh side. The term vellum means parchment made from the skin of a still-born calf. In practice, it is used to mean parchment of high quality, but the standards for judging what is high-quality parchment are applied so arbitrarily and unevenly that the term is essentially devoid of meaning. Fortunately, and deservedly, it has almost completely vanished from the technical vocabulary. Paper is, of course, made from vegetable matter, and the chief means used to identify and date it is the watermark that papermakers fix on their product by thinning the paper slightly in a design.

Jan LaRue, "Watermarks and Musicology," *Acta Musicologica*, 33 (1961), 120–46.

idem, "Classification of Watermarks for Musicological Purposes," *Fontes Artis Musicae*, 13 (1966), 59–63.

Theo Gerardy, "Datierung mit Hilfe des Papiers," in *Quellenstudien zur Musik der Renaissance*, II, *Datierung und Filiation von Musikhandschriften der Josquin-Zeit*, ed. Ludwig Finscher, Wolfenbütteler Forschungen, 26 (Wiesbaden, 1983), pp. 217–28.

Alan Tyson, "The Problem of Beethoven's 'First' *Leonore* Overture," *Journal of the American Musicological Society*, 28 (1975), 292–334. A particularly important example of the use of watermarks in research, with an Appendix entitled "Ground Rules for the Description of Watermarks," pp. 332–34.

In many manuscripts, the staves are drawn by hand, and, in the case of the earliest manuscripts on parchment up to about 1200, with a sharp stylus that scratches a line in the surface of the parchment without any pigmentation. Such lines are called drypoint. Furthermore, in manuscripts where all the ruling is done by hand, the margins are established at either side of the page by hand-drawn vertical lines. These vertical rules and the top and bottom horizontal rules together form the writing frame. The position of the horizontal rules is often established by prick marks that are sometimes still visible at the outer edge of the pages. Hand-drawn staves are often done with a rastrum, a multi-pointed pen that permits the ruling of a complete staff with one pass;

Systems for Designating Recto and Verso

	recto	verso
(1)	e.g., fol. 8a	8b
(2)	8	8′
(3)	8	8v
(4)	8r	8v

in the eighteenth and early nineteenth centuries, multistave rastra, with which two or more staves could be ruled simultaneously, became common.

Jean K. and Eugene K. Wolf, "Rastrology and Its Use in Eighteenth-Century Manuscript Studies," in *Studies in Musical Sources and Style: Essays in Honor of Jan LaRue*, ed. Eugene K. Wolf and Edward H. Roesner (Madison, 1990), pp. 237–91.

Paper with printed staves, on which music could be written in manuscript, began to appear in the second half of the sixteenth century, although its use did not become widespread until around 1800. This is often called "manuscript paper."

Iain Fenlon and John Milsom, "'Ruled Paper Imprinted': Music Paper and Patents in Sixteenth-Century England," *Journal of the American Musicological Society*, 37 (1984), 139–63.

A leaf is a single piece of paper or parchment in a book. When the leaves of a source are numbered such that each leaf bears one number, which then refers to the entire leaf, front and back, that numbering is called foliation. When front and back each bear their own number, the numbering is termed, of course, pagination. Hence one leaf equals one folio, or two pages, because a single folio consists of front and back surfaces. When foliation is used, the folio numbers are supplemented by the suffix *r* (recto, or front side) and *v* (verso, or back side). If the source is written or printed in parallel columns, lower-case letters beginning with *a* refer to the columns on folios or pages: hence fol. 141vb means the second column on the verso of fol. 141; p. 158a the first column on p. 158. In practice, the conventions used to cite folio numbers vary.

The first two systems in the Table on p. 221 are now obsolete, but one meets them, of course, in older publications. The two chief competing conventions are listed as numbers 3 and 4 in the Table. The principal advantage of the latter is that it leaves free the folio number without suffix (e.g., fol. 8) to designate the entire folio, recto and verso, whereas this can only be indicated in the former system by fol. 8–v, or fol. 8–8v. Further complexity arises when a series of conjunct folios is cited. The reference fols. 8–12 would mean, in system 3, fols. 8r–12r, and, in system 4, fols. 8r–12v. Perhaps the most economical compromise would be to incorporate the appropriate suffix for recto, verso or column, whenever appropriate. Thus, the entire folio would be indicated by the reference fol. 8r–v, and the citation of conjunct folios (e.g., fols. 12ra–18vb) would be unequivocal.

An opening consists of the verso of one leaf and the recto of the immediately following leaf: in other words, exactly what one sees when the book is opened. This term is especially useful when describing the physical layout of the book, particularly when dealing with music books; often their layout is determined by the practical issue of how much music needs to be visible in a single opening in order that the book be usable in performance. The term is also convenient when describing photographic reproductions, where often a single exposure is used for an entire opening, rather than individual exposures for each page.

A bifolium is a sheet of paper or parchment that is folded in the middle to form two leaves or folios. This is the basic physical unit of most books. The next largest unit is the gathering, which usually consists of several bifolia folded one inside another to form a series of leaves. Older writers, and some more recent, on codicology in English call this unit a quire. This word ultimately derives from the Latin *quater*, which means "four times," and refers to a gathering that consists of four bifolia. Although it has acquired the generic meaning "gathering," not all gatherings consist of four bifolia, and it seems perverse to make reference to "a quire of five (or any other number) bifolia," when quire carries in its etymological makeup the quantity four. As I demonstrate below, other words that specify the quantity of bifolia in a gathering have entered codicological parlance, and so it seems preferable to abandon quire as the generic term.

Often a gathering is made from a single sheet: it is folded several times to create leaves of the correct size, and then cut along the edges to create the individual leaves. The fold at the inside of the gathering is not cut, and so the gathering becomes a series of bifolia. The gathering is then sewn along the inside fold, and eventually it is sewn together with other gatherings to form a codex. This procedure of folding a single sheet to create a gathering is the source of the terms folio, quarto, octavo, and so on, which now generally are taken to refer to a specific size of book.

In fact, they refer to the number of leaves created in the folding of a single sheet. Therefore folio indicates that one fold was made in each sheet to create two leaves; quarto, two folds for four leaves; octavo, three for eight leaves. These terms are normally reserved, then, to describe those gatherings whose folding pattern can be determined. Gatherings are characterized by the number of bifolia they contain: binio, ternio, quaternio, quinio mean gatherings of two to five bifolia, respectively. A quaternio, then, contains four bifolia, eight leaves or folios, and sixteen pages, and, if it is made from a single sheet folded three times, it can be designated octavo.

Printers and scribes use various devices to ensure that, when the gatherings are assembled to form the codex, the correct order is retained. Most common is the signature. This can consist of anything from a single letter or number to a complex formula that sometimes includes the composer's name or the title of the piece. Within a given codex, it usually appears in the same place; the most frequently met is the bottom of the gathering's first page. The position, however, can change from codex to codex. Another device, seen occasionally in certain literary texts but never, to the best of my knowledge, in music, is the pecia. In the Middle Ages, university texts were made available to students one gathering at a time. The students then made their own copies, in which the end of each gathering from the exemplar is indicated by a pecia mark.[1] Music did not circulate in this fashion in the Middle Ages, and no known music manuscript contains pecia marks.

[1] Destrez, *La pecia*; and Bataillon, Guyot and Rouse, eds., *La production du livre universitaire au moyen âge*.

Also commonly found in literary texts, and occasionally in texted vocal music, is the catchword. This is the first word of a page printed also at the bottom of the preceding page to act as a cue to what follows; in some books a catchword appears at the bottom of each page, in others just on the last page of a gathering. A similar device, although it links succeeding lines rather than pages or gatherings, is often found in music, and that is the *custos* (plural *custodes*) or direct, a cue that occurs at the end of a line of music and gives the pitch of the first note of the following line.

Thus the typical source consists of a series of gatherings, each made up of one or more bifolia, sewn together. The existing state of the source, however, might be quite different from its original condition. Ragged leaves are trimmed, sometimes with a loss of marginalia, sometimes of main text; bindings are replaced; single leaves, bifolia and gatherings are lost or added; and the original order is shuffled. Occasionally gatherings that were originally unrelated are bound together into a single codex. The best term to describe these independent units is libellus ("little book," plural libelli), and they can consist of one or several gatherings. Librarians, in the Middle Ages and the modern period, collected, and continue to collect, small booklets of the same (or nearly the same) size leaves, irrespective of their content, to form larger bound codices for ease of storage. The monastic librarians at the Abbey of Saint Martial in Limoges followed this practice throughout the twelfth and thirteenth centuries,[2] and at least one codex among the nouvelles acquisitions latines in the Bibliothèque Nationale in Paris is the result of a modern application of this procedure (MS 2073).

Sometimes the content of a manuscript is divided up into discrete sections in the initial stages of planning and execution, and each section is organized in such a way that it begins with a new gathering. The term libellus is also to be used for these independent sections within a uniform manuscript.[3] Many music manuscripts of the medieval and Renaissance periods contain several types of pieces, which are then assembled in individual sections. A well-known example is the Notre Dame manuscript F (Florence, Biblioteca Medicea-Laurenziana, MS pluteo 29,1), whose libelli are organized according to number of voices and genre. For such independent units within a codex, Charles Hamm uses the term fascicle-manuscripts,[4] but libellus is now well established in the codicological literature and so should be preferred.

Technical terms are commonly used for certain types of texts that precede or follow items in the main body of the source, or that give extra-textual information at the beginning or in the course of an item. The latter is called a rubric, so-named because it is often written in red. Liturgical books, in particular, transmit numerous rubrics that furnish information on such matters as performance and liturgical assignment. Introductory and closing materials are called, respectively, incipits (from the Latin: literally "it begins") and explicits ("it ends"). The latter are sometimes expanded to include such information as the scribe's or printer's name, the date and place in which the book was copied or printed, and occasionally, in manuscripts, a personal statement by the scribe. These expanded texts are usually called colophons.

At the beginning and end of a codex there is often material that needs special consideration. Flyleaves are the few leaves that occur at either end of the codex to protect the main text. End-papers are bifolia one leaf of which is pasted to the inside covers of the codex,

[2] Grier, "Some Codicological Observations," pp. 7–16.

[3] Huglo, "Les *Libelli* de tropes"; and *Les livres de chant liturgique*, pp. 64–75.

[4] Hamm, "Manuscript Structure in the Dufay Era."

front and back, and is called a paste-down. Sometimes end-papers and flyleaves are borrowed from a discarded manuscript, and, as mentioned above, obsolete music manuscripts are often recycled in this way. Paste-downs create some frustration because the pasted surface is no longer visible. Parts of music manuscripts also turn up as binding material, used to stiffen the spine or covers of the codex. The disposition of all of these materials within a given source is the concern of the tasks of inspection and description.

The process of inspection is the editor's opportunity to discover as much as possible about the material and physical state of each of the sources. Any individual piece of evidence may seem irrelevant, but, taken in context, may illuminate some aspect of the source's history. The following list is not intended to be complete, but functions as a suggestion of the kinds of information an editor might seek. Most apply to both manuscript and printed sources. Starting from the outside of the source, the editor records the materials and colours used in the bindings and covers, along with any identifying marks, such as a coat of arms or shelfmarks. Such marks might also appear on the flyleaves or the first few leaves of the book. In these places there might also be other information that could help in identifying previous owners. In the case of printed books, the editor also records the title page data, as well as any other identifying information, such as the library shelfmark or -marks for the copy used.

Many prints of music do not carry a date of publication, but this may sometimes be inferred from other evidence. First, publishers identify the plates from which a particular edition is made by a number that usually appears at the foot of the printed page and occasionally on the title page. The sequence of numbers does not necessarily reflect the chronological sequence of the plate's production, but some publishers keep records that do permit the dating of the plates.[5]

Otto Erich Deutsch, *Musikverlagsnummern: Eine Auswahl von 40 datierten Listen*, 2nd edn. (Berlin, 1961; rev. edn. and trans. of *Music Publishers' Numbers: A Selection of 40 Dated Lists, 1710–1900* [London, 1946]). D-K 2630.

Alexander Weinmann, *Beiträge zur Geschichte des Alt-Wiener Musikverlages*, series 2, *Verleger*, 24 vols. (Vienna, 1950–85).[6] D-K 2638–62.

O. W. Neighbour and Alan Tyson, *English Music Publishers' Plate Numbers in the First Half of the Nineteenth Century* (London, 1965). D-K 2701.

Wolfgang Matthäus, *Johann André Musikverlag zu Offenbach am Main: Verlagsgeschichte und Bibliographie 1772–1800* (Tutzing, 1973). D-K 2692.

Hans-Christian Müller, *Bernhard Schott, Hofmusikstecher in Mainz: Die Frühgeschichte seines Musikverlages bis 1797 mit einem Verzeichnis der Verlagswerke 1779–1797*, Beiträge zur Mittelrheinischen Musikgeschichte, 16 (Mainz, 1977). D-K 2699.

Anik Devriès and François Lesure, *Dictionnaire des éditeurs de musique français*, 2 vols. in 3, Archives de l'Édition Musicale Française, 4 (Geneva, 1979–88). D-K 2634.

Agostina Zecca Laterza, *Il catalogo numerico Ricordi 1857 con date e indici*, Bibliotheca Musicae, 8, Cataloghi Editoriali, 1 (Rome, 1984; repr. of *Catalogo (in ordine numerico) delle opere publicate* [Milan, 1857]). D-K 2617.

[5] In general, see Squire, "Publisher's Numbers." D-K 2725. And Krummel, comp., *Guide for Dating Early Published Music*, pp. 53–64. D-K 2679. The most important inventories of plate numbers are listed below; for others, see Krummel, *The Literature of Music Bibliography*, nos. 758, 799, 812, 821, 840, 848, pp. 272, 281, 290, 292, 296–97, 299.

[6] For a synopsis of the contents of this important series, see Krummel, *The Literature of Music Bibliography*, no. 800, pp. 281–83.

Hans Schneider, *Der Musikverleger Heinrich Philipp Bossler 1744–1812* (Tutzing, 1985).
idem, *Der Musikverleger Johann Michael Götz (1740–1810) und seine kurfürstlich privilegierte Notenfabrique*, 2 vols. (Tutzing, 1989).
idem, *Makarius Falter (1762–1843) und sein münchner Musikverlag (1796–1888)* (Tutzing, 1993).

It is important to differentiate between the plate number and the publisher's number, something not all scholars accomplish, as the titles listed above show. The publisher's number appears on the cover and the title page, and identifies a particular form of the published work, as opposed to the plates from which it was printed. It is possible for composite editions to bear several plate numbers, because several sets of plates, each set with its own number, were used to print the edition, to which the publisher then assigned a single publisher's number for the entire volume. In many cases, however, the practical distinction is not so clear. Publishers' numbers, also, do not necessarily reflect the chronological sequence of publication.

The next concern of the editor is the composition of the source, which is examined gathering by gathering in order to record the number of leaves in each, as well as which leaves constitute bifolia, and to note any stubs, indicating where leaves have been removed, or added bifolia or leaves. If the writing surface is parchment, one often finds a regular arrangement of the hair and flesh surfaces: a common system is to organize the parchment so that each opening consists of a like surface (i.e., hair faces hair, smooth side faces smooth side). In any event, the structure of each source may differ. If, however, a regular pattern is discerned, any disruption might indicate the loss or addition of a leaf. The folding pattern used to create the gathering can be identified by matching accidents, such as tears or holes, on edges of the paper or parchment that were originally attached and then cut when the book was first used. The pattern of grain in parchment can provide the same clue, as can the location of the watermark on paper.

The sequence and location of signatures and catchwords show the order of the gatherings that make up a source. Any interruption in that sequence, or the presence of catchwords and signatures in a different location on the page or in a different format, indicates the addition or loss of gatherings or individual leaves, as well as any disruption in their order. Many manuscript descriptions include the size of leaves, and by measuring them, the editor can confirm whether any differ in size. In many cases, however, the leaves have been trimmed when the book was bound or rebound, and so their present size does not tell us much about their original state. More fruitful is the measurement of the writing frame. This, at least, cannot be altered by binders.

Watermarks in a paper source and their location often offer valuable evidence for dating, provenance and the physical makeup of the source. The presence of a different watermark might indicate the addition of a leaf or gathering, and the location of the watermark might reveal the folding pattern by which the gatherings were produced. If the source is a manuscript written on printed music paper, the number and arrangement of the staves can help to date and identify it, as well as other marks, such as the name and address of the manufacturer, product number or name, and of course the watermark. In the case of ruling by hand, similar evidence for dating and provenance is provided by the method of ruling and pricking; where a rastrum has been used, the distance between lines of the staff and between staves, as well as the thickness of the lines and any irregularities in the staving, can help to identify the type of rastrum used.

The history of the source can be further illuminated by changes in format, in hand or, in a printed book, font, by changes in the writing material between parchment and paper, and any changes in the colour of the ink. The specific characteristics of the hand or font, both musical and textual, provide important evidence for dating and provenance, as does the presence of clefs, staves, key signatures, time signatures, mensuration and proportion signs, accidentals, coloration and *custodes*, where they appear. It is very unlikely that a musical source would contain pecia marks, but if they occur, they should be noted. Any illustrations, such as decorated initials or woodcuts, are also noteworthy. The final stage in the inspection is a complete inventory of the contents, complete with any incipits, explicits and colophons. Other details will certainly arise in most cases, but this list serves as a starting point.

Appendix C

The sources: description

All users of an edition, no matter how knowledgeable and sophisticated, appreciate a clear statement and description of the sources on which it is based. The form of the description should suit the nature of the source, and the following recommendations are intended to function as points of departure for the varying types of sources that the editor will confront in practice. In general terms, they divide between manuscript and printed sources. The former are all unique, and the description reflects that fact, focusing on the positive identification of the source according to its location. Printed sources are more difficult to identify. Music publishers often omit important facts of publication, like place and date, and they do not necessarily make the same distinctions between impressions and editions as book publishers.[1] And, as noted above in Chapter 2, not all copies of the same impression are identical in text. Therefore, editors usually consult as many copies of a printed source as is practicable, and, when dealing with rare prints, they record exactly which copies they consulted.

The form for describing manuscripts is adapted from that used by Leonard Boyle in his codicological studies, as is the format advocated for transcription and collation below. It bears repeating that the editor might not find it necessary to provide information in each category, and inevitably other categories will suggest themselves in many cases, but this form is a starting point. Many of the technical details, such as the description of bindings, text hands or fonts and illustrations, might be beyond the expertise of the editor. Nevertheless, even a brief reference could lead scholars in these specialized fields to the sources used in the edition.[2]

Identity

1. Siglum for codex used in edition.
2. Location (city, town, precise name of library).

[1] Hoboken, "Probleme der musikbibliographischen Terminologie." D-K 3122. Krummel, comp., *Guide for Dating Early Published Music*, pp. 30–48. Weinhold, "Die Erst- und Frühdrucke von Beethovens Werken. 2. Zur Definition der Ausgabe-Typen; 3. Die Gestalt des Titelblatters und ihre Veränderung."

[2] A good model for the description of early music manuscripts is Husmann, *Tropen- und Sequenzenhandschriften*; for modern manuscripts, the Critical Commentaries of the Verdi edition (Chicago, London and Milan, 1983–).

3. Present shelfmark (and alternative, if there is one).
4. Brief statement of contents (detailed comes later).
5. Date.
6. Copyist(s).
7. Ownership (all owners, contemporary, modern). Origin.

Material

8. Description of musical notation.
9. Number of folios and flyleaves. Presence of paste-downs.
10. Collation of gatherings. Presence, location and description of signatures.
11. Presence of independent libelli (original or added).
12. Layout of the page: dimensions of full page, writing frame and columns.
13. Pricking, ruling, and number and arrangement of lines to page or column.
14. Number and arrangement of staves (ruled freehand, with a rastrum, or printed).
15. Number and arrangement of systems, presence and type of braces.
16. Watermarks.
17. Manufacturer of manuscript paper and product identification.
18. Presence of pecia marks and catchwords.
19. Decoration.
20. Binding.

Contents (item by item)

21. Composer; author of text in vocal music.
22. Title.
23. Incipit and folios that contain the item.
24. Published editions.
25. Bibliography of item(s).
26. Bibliography of codex.

The positive identification of a printed source depends upon the bibliographic facts of publication. This begins with a full transcription of the title page, but includes other information, such as the publisher's number and the plate number.[3] Again, the following template is intended as a starting point.[4]

Identity

1. Siglum for print used in edition. RISM siglum.
2. Complete transcription of title page, showing line divisions.
3. Publisher's number, including location.
4. Plate number(s), including location.
5. Date (if not given on title page, but can be inferred).

[3] For a discussion of the history and principles of bibliographic citations of printed music, see Krummel, "Citing the Score."

[4] A good model for the description of printed sources is found in the Critical Commentaries of the Verdi edition.

6. Copies consulted: location (city, town, precise name of library); present shelfmark (and alternative, if there is one).

Material

7. Description of musical notation.
8. Number of folios or pages and flyleaves.
9. Collation of gatherings. Presence, location and description of signatures.
10. Layout of the page: dimensions of full page, printed surface and columns.
11. Number and arrangement of staves and systems to page or column.
12. Watermarks.
13. Decoration.
14. Binding.
15. Special physical characteristics of individual copies consulted.

Contents (item by item)

16. Composer; author of text in vocal music.
17. Title.
18. Incipit and folios (pages) that contain the item.
19. Bibliography of item(s).
20. Bibliography of print.

An attractive and easily comprehensible layout is a key feature of the successful description. Users of the edition will consult it for reference and for the information that is of importance to them. The easier it is for them to find the information they need, the more use they will make of the description. Naturally editors will want to be critical and selective about what data they present. Too full a description will antagonize all but the most dedicated readers. Nevertheless, if the editor feels any uncertainty about whether to include a particular detail, it is always better to err on the side of too much information rather than too little.

Appendix D

The sources: transcription

In Chapter 2 above, I discuss the issue of diplomatic transcriptions and the relationship between transcription and interpretation. No matter what method of transcription the editor adopts, the priority is to record as many details from each source as possible. As at the stage of inspection, transcription belongs to the process of collecting the data. The more evidence editors gather at these two stages, the better informed will their judgements be later. Consequently, clefs, key and time signatures, accidentals, mensuration signs, proportional symbols and coloration are transcribed as they appear in the source, together with any expression markings, like tempo markings, metronome settings, dynamics, indications for breathing, slurs and other marks that govern attacks. In vocal music, text underlay is noted exactly as it occurs in the source, retaining spelling, capitalization and punctuation. Other important details to be included in the transcription are indications where lines and leaves end, and any *custodes* that occur in the source. Such information might prove useful when sources are compared.

Finally, any irregularities in the way information is presented in the source is recorded: additions in the margin, above or below the line, in a second or subsequent hand, over an erasure, in a different colour ink, and any erased text that can be read. Ultra-violet light usually facilitates reading such erasures, but this task can only be done *in situ*, of course. The following is a suggested list of abbreviations that can be used to indicate these irregularities. Whatever form of abbreviation the editor adopts for the transcriptions can also eventually be used in the edition's critical apparatus.

add.	added
in marg.	in the margin
b. l.	below the line
a. l.	above the line
h^1, h^2, h^3	in the first, second, third hand
in eras.	over an erasure
eras.	erased
can.	cancelled
exp.	expunged
ink^1, ink^2, ink^3	in the first, second, third ink
om.	omitted

Not all this information will necessarily be reported in the edition, but it is essential to record as many details as possible at the stage of transcription. When the stages of classifying the sources and of establishing the text are reached, then, editors have at their disposal the maximum amount of data, which in turn contributes to their making informed decisions.

There are two principal procedures for transcription. The first is to take an existing copy, usually a print, and compare all sources to it. Any differences are marked, either in the master copy or in some kind of notebook. Only those details in which the source differs from the master are recorded. This method has the potential to be relatively fast and efficient. It has two significant drawbacks, however. First it is difficult to be precise about the nature of the difference in many cases. For example, a dynamic mark may occur a note or two earlier or later in the source being collated than in the master. It may be difficult to express that circumstance with precision in a note. As situations of this sort multiply, the second drawback emerges, and that is that it becomes easier for the editor to rationalize what might appear to be minor differences into no differences at all. One begins with good intentions, and it is certainly possible to produce good, clear and useful collations with this method, but the temptation often arises to concentrate on what seem to be major variations and disregard minor details. It is precisely these details that might reveal the value and importance of the source, or assist in determining the filiation.

The second method is hardly foolproof, but it at least encourages the editor to make fuller notes concerning variations. To begin, one source is selected to serve as the base, against which others are to be compared. The selection of a source has absolutely no bearing on its value in the piece's tradition and vice versa. Editors might choose the most complete source, if other versions are abridged, so that they will have to record fewer additions; or they might choose the easiest source to read so that the initial transcription can be expedited. The editor might also consider the possibility of using a printed edition for this purpose, for reasons that will become clear below.

This base text, then, is transcribed in full, and in the fullest detail, beginning on the recto of the second leaf of a notebook, and continues, using only the top staves of each recto page. If a printed source is used, a photocopy of it could be made, and then affixed, one line at a time, across the top of each recto page. Then the base transcription is divided into some kind of intelligible units. Pieces in modern rhythmic notation can be divided into bars, and syllables in the text of unmeasured vocal music or, especially in melismatic settings, individual neumes can serve as the unit. Solid vertical lines are drawn between such units. Music in mensural notation requires a slightly different layout. The unit will probably be the *prolatio* or *tempus*, but because individual notes often bridge two units of *prolatio* or *tempus*, solid vertical lines will cause such notes to be tied over to the next unit. I recommend that vertical lines between, but not on, the staves be used. These are the equivalent of the *Mensurstrich*, whose employment in the edition of early mensural music is discussed above in Chapter 4. On completion of this initial transcription, the page resembles a grid with the base text running across the top.

Now the collation of this text with the other sources can begin. Each new source is given a new line and is compared with the base text one unit at a time. If it agrees with the base text in all details, the box for that unit is left blank. Any differences between the new source and the base text are recorded in the box for that unit. The least ambiguous method of recording is to write the entire unit. This has the advantage of leaving no doubt about the disposition of all the symbols for the unit in the new source. Its efficiency, however, is not optimal because much information is repeated and it is not easy to tell at a glance how the various sources align themselves on a particular reading. In some cases, then, where it is possible to record the information unambiguously, the editor may avoid writing out the entire unit. For example, if the unit contains a single note, a variant, such as an accidental, may be noted without repeating the rest of the unit.

Nevertheless, I recommend writing out the full unit so that, when the editor returns to the transcription, sometimes months later, there is no doubt about the reading. If any detail in the base text is not found in the new source, it is noted as being omitted by the abbreviation *om*. The abbreviation *om*. by itself in the box denotes that all information in the unit has been omitted. Sometimes more detailed observations are recorded, in particular added material not found in the base text, and here editors have at their disposal the facing verso of the notebook, which hitherto has been left blank. When transcribing from a photographic reproduction, the editor might find it useful to make a list of details to check in the source itself where there are any uncertainties in reading the reproduction.

Up to this point I have treated the piece to be transcribed as if it were a single line, requiring a single staff for each source. Because most Western art music is polyphonic, most pieces will require the use of two or more staves. This system of grids works for pieces that require up to about six staves (enough, e.g., for a piano quintet). I refrain from creating an arbitrary limit because editors will have to judge for themselves how many can be managed. The base source is transcribed in score with the parts in the order of the base source; then the same number of staves is allotted each source to be collated, whose parts will be distributed in the same order as the base source, with any differences from the base source being recorded. Thus the page will have the appearance of several systems in score; on each system will be recorded a discrete source.

For pieces that require more than about six staves, the score is divided into manageable groups. Pieces for larger chamber groups or less complex orchestral scores can be arranged according to instrumental families (i.e., woodwinds, brass, percussion, strings) as they would be in full score. Larger and more complex orchestral scores (e.g., Mahler or Richard Strauss) might need even further division, down as far as individual instruments: flute and piccolo, oboe and English horn, clarinet family, bassoon and contrabassoon, among the woodwinds, would form a total of four groups. The determining factor in creating these groups is how many individual lines of music the editor can handle simultaneously when comparing readings between sources.

This system is somewhat cumbersome, especially for complex scores. Nevertheless, its chief advantage is that it encourages the recording of detail, and the more detail editors have at their disposal in the course of producing their editions, the better informed will their decisions be.

Bibliography

Manuscripts

Berlin, Deutsche Staatsbibliothek, MS Am. B. 78. Autograph of Johann Sebastian Bach, *Brandenburg* Concertos, BWV 1046–51. Facsimile: Johann Sebastian Bach, *Brandenburgische Konzerte* (Leipzig, n.d.).

Berlin, Staatsbibliothek Preußischer Kulturbesitz:

Mus. ms. Bach P 180. Autograph of Johann Sebastian Bach, Mass in B Minor, BWV 232. Facsimile: *Messe in H-moll BWV 232*, ed. Alfred Dürr (Kassel, Basel, Paris, London and New York, 1965).

Mus. ms. Bach P 268. Anna Magdalena Bach's copy of Johann Sebastian Bach, Sonatas and Partitas for Violin Solo, BWV 1001–6.

Mus. ms. Bach P 269. Anna Magdalena Bach's copy of Johann Sebastian Bach, Suites for Violoncello Solo, BWV 1007–12. Facsimile: Hans Eppstein, ed., *Sechs Suiten für Violoncello solo BWV 1007–1012: Die vier Quellen in verkleinerter Wiedergabe, Faksimile-Beiband zum kritischen Bericht*, Neue Ausgabe Sämtlicher Werke, ser. 6, 2 (Kassel, Basel, London and New York, 1991), pp. 7–48.

Mus. ms. Bach P 289. Copy of Johann Sebastian Bach, Suites for Violoncello Solo, BWV 1007–12, possibly once part of Johann Christoph Westphal's collection. Facsimile: Eppstein, ed., *Sechs Suiten für Violoncello solo ... Faksimile-Beiband*, pp. 79–124.

Mus. ms. Bach P 804. Johann Peter Kellner's copy of Johann Sebastian Bach, Suites for Violoncello Solo, BWV 1007–12. Facsimile: Eppstein, ed., *Sechs Suiten für Violoncello solo ... Faksimile-Beiband*, pp. 49–78.

Mus. ms. Bach P 967. Autograph of Johann Sebastian Bach, Sonatas and Partitas for Violin Solo, BWV 1001–6. Facsimile: Johann Sebastian Bach, *Sei solo a violino senza basso accompagnato*, Monumenta Musicae Reuocata, 2 (Florence, 1985).

Brussels, Bibliothèque Royale, MS II.4085. Autograph of Johann Sebastian Bach, Suite in G Minor for Lute, BWV 995, arranged from Suite no. 5 for Violoncello Solo, BWV 1011. Facsimile: Hermann Scherchen, ed., *Musica viva*, no. 3, supplement (1936).

Budapest, Országos Széchényi Könyvtár, MS K 1148. Parts for Joseph Haydn, String Quartets, Op. 33, Hob. III:37–42.

Chartres, Bibliothèque de la Ville, MS 520. Twelfth- or thirteenth-century noted missal from the Cathedral of Chartres. Facsimile: *Missale Carnotense (Chartres Codex 520)*, 2 vols., ed. David Hiley, Monumenta Monodica Medii Aeui, 4 (Kassel, Basel, London, New York and Prague, 1992).

Chicago, Newberry Library, MS 54.1. Fourteenth-century collection of music treatises.

Donaueschingen, Fürstlich Fürstenbergische Hofbibliothek, MSS S.B. 2/9. Instrumental parts for Wolfgang Amadeus Mozart, Symphony no. 36 in C Major K. 425 (*Linz*).

Florence, Biblioteca Medicea-Laurenziana, MS Pluteo 29.1. Thirteenth-century collection of polyphony associated with Notre Dame de Paris. Facsimile: Luther Dittmer, ed., *Firenze, Biblioteca Mediceo-Laurenziana, Pluteo 29,1*, 2 vols., Veröffentlichungen Mittelalterlicher Musikhandschriften, 10–11 (Brooklyn, n.d.).

London, British Library:

Additional MS 19583. Sixteenth-century collection of polyphony, alto partbook.

Additional MS 36881. Twelfth-century Aquitanian *uersaria*. Facsimile: Bryan Gillingham, ed., *Paris B.N., fonds latin 3549 and London, B.L. Add. 36,881*, Veröffentlichungen Mittelalterlicher Musikhandschriften, 16 (Ottawa, 1987), pp. 43–101.

Madrid, Biblioteca Nacional, MS 20486. Thirteenth-century collection of polyphony associated with Notre Dame de Paris. Facsimile: Luther Dittmer, ed., *Madrid 20486*, Veröffentlichungen Mittelalterlicher Musikhandschriften, 1 (Brooklyn, 1957).

Melk, Benediktinerstift, Musikarchiv, MSS VI, 736–39. Parts for Joseph Haydn, String Quartets, Op. 33, Hob. III:37–42.

Modena, Biblioteca Estense, MS α F 2.29. Sixteenth-century collection of polyphony, tenor or bass partbook.

Montpellier, Bibliothèque de l'École de Médecine, MS H. 159. Eleventh-century tonary of Mass chants. Facsimile: *Antiphonarium tonale missarum, XIe siècle, Codex H. 159 de la Bibliothèque de l'École de Médecine de Montpellier*, 2 vols., Paléographie Musicale, ser. 1, 7–8 (Tournai, 1900–5).

Naples, Conservatorio di Musica S Pietro a Majella, MS Rari 6.4.1. Copy of Claudio Monteverdi, *L'incoronazione di Poppea*.

New York, Pierpont Morgan Library, Cary Music Collection. Autograph instrumental parts for Franz Schubert, Mass in F major, D. 105.

New York, Wildenstein Galleries, no shelfmark; *olim* private collection of the Marquis de Vogüé. Fourteenth-century copy of the works of Machaut.

Paris, Bibliothèque-Musée de l'Opéra, A 619, I–IV. Conductor's copy of Giuseppe Verdi, *Don Carlos* for first production in Paris.

Paris, Bibliothèque Nationale, fonds français:

MS 1585. Fourteenth-century copy of the works of Guillaume de Machaut.

MS 9221. Fourteenth-century copy of the works of Guillaume de Machaut.

Paris, Bibliothèque Nationale, fonds latin:

MS 743. Eleventh-century breviary from Saint Martial de Limoges.

MS 778. Twelfth-century Aquitanian troper-proser.

MS 821. Eleventh-century sacramentary associated with Saint Martial de Limoges.

MS 822. Eleventh-century sacramentary from Saint Martial de Limoges.

MS 887. Eleventh-century Aquitanian troper-proser.
MS 890. Thirteenth- or fourteenth-century lectionary from Saint Martial de Limoges.
MS 909. Eleventh-century Aquitanian troper-proser, with music written in the hand of Adémar de Chabannes.
MS 1084. Tenth- or eleventh-century Aquitanian troper-proser.
MS 1085. Eleventh-century antiphoner from Saint Martial de Limoges.
MS 1086. Twelfth-century Aquitanian troper-proser.
MS 1088. Thirteenth- or fourteenth-century antiphoner from Saint Martial de Limoges.
MS 1118. Tenth- or eleventh-century Aquitanian troper-proser.
MS 1119. Eleventh-century Aquitanian troper-proser.
MS 1120. Eleventh-century Aquitanian troper-proser.
MS 1121. Eleventh-century Aquitanian troper-proser.
MS 1132. Eleventh-century Aquitanian gradual-proser.
MS 1133. Eleventh-century Aquitanian troper-proser.
MS 1134. Eleventh-century Aquitanian troper-proser.
MS 1135. Eleventh-century Aquitanian troper-proser.
MS 1136. Eleventh-century Aquitanian troper-proser.
MS 1137. Eleventh-century Aquitanian troper-proser.
MS 1139. Miscellany that includes two twelfth-century Aquitanian *uersaria.* Facsimile: Bryan Gillingham, ed., *Paris Bibliothèque Nationale, fonds latin 1139*, Veröffentlichungen Mittelalterlicher Musikhandschriften, 14 (Ottawa, 1987).
MS 1240. Tenth-century Aquitanian troper-proser.
MS 1253. Eleventh-century breviary from Saint Martial de Limoges.
MS 1978. Commentary on the Psalms by Saint Augustine; endleaves contain music copied in the hand of Adémar de Chabannes.
MS 3549. Miscellany that includes one twelfth-century Aquitanian *uersarium.* Facsimile: Bryan Gillingham, ed., *Paris B.N., fonds latin 3549 and London, B.L. Add. 36,881*, Veröffentlichungen Mittelalterlicher Musikhandschriften, 16 (Ottawa, 1987), pp. 1–44.
MS 3719. Miscellany that includes four twelfth-century Aquitanian *uersaria.* Facsimile: Bryan Gillingham, ed., *Paris Bibliothèque Nationale, fonds latin 3719*, Veröffentlichungen Mittelalterlicher Musikhandschriften, 15 (Ottawa, 1987).

Paris, Bibliothèque Nationale, Mus. MS 17669. Print of Johann Sebastian Bach, *Goldberg Variations*, published by Balthasar Schmid in Nürnberg probably in 1741, with autograph annotations and corrections by the composer.

Paris, Bibliothèque Nationale, Mus. Rés. MSS 1072–74. Autograph of Giuseppe Verdi, *Don Carlos*.

Paris, Bibliothèque Nationale, nouvelles acquisitions latines:
MS 1177. Eleventh-century Aquitanian troper-proser.
MS 1871. Eleventh-century Aquitanian troper-proser.

Perugia, Biblioteca Comunale Augusta, MS 1013 (*olim* M 36). Fifteenth-century collection of music treatises.

Rome, Biblioteca Apostolica Vaticana, Cappella Sistina, MS 23. Fifteenth- or sixteenth-century collection of polyphonic settings of the Ordinary of the Mass.

Rome, Biblioteca Apostolica Vaticana, MS Ottob. lat. 3025. Miscellany containing the Vatican organum treatise.

Rostock, Bibliothek der Wilhelm-Pieck-Universität, MS Mus. Saec. XVI-40 (1–5). Sixteenth-century collection of polyphonic settings of the Ordinary of the Mass.

Salzburg, Internationale Stiftung Mozarteum, MSS Rara 425/1. Instrumental parts for Wolfgang Amadeus Mozart, Symphony no. 36 in C Major K. 425 (*Linz*).

Trent, Museo Diocesano, MS BL (commonly known as Trent 93). Fifteenth-century collection of polyphony. Facsimile: *Codex tridentinus 93* (Rome, 1970).

Trent, Museo Provinciale d'Arte, Castello del Buon Consiglio, MS 90. Fifteenth-century collection of polyphony. Facsimile: *Codex tridentinus 90* (Rome, 1970).

Venice, Biblioteca Nazionale Marciana, MS It. IV 439 (= 9963). Copy of Claudio Monteverdi, *L'incoronazione di Poppea.*

Vienna, Österreichische Nationalbibliothek, MS ohne Signatur. Autograph of Joseph Haydn, Concerto for Violoncello and Orchestra in D Major, Hob. VIIb:2.

Vienna, Österreichische Nationalbibliothek, Mus. Hs. 5007. Copy of Johann Sebastian Bach, Suites for Violoncello Solo, BWV 1007–12, possibly once part of Johann Traeg's collection. Facsimile: Hans Eppstein, ed., *Sechs Suiten für Violoncello solo BWV 1007–1012: Die vier Quellen in verkleinerter Wiedergabe, Faksimile-Beiband zum kritischen Bericht*, Neue Ausgabe Sämtlicher Werke, ser. 6, 2 (Kassel, Basel, London and New York, 1991), pp. 125–70.

Vienna, Stadt- und Landesbibliothek, MS MH 13. Autograph score of Franz Schubert, Mass in F major, D. 105.

Wolfenbüttel, Herzog-August-Bibliothek:

MS Helmstedt 628. Thirteenth-century collection of polyphony associated with Notre Dame de Paris. Facsimile: J. H. Baxter, ed., *An Old St. Andrews Music Book (Cod. Helmst. 628)*, St Andrews University Publications, 30 (London and Paris, 1931; repr. New York, 1973).

MS Helmstedt 1099. Thirteenth-century collection of polyphony associated with Notre Dame de Paris. Facsimile: Luther Dittmer, ed., *Wolfenbüttel 1099 (1206)*, Veröffentlichungen Mittelalterlicher Musikhandschriften, 2 (Brooklyn, 1960; repr. Brooklyn, 1969).

Editions of music

Adam of Saint Victor. *Les proses d'Adam de Saint-Victor*, ed. E. Misset and Pierre Aubry. Mélanges de Musicologie Critique. Paris, 1900.

Bach, Johann Sebastian. *Einzeln überlieferte Klavierwerke II und Kompositionen für Lauteninstrumente*, ed. Hartwig Eichberg and Thomas Kohlhase. Johann Sebastian Bach: Neue Ausgabe Sämtlicher Werke, ser. 5, 10. Kassel, Basel, Tours and London, 1976. *Kritischer Bericht.* Kassel, Basel and London, 1982.

Sechs Brandenburgische Konzerte, ed. Heinrich Besseler. Johann Sebastian Bach: Neue Ausgabe Sämtlicher Werke, ser. 7, 2. Kassel and Basel, 1956. *Kritischer Bericht.* Kassel and Basel, 1956.

Sechs Suiten für Violoncello solo BWV 1007–1012, ed. Hans Eppstein. Johann Sebastian Bach: Neue Ausgabe Sämtlicher Werke, ser. 6, 2. Kassel, Basel, London and New York, 1988. *Kritischer Bericht.* Kassel, Basel, London and New York, 1990. *Die vier Quellen in verkleinerter Wiedergabe: Faksimile-Beiband zum kritischen Bericht.* Kassel, Basel, London and New York, 1991.

Six Suites for Unaccompanied Violoncello, ed. Janos Starker. New York and Hamburg, 1971.

Zweiter Teil der Klavierübung, BWV 971, 831, 831a; Vierter Teil der Klavierübung, BWV 988; Vierzehn Kanons BWV 1087, ed. Walter Emery, and Christoph Wolff. Johann Sebastian Bach: Neue Ausgabe Sämtlicher Werke, ser. 5, 2. Kassel, Basel, Tours and London, 1977. *Kritischer Bericht*. Kassel, Basel and London, 1981.

Beethoven, Ludwig van. *Drei Skizzenbücher zur Missa solemnis*, I, *Ein Skizzenbuch aus den Jahren 1819/20*, ed. Joseph Schmidt-Görg. Veröffentlichungen des Beethovenhauses in Bonn, Skizzen und Entwürfe. Bonn, 1952.

Drei Skizzenbücher zur Missa solemnis, I, *Ein Skizzenbuch aus den Jahren 1819/20*, part 2, *Faksimile*, ed. Joseph Schmidt-Görg. Veröffentlichungen des Beethovenhauses in Bonn, Skizzen und Entwürfe, 34. Bonn, 1968.

Drei Skizzenbücher zur Missa solemnis, II, *Ein Skizzenbuch zum Credo*, 2 vols., ed. Joseph Schmidt-Görg. Veröffentlichungen des Beethovenhauses in Bonn, Skizzen und Entwürfe, 35. Bonn, 1968–70.

Drei Skizzenbücher zur Missa solemnis, III, *Ein Skizzenbuch zum Benedictus und zum Agnus dei*, 2 vols., ed. Joseph Schmidt-Görg. Veröffentlichungen des Beethovenhauses in Bonn, Skizzen und Entwürfe, 36. Bonn, 1968–70.

Die letzten fünf Sonaten von Beethoven: Kritische Ausgabe mit Einführung und Erläuterung, 4 vols. (numbered 1, 3–5), ed. Heinrich Schenker. Vienna, 1913–21.

Sämtliche Klaviersonaten, 4 vols., ed. Heinrich Schenker. Vienna, 1934.

Ein Skizzenbuch zu den Diabelli-Variationen und zur Missa solemnis, 2 vols., ed. Joseph Schmidt-Görg. Veröffentlichungen des Beethovenhauses in Bonn, Skizzen und Entwürfe, 33. Bonn, 1968–72.

Ein Skizzenbuch zur Chorfantasie op. 80 und zu anderen Werken, ed. Dagmar Weise. Veröffentlichungen des Beethovenhauses in Bonn, Neue Folge, Reihe 1, Skizzen und Entwürfe. Bonn, 1957.

Ein Skizzenbuch zur Pastoralsymphonie op. 68 und zu den Trios op. 70, 1 und 2, 2 vols., ed. Dagmar Weise. Veröffentlichungen des Beethovenhauses in Bonn, Neue Folge, Reihe 1, Skizzen und Entwürfe. Bonn, 1961.

32 Sonatas for the Pianoforte, 2 vols., ed. Artur Schnabel. New York, 1935.

Bent, Margaret, ed. *Fifteenth-Century Liturgical Music*, II, *Four Anonymous Masses*. Early English Church Music, 22. London, 1979.

Boe, John, ed. *Beneventanum troporum corpus*, II, *Ordinary Chants and Tropes for the Mass from Southern Italy, A.D. 1000–1250*, part 1, *Kyrie eleison*, part 2, *Gloria in excelsis*. 4 vols. Recent Researches in Music of the Middle Ages and Early Renaissance, 19–24. Madison, 1989–90.

Cage, John. *4'33"*. New York, 1952.

Chopin, Frédéric. *Ballades*, ed. Alfred Cortot. Paris, 1929.

Complete Works, XVI, *Chamber Music*, ed. I. J. Paderewski, L. Bronarski and J. Turczyński. Warsaw and Cracow, 1961.

Pièces diverses, ed. Alfred Cortot. Paris, 1936.

Polonaise Brillante Opus 3, arr. Emanuel Feuermann, ed. Leonard Rose. New York, 1960.

24 préludes, ed. Alfred Cortot. Paris, 1926.

Corelli, Arcangelo. *Les Œuvres de Arcangelo Corelli*, III, part 1, *VI Sonate a violino solo e violone o cimbalo, Op. 5, I*, part 2, *Preludii, Allemande, Correnti, Gighe, Sarabande,*

Gavotte e Follia a violino solo e violone o cimbalo, Op. 5, II, ed. J. Joachim and F. Chrysander. London, 1890.

Dobson, E. J., and F. Ll. Harrison, eds. *Medieval English Songs*. London and Boston, 1979.

Dunstable, John. *The Works of John Dunstable*, ed. Manfred F. Bukofzer, 2nd rev. edn., ed. Margaret Bent, Ian Bent and Brian Trowell. Musica Britannica, 8. London, 1970.

Dutilleux, Henri. *"Tout un monde lointain ..."*. Paris, 1973.

Gillingham, Bryan, ed. *Saint-Martial Mehrstimmigkeit*. Wissenschaftliche Abhandlungen, 44. Henryville, Ottawa and Binningen, 1984.

Graduale sacrosanctae romanae ecclesiae de tempore et de sanctis. Rome, 1908.

Graduale triplex. Solesmes, 1979.

Hansen, Finn Egeland. *H 159 Montpellier: Tonary of St Bénigne of Dijon*. Studier og Publikationer fra Musikvidenskabeligt Institut Aarhus Universitet, 2. Cophenhagen, 1974.

Haydn, Joseph. *Concert in D dur für Violoncell und Orchester*, arr. F. A. Gevaert. Leipzig, 1890 (Breitkopf & Härtel No. 18380).

Concerto in D major for Cello and Orchestra, piano reduction by F. A. Gevaert, ed. Leonard Rose. New York, 1960.

Konzerte für Violoncello und Orchester, ed. Sonja Gerlach. Joseph Haydn Werke, ser. 3, 2. Munich, 1981.

Streichquartette "opus 20" und "opus 33", ed. Georg Feder and Sonja Gerlach. Joseph Haydn Werke, ser. 12, 3. Munich, 1974. *Kritischer Bericht*. Munich, 1974.

Hertzmann, Erich, Cecil B. Oldman, Daniel Heartz and Alfred Mann, eds. *Thomas Attwoods Theorie- und Kompositionsstudien bei Mozart*. Wolfgang Amadeus Mozart: Neue Ausgabe Sämtlicher Werke, ser. 10, Supplement, Werkgruppe 30, Band 1. Kassel, Basel, Paris, London and New York, 1965.

Hindemith, Paul. *Das Marienleben*. Mainz, 1948.

Hoppin, Richard H., ed. *Anthology of Medieval Music*. The Norton Introduction to Music History. New York, 1978.

Josquin des Prez, *Werken*, 13 vols., ed. A Smijers, *et al.* Amsterdam, 1921–69.

Lowinsky, Edward E., ed. *The Medici Codex of 1518: A Choirbook of Motets Dedicated to Lorenzo de' Medici, Duke of Urbino*. 3 vols. Monuments of Renaissance Music, 3–5. Chicago, 1968.

Monteverdi, Claudio. *L'incoronazione di Poppea*, ed. Alan Curtis. London and Sevenoaks, 1989.

Mozart, Wolfgang Amadeus. *Sinfonie in C ("Linzer Sinfonie") KV 425*, ed. Friedrich Schnapp. Wolfgang Amadeus Mozart: Neue Ausgabe Sämtlicher Werke, ser. 4, Orchesterwerke, Werkgruppe 11, Sinfonien, 8. Kassel, Basel, Tours and London, 1971; repr. Kassel, Basel, London and New York, 1986, pp. 3–62.

Symphonien. Wolfgang Amadeus Mozart's Werke: Kritisch durchgesehene Gesammtausgabe, ser. 8, 3. Leipzig, 1880.

Symphony in C Major No. 36 K. 425 "Linz", ed. Cliff Eisen. London, 1992.

Offertoriale triplex cum uersiculis. Solesmes, 1985.

Penderecki, Krzysztof. *Threnody for the Victims of Hiroshima*. Melville, NY, 1961.

Rosenberg, Samuel N., and Hans Tischler, eds. *Chanter m'estuet: Songs of the Trouvères*. Bloomington, 1981.

———, eds. *The Monophonic Songs in the Roman de Fauvel*. Lincoln, NB, and London, 1991.

Schlager, Karlheinz, ed. *Alleluia-Melodien*, I, *bis 1100*. Monumenta Monodica Medii Aeui, 7. Kassel, Basel, Paris, London and New York, 1968.

Schönberg, Arnold. *Fünf Orchesterstücke Opus 16*, in *Orchesterwerke I*, ed. Nikos Kokkinis. Arnold Schönberg Sämtliche Werke, Abteilung 4, Orchesterwerke, Reihe A, Band 12. Mainz and Vienna, 1980, pp. 1–69.

A Survivor from Warsaw, Op. 46. New York, 1949.

A Survivor from Warsaw, Op. 46, rev. edn., ed. Jacques-Louis Monod. Hillsdale, NY, 1974.

A Survivor from Warsaw Opus 46, in *Chorwerke II*, ed. Josef Rufer and Christian Martin Schmidt. Arnold Schönberg Sämtliche Werke, Abteilung 5, Chorwerke, Reihe A, 19. Mainz and Vienna, 1975, pp. 91–120. *Kritischer Bericht, Skizzen, Fragment*, ed. Christian Martin Schmidt. Mainz and Vienna, 1977.

Schubert, Franz. *Messe in F*, ed. Talia Pecker Berio. Franz Schubert: Neue Ausgabe Sämtlicher Werke, ser. 1, band 1a. Kassel, Basel and London, 1990.

Phantasie, Impromptus und andere Stücke. Franz Schubert's Werke: Kritisch durchgesehene Gesammtausgabe, ser. 11, no. 5. Leipzig, 1888. *Revisionsbericht*, ed. Jules Epstein. Leipzig, 1897.

Solesmes, Les Moines de. *Le graduel romain: Édition critique*, II, *Les sources*. Solesmes, 1957. IV, *Le texte neumatique*, part 1, *Le groupement des manuscrits*. Solesmes, 1960. Part 2, *Les relations généalogiques des manuscrits*. Solesmes, 1962.

Stockhausen, Karlheinz. *Nr. 2 Klavierstücke I–IV*. Vienna, 1954.

Stoltzer, Thomas. *Ausgewählte Werke*, II, *Sämtliche Psalmmotetten*, ed. Lothar Hoffmann-Erbrecht. Das Erbe Deutscher Musik, 66. Frankfurt, 1969.

Taruskin, Richard, ed. *Coment peult avoir joye/Wohlauf gut Gesell von hinnen*. Ogni Sorte Editions, RS 1. Miami, 1978.

Verdi, Giuseppe. *Don Carlos*, 2 vols., ed. Ursula Günther. Milan, 1980.

Weiß, Günther, ed. *Introitus-tropen*, I, *Das Repertoire der südfranzösischen Tropare des 10. und 11. Jahrhunderts*. Monumenta Monodica Medii Aeui, 3. Kassel, Basel, Tours and London, 1970.

Articles and books

Abbate, Carolyn. "The Parisian 'Vénus' and the 'Paris' *Tannhäuser*." *Journal of the American Musicological Society*, 36 (1983), 73–123.

Abravanel, Claude. "A Checklist of Music Manuscripts in Facsimile Edition." *Notes: Journal of the Music Library Association*, 34 (1977–78), 557–70.

Adams, Robert. "Editing *Piers Plowman B*: The Imperative of an Intermittently Critical Edition." *Studies in Bibliography*, 45 (1992), 31–68.

Adler, Guido. *Methode der Musikgeschichte*. Leipzig, 1919.

Der Stil in der Musik. 2nd edn. Leipzig, 1929.

Verzeichniss der musikalischen Autographe von Ludwig van Beethoven … im Besitze von A. Artaria in Wien. Vienna, 1890.

Alain, Olivier. "Un supplément inédit aux *Variations Goldberg* de J. S. Bach." *Revue de Musicologie*, 61 (1975), 244–94.

Allrogen, Gerhard, and Detlef Altenburg, eds. *Festschrift Arno Forchert zum 60.*

Geburtstag am 29. Dezember 1985. Kassel, Basel, London and New York, 1986.

Altmann, Wilhelm. "Ist die Originalhandschrift oder der Erstdruck maßgebend?" *Allgemeine Musikzeitung*, 67 (1940), 243b–44b.

Anglès, Higini. "La música del Ms. de Londres, Brit. Museum Add. 36881." *Butlletí de la Biblioteca de Catalunya*, 8 (1928–32), 301–14 . Reprinted in Hygini Anglés. *Scripta musicologica*, 3 vols., ed. Iosephi López-Calo. Storia e Letteratura, Raccolta di Studi e Testi, 131–33. Rome, 1975–76, III, 1051–66.

Atlas, Allan. *The Cappella Giulia Chansonnier (Rome, Biblioteca Apostolica Vaticana, C. G. XIII.27).* 2 vols. Wissenschaftliche Abhandlungen, 27. Brooklyn, 1975–76.

"Conflicting Attributions in Italian Sources of the Franco-Netherlandish Chanson, *c.* 1465– *c.* 1505: A Progress Report on a New Hypothesis," in *Music in Medieval and Early Modern Europe*, ed. Fenlon, pp. 249–93.

Babcock, Robert G. *Reconstructing a Medieval Library: Fragments from Lambach.* New Haven, 1993.

Badura-Skoda, Eva. "Textual Problems in Masterpieces of the 18th and 19th Centuries," trans. Piero Weiss. *The Musical Quarterly*, 51 (1965), 301–17.

Badura-Skoda, Eva, and Paul Badura-Skoda. *Mozart-Interpretation.* Vienna, 1957. English translation: *Interpreting Mozart on the Keyboard*, trans. Leo Black. London, 1962.

Badura-Skoda, Paul. "Noch einmal zur Frage Ais oder A in der Hammerklaviersonate opus 106 von Beethoven," in *Musik–Edition–Interpretation*, ed. Bente, pp. 53–81.

Baltzer, Rebecca A. "Thirteenth-Century Illuminated Miniatures and the Date of the Florence Manuscript." *Journal of the American Musicological Society*, 25 (1972), 1–18.

Baron, Carol K. "Dating Charles Ives's Music: Facts and Fictions." *Perspectives of New Music*, 28 (1990), 20–56.

Bataillon, Louis J., Bertrand G. Guyot and Richard H. Rouse, eds. *La production du livre universitaire au moyen âge: Exemplar et pecia.* Paris, 1988.

Baumann, Dorothea. "Silben- und Wortwiederholungen im italienischen Liedrepertorie des späten Trecento und frühen Quattrocento," in *Musik und Text*, ed. Günther and Finscher, pp. 77–91.

Bédier, Joseph. "La tradition manuscrite du Lai de l'Ombre: Réflexions sur l'art d'éditer les anciens textes." *Romania*, 54 (1928), 161–96, 321–56. Repr. separately Paris, 1929 and 1970.

Bédier, Joseph, ed. *Le Lai de L'Ombre par Jean Renart.* Société des Anciens Textes Français. Paris, 1913.

Bennwitz, Hanspeter, Georg Feder, Ludwig Finscher and Wolfgang Rehm, eds. *Musikalisches Erbe und Gegenwart: Musiker-Gesamtausgaben in der Bundesrepublik Deutschland.* Kassel, Basel, Tours and London, 1975.

Bent, Margaret. "Editing Music: The Dilemma of Translation." *Early Music*, 22 (1994), 373–92.

"Fact and Value in Contemporary Musical Scholarship," in The College Music Society, *CMS Proceedings: The National and Regional Meetings 1985*, ed. William E. Melin. Boulder, CO, 1986, pp. 3–9. Also published as "Fact and Value in Contemporary Scholarship." *Musical Times*, 127 (1986), 85a–89c.

"The Machaut Manuscripts *Vg*, *B* and *E*." *Musica Disciplina*, 37 (1983), 53–82.

"Some Criteria for Establishing Relationships between Sources of Late-Medieval Polyphony," in *Music in Medieval and Early Modern Europe*, ed. Fenlon, pp. 295–317.

"Text Setting in Sacred Music of the Early 15th Century: Evidence and Implications," in *Musik und Text*, ed. Günther and Finscher, pp. 291–326.

"Trent 93 and Trent 90: Johannes Wiser at Work," in *I codici musicali trentini a cento anni dalla loro riscoperta: Atti del Convegno Laurence Feininger, la musicologia come missione*, ed. Nino Pirrotta and Danilo Curti. Trent, 1986, pp. 84–111.

Bente, Martin. "Ermittlung und Vermittlung: Zum Begriff 'Urtext'." *Österreichische Musikzeitschrift*, 46 (1991), 528–31.

———, ed. *Musik–Edition–Interpretation: Gedenkschrift Günter Henle*. Munich, 1980.

Bentley, Gerald Eades. *The Profession of Dramatist in Shakespeare's Time 1590–1642*. Princeton, 1971.

Berger, Anna Maria Busse. *Mensuration and Proportion Signs: Origins and Evolution*. Oxford Monographs on Music. Oxford, 1993.

Bergeron, Katherine. "A Lifetime of Chants," in *Disciplining Music*, ed. Bergeron and Bohlman, pp. 182–96.

"Representation, Reproduction, and the Revival of Gregorian Chant at Solesmes." Unpublished Ph.D. dissertation, Cornell University, 1989.

Bergeron, Katherine, and Philip V. Bohlman, eds. *Disciplining Music: Musicology and Its Canons*. Chicago, 1992.

Berke, Dieter. "Urtext zwischen Wissenschaftsanspruch und Praxisnähe: Die modernen Musiker-Gesamtausgaben." *Österreichische Musikzeitschrift*, 46 (1991), 531–35.

Bibliothèque Nationale, Département des Manuscrits. *Catalogue général des manuscrits latins*. 7 vols. to date. Paris, 1939–.

Blackburn, Bonnie J. "Josquin's Chansons: Ignored and Lost Sources." *Journal of the American Musicological Society*, 29 (1976), 30–76.

"A Lost Guide to Tinctoris's Teachings Recovered." *Early Music History*, 1 (1981), 29–116.

Blacking, John. *How Musical is Man?* John Danz Lectures. Seattle and London, 1973.

Blecua, Alberto. *Manual de crítica textual*. Literatura y Sociedad, 33. Madrid, 1983.

Bohlman, Philip V. "Musicology as a Political Act." *Journal of Musicology*, 11 (1993), 411–36.

Boorman, Stanley. "The 'First' Edition of the *Odhecaton A*." *Journal of the American Musicological Society*, 30 (1977), 183–207.

"Limitations and Extensions of Filiation Technique," in *Music in Medieval and Early Modern Europe*, ed. Fenlon, pp. 319–46.

"Notational Spelling and Scribal Habit," in *Quellenstudien zur Musik der Renaissance*, II, *Datierung und Filiation*, ed. Finscher, 65–109.

"Petrucci's Type-Setters and the Process of Stemmatics," in *Quellenstudien zur Musik der Renaissance*, I, *Formen und Probleme*, ed. Finscher, 245–80.

"The Uses of Filiation in Early Music." *Text: Transactions of the Society for Textual Scholarship*, 1 (1984), 167–84.

Boretz, Benjamin, and Edward T. Cone, eds. *Perspectives on Notation and Performance*. Perspectives of New Music. New York, 1976.

Bosse, Detlev. *Untersuchung einstimmiger mittelalterlicher Melodien zum "Gloria in excelsis deo"*. Forschungsbeiträge zur Musikwissenschaft, 2. Regensburg, 1955.

Bowers, Fredson. "Current Theories of Copy-Text." *Modern Philology*, 48 (1950–51), 12–20.

"Greg's 'Rationale of Copy-Text' Revisited." *Studies in Bibliography*, 31 (1978), 90–161.

"Some Principles for Scholarly Editions of Nineteenth-Century American Authors." *Studies in Bibliography*, 17 (1964), 223–28.

Bowers, Roger, and Andrew Wathey, compilers. "New Sources of English Fifteenth- and Sixteenth-Century Polyphony." *Early Music History*, 4 (1984), 297–346.

———, compilers. "New Sources of English Fourteenth- and Fifteenth-Century Polyphony." *Early Music History*, 3 (1983), 123–73.

Boyden, David D. "The Corelli 'Solo' Sonatas and Their Ornamental Additions by Corelli, Geminiani, Dubourg, Tartini, and the 'Walsh Anonymous'," in *Musica antiqua*, III, *Acta scientifica*, ed. Jerzy Wiśniowski. Bydgoszcz, 1972, pp. 591–606.

Boyle, Leonard E., O. P. "Optimist and Recensionist: 'Common Errors' or 'Common Variations'?" in *Latin Script and Letters A.D. 400–900: Festschrift Presented to Ludwig Bieler on the Occasion of his 70th Birthday*, ed. John J. O'Meara and Bernd Naumann. Leiden, 1976, pp. 264–74.

Brandenburg, Sieghard, William Drabkin, and Douglas Johnson. "On Beethoven Scholars and Beethoven Sketches." *19th Century Music*, 2 (1978–79), 270–79.

Brett, Philip. "Text, Context, and the Early Music Editor," in *Authenticity and Early Music: A Symposium*, ed. Nicholas Kenyon. Oxford and New York, 1988, pp. 83–114.

Brewer, Charlotte. "The Textual Principles of Kane's A Text." *Yearbook of Langland Studies*, 3 (1989), 67–90.

Brooks, Jeanice. "Jean de Castro, the Pense Partbooks and Musical Culture in Sixteenth-Century Lyons." *Early Music History*, 11 (1992), 91–149.

Broude, Ronald. "When Accidentals Are Substantive: Applying Methodologies of Textual Criticism to Scholarly Editions of Music." *Text: Transactions of the Society for Textual Scholarship*, 5 (1991), 105–20.

Brown, Howard Mayer. "Editing," in *The New Grove Dictionary of Music and Musicians*, 20 vols., ed. Stanley Sadie. London, 1980, V, 839b–48a.

"In Alamire's Workshop: Notes on Scribal Practice in the Early Sixteenth Century," in *Quellenstudien zur Musik der Renaissance*, II, *Datierung und Filiation*, ed. Finscher, 15–63.

"Words and Music in Early 16th-Century Chansons: Text Underlay in Florence, Biblioteca del Conservatorio, Ms Basevi 2442," in *Quellenstudien zur Musik der Renaissance*, I, *Formen und Probleme*, ed. Finscher, pp. 97–141.

Brown, Julian, Sonia Patterson and David Hiley. "Further Observations on W_1." *Journal of the Plainsong & Mediaeval Music Society*, 4 (1981), 53–80.

Brown, Maurice J. E. "Recent Schubert Discoveries." *Music & Letters*, 32 (1951), 349–62.

Butt, John. *Bach Interpretation: Articulation Marks in Primary Sources of J. S. Bach*. Cambridge Musical Texts and Monographs. Cambridge, 1990.

Music Education and the Art of Performance in the German Baroque. Cambridge Musical Texts and Monographs. Cambridge, 1994.

Caldwell, John. *Editing Early Music*. Early Music Series, 5. Oxford, 1985.
Carroll, William C. "New Plays vs. Old Readings: *The Division of the Kingdoms* and Folio Deletions in *King Lear*." *Studies in Philology*, 85 (1988), 225–44.
Catalogus codicum manuscriptorum Bibliothecae regiae parisiensis. 4 vols. Paris, 1744.
Census-Catalogue of Manuscript Sources of Polyphonic Music 1400–1550. 5 vols. Renaissance Manuscript Studies, 1. Neuhausen–Stuttgart, 1979–88.
Chailley, Jacques. "Les anciens tropaires et séquentiaires de l'école de Saint-Martial de Limoges (Xe–XIe s.)." *Études Grégoriennes*, 2 (1957), 163–88.
L'école musicale de Saint Martial de Limoges jusqu'à la fin du XIe siècle. Paris, 1960.
Chiarelli, Alessandra. "*L'Incoronazione di Poppea* o *Il Nerone*: Problemi di filologia testuale." *Rivista Italiana di Musicologia*, 9 (1974), 117–51.
Cohen, Philip, ed. *Devils and Angels: Textual Editing and Literary Theory*. Charlottesville and London, 1991.
Cole, Hugo. *Sounds and Signs: Aspects of Musical Notation*. London, 1974.
Collomp, P. *La critique des textes*. Publications de la Faculté des Lettres de l'Université de Strasbourg, Initiation Méthode, 6. Paris, 1931.
Combe, Pierre. *Histoire de la restauration du chant grégorien d'après des documents inédits: Solesmes et l'Édition Vaticane*. Abbaye de Solesmes, 1969. Revised version of "La réforme du chant et des livres de chant grégorien à l'Abbaye de Solesmes, 1833–1883: Dom Guéranger, dom Jausions et dom Pothier." *Études Grégoriennes*, 6 (1963), 185–234. "Les préliminaires de la réforme grégorienne de S. Pie X: I. Dom André Mocquereau, II. Le P. de Santi et Mgr Carlo Respighi." *Ibid.*, 7 (1967), 63–145. "La restauration du chant grégorien: III. L'œuvre de S. Pie X." *Ibid.*, 8 (1967), 137–98. "La restauration du chant grégorien: III. L'œuvre de S. Pie X [suite]." *Ibid.*, 9 (1968), 47–100.
Cooke, Deryck. "The Bruckner Problem Simplified." *Musical Times*, 110 (1969), 20–22, 142–44, 362–65, 479–82, 828.
Coover, James. "Composite Music Manuscripts in Facsimile." *Notes: Journal of the Music Library Association*, 38 (1981–82), 275–95.
Crocker, Richard Lincoln. "The Repertoire of Proses at Saint Martial de Limoges (Tenth and Eleventh Centuries)." 2 vols. Unpublished Ph.D. dissertation, Yale University, 1957.
Curtis, Alan. "*La Poppea Impasticciata* or, Who Wrote the Music to *L'Incoronazione* (1643)?" *Journal of the American Musicological Society*, 42 (1989), 23–54.
Dadelsen, Georg von. "Die Crux der Nebensache: Editorische und praktische Bemerkungen zu Bachs Artikulation." *Bach-Jahrbuch*, 64 (1978), 95–112.
"Die 'Fassung letzter Hand' in der Musik." *Acta Musicologica*, 33 (1961), 1–14.
"Über das Wechselspiel von Musik und Notation," in *Festschrift Walter Gerstenberg zum 60. Geburtstag*, ed. Georg von Dadelsen and Andreas Holschneider. Wolfenbüttel and Zürich, 1964, pp. 17–25.
"Über den Wert musikalischer Textkritik," in *Quellenstudien zur Musik: Wolfgang Schmieder zum 70. Geburtstag*, ed. Georg von Dadelsen and Kurt Dorfmüller. Frankfurt, London and New York, 1972, pp. 41–45.
"Zur Geltung der Legatobögen bei Bach: Eine Studie für Artikulationsfanatiker und Editoren," in *Festschrift Arno Forchert*, ed. Allrogen and Altenburg, pp. 114–22.
———, ed. *Editionsrichtlinien musikalischer Denkmäler und Gesamtausgaben*.

Musikwissenschaftliche Arbeiten Herausgegeben von der Gesellschaft für Musikforschung, 22. Kassel, Basel, Paris, London and New York, 1967.

Dahlhaus, Carl. "Ästhetik und Musikästhetik," in *Systematische Musikwissenschaft*, ed. Carl Dahlhaus and Helga de la Motte-Haber. Neues Handbuch der Musikwissenschaft, 10. Wiesbaden and Laaber, 1982, pp. 81–108.

Musikästhetik. Musik-Taschen-Bücher, Theoretica, 8. Cologne, 1967. English translation: *Esthetics of Music*, trans. William Austin. Cambridge, 1982.

"Philologie und Rezeptionsgeschichte: Bemerkungen zur Theorie der Edition," in *Festschrift Georg von Dadelsen zum 60. Geburtstag*, ed. Thomas Kohlhase and Volker Scherliess. Neuhausen–Stuttgart, 1978, pp. 45–58.

"Urtextausgaben." *Neue Zeitschrift für Musik*, 134 (1973), 334a–b.

"Zur Ideengeschichte musikalischer Editionsprinzipien." *Fontes Artis Musicae*, 25 (1978), 19–27.

Dart, Thurston. *The Interpretation of Music*. London, 1954.

Dart, Thurston, Walter Emery and Christopher Morris. *Editing Early Music: Notes on the Preparation of Printer's Copy*. London, 1963.

Dearing, Vinton A. *A Manual of Textual Analysis*. Berkeley and Los Angeles, 1959.

Principles and Practice of Textual Analysis. Berkeley and Los Angeles, 1974.

Delisle, Léopold. *Le cabinet de manuscrits de la Bibliothèque impériale*. 4 vols. Histoire Générale de Paris. Paris, 1868–81; repr. Amsterdam, 1969, and New York, 1974.

"Inventaire des manuscrits conservés à la Bibliothèque impériale sous les nos 8823–11503 du fonds latin." *Bibliothèque de l'École des Chartes*, 23 (1862), 277–308, 469–512; *ibid.*, 24 (1863), 185–236.

Inventaire des manuscrits latins conservés à la Bibliothèque nationale sous les numéros 8823–18613. Paris, 1863–71.

"Inventaire des manuscrits latins de la Sorbonne conservés à la Bibliothèque impériale sous les numéros 15176–16718 du fonds latin." *Bibliothèque de l'École des Chartes*, 31 (1870), 1–50, 135–61.

"Inventaire des manuscrits latins de Notre-Dame et d'autres fonds conservés à la Bibliothèque impériale sous les numéros 16719–18613." *Bibliothèque de l'École des Chartes*, 31 (1870), 463–565.

"Inventaire des manuscrits latins de Saint-Germain-des-Prés." *Bibliothèque de l'École des Chartes*, 26 (1865), 185–214; *ibid.*, 28 (1867), 343–76, 528–56; *ibid.*, 29 (1868), 220–60.

"Inventaire des manuscrits latins de Saint-Victor conservés à la Bibliothèque impériale sous les numéros 14232–15175." *Bibliothèque de l'École des Chartes*, 30 (1869), 1–79.

"Notice sur les manuscrits originaux d'Adémar de Chabannes." *Notices et extraits des manuscrits de la Bibliothèque Nationale et autres bibliothèques*, 35 (1896), 241–358.

Dennery, Annie. *Le chant postgrégorien: Tropes, séquences et prosules*. Musique–Musicologie, 19. Paris, 1989.

Destrez, Jean. *La pecia dans les manuscrits universitaires du XIIIe siècle et du XIVe siècle*. Paris, 1935.

Deutsch, Otto Erich. *Franz Schubert: Thematisches Verzeichnis seiner Werke in chronologischer Folge*, new edn., ed. Werner Aderhold. Franz Schubert: Neue Ausgabe Sämtlicher Werke, ser. 8, supplement vol. 4. Kassel, Basel, Tours and London, 1978.

Dinter, Peter, ed. *Liber tramitis aeui Odilonis abbatis*. Corpus Consuetudinum Monasticarum, 10. Siegburg, 1980.

Dorfmüller, Kurt, ed. *Beiträge zur Beethoven-Bibliographie: Studien und Materialien zum Werkverzeichnis von Kinsky-Halm*. Munich, 1978.

Dreves, Guido Maria, Clemens Blume and Henry M. Bannister, eds. *Analecta hymnica*. 55 vols. Leipzig, 1886–1922.

Duckles, Vincent H., and Michael A. Keller. *Music Reference and Research Materials: An Annotated Bibliography*. 4th edn. New York and London, 1988.

Dunsby, Jonathan. "Music and Semiotics: The Nattiez Phase." *The Musical Quarterly*, 69 (1983), 27–43.

Duplès-Agier, H. ed. *Chroniques de Saint-Martial de Limoges*. Paris, 1874.

Earp, Lawrence. "Machaut's Role in the Production of Manuscripts of His Works." *Journal of the American Musicological Society*, 42 (1989), 461–503.

Eisen, Cliff. "The Mozarts' Salzburg Copyists: Aspects of Attribution, Chronology, Text, Style, and Performance Practice," in *Mozart Studies*, ed. Cliff Eisen. Oxford, 1991, pp. 253–307.

"New Light on Mozart's 'Linz' Symphony, K.425." *Journal of the Royal Musical Association*, 113 (1988), 81–96.

"The Old and New Mozart Editions." *Early Music*, 19 (1991), 513–32.

Eklund, Sten. "On Errors and Contamination." *Kungl. Humanistiska Vetenskaps-Samfundet i Uppsala, Årsbok* (1975–76), 73–83.

"The Traditional or the Stemmatic Editorial Technique." *Kungl. Humanistiska Vetenskaps-Samfundet i Uppsala, Årsbok* (1987–88), 33–49.

Emerson, John A. "Two Newly Identified Offices for Saints Valeria and Austriclinianus by Adémar de Chabannes (MS Paris, Bibl. Nat., Latin 909, FOLS. 79–85v)." *Speculum*, 40 (1965), 31–46.

Emery, Walter. *Editions and Musicians*. London, 1957.

England, Nicholas M., Robert Garfias, Mieczylaw Kolinski, George List, Willard Rhodes and Charles Seeger. "Symposium on Transcription and Analysis: A Hukwe Song with Musical Bow." *Ethnomusicology*, 8 (1964), 223–77.

"Das Erbe deutscher Music. Herausgegeben von der Musikgeschichtlichen Kommission e. V.," in *Editionsrichtlinien*, ed. Dadelsen, pp. 19–54.

Escudier, Denis. "Des notations musicales dans les manuscrits non liturgiques antérieurs au XIIe siècle." *Bibliothèque de l'École des Chartes*, 129 (1971), 27–48.

Evans, Paul. *The Early Trope Repertory of Saint Martial de Limoges*. Princeton Studies in Music, 2. Princeton, 1970.

Everist, Mark. "From Paris to St. Andrews: The Origins of W_1." *Journal of the American Musicological Society*, 43 (1990), 1–42.

Fassler, Margot E. "The Office of the Cantor in Early Western Monastic Rules and Customaries: A Preliminary Investigation." *Early Music History*, 5 (1985), 29–51.

Feder, Georg. "Das Autograph als Quelle wissenschaftlicher Edition," in *Internationales Symposium Musikerautographe*, ed. Hilmar, pp. 115–44.

"Gedanken über den kritischen Apparat aus der Sicht der Haydn-Gesamtausgabe," in *Colloquium amicorum: Joseph Schmidt-Görg zum 70. Geburtstag*, ed. Siegfried Kross and Hans Schmidt. Bonn, 1967, pp. 73–81.

Musikphilologie: Eine Einführung in die musikalische Textkritik, Hermeneutik und

Editionstechnik. Die Musikwissenschaft: Einführungen in Gegenstand, Methoden und Ergebnisse ihrer Disziplinen. Darmstadt, 1987.

"Textkritische Methoden: Versuch eines Überblicks mit Bezug auf die Haydn-Gesamtausgabe." *Haydn-Studien*, 5 (1982–83), 77–109.

Feder, Georg, and Hubert Unverricht. "Urtext und Urtextausgaben." *Musikforschung*, 12 (1959), 432–54.

Fellerer, Karl Gustav. "Werk–Edition–Interpretation," in *Musik–Edition–Interpretation*, ed. Bente, pp. 180–92.

Fenlon, Iain, ed. *Music in Medieval and Early Modern Europe: Patronage, Sources and Texts*. Cambridge, 1981.

Finscher, Ludwig. "Gesamtausgabe–Urtext–Musikalische Praxis: Zum Verhältnis von Musikwissenschaft und Musikleben," in *Musik–Edition–Interpretation*, ed. Bente, pp. 193–98.

"Musikalische Denkmäler und Gesamtausgaben," in *Musikalisches Erbe und Gegenwart*, ed. Bennwitz, *et al.*, pp. 1–13.

———, ed. *Quellenstudien zur Musik der Renaissance*, I, *Formen und Probleme der Überlieferung mehrstimmiger Musik im Zeitalter Josquins Desprez*. Wolfenbütteler Forschungen, 6. Munich, 1981.

———, ed. *Quellenstudien zur Musik der Renaissance*, II, *Datierung und Filiation von Musikhandschriften der Josquin-Zeit*. Wolfenbütteler Forschungen, 26. Wiesbaden 1983.

Finson, Jon W. "Schumann, Popularity, and the *Ouverture, Scherzo, und Finale*, Opus 52." *The Musical Quarterly*, 69 (1983), 1–26.

Friedländer, Max. *Ueber musikalische Herausgeberarbeit*. Weimar, 1922. Revised version of "Über die Herausgabe musikalischer Kunstwerke." *Jahrbuch der Musikbibliothek Peters*, 14 (1907), 13–33.

Froger, J. *La critique des textes et son automatisation*. Initiation aux Nouveautés de la Science, 7. Paris, 1968.

"The Critical Edition of the Roman Gradual by the Monks of Solesmes." *Journal of the Plainsong & Mediaeval Music Society*, 1 (1978), 81–97.

Frye, Northrop. *Anatomy of Criticism: Four Essays*. Princeton, 1957.

Fux, Johann Joseph. *Gradus ad Parnassum*, ed. Alfred Mann. Johann Joseph Fux: Sämtliche Werke, ser. 7, 1. Kassel, Basel, Paris, London, New York and Graz, 1967.

Gaborit-Chopin, D. *La décoration des manuscrits à Saint-Martial de Limoges et en Limousin du IXe au XIIe siècle*. Mémoires et Documents Publiés par la Société de l'École des Chartes, 17. Paris and Geneva, 1969.

Gaskell, Philip. *From Writer to Reader: Studies in Editorial Method*. Oxford, 1978.

"Night and Day: The Development of a Play Text," in *Textual Criticism and Literary Interpretation*, ed. McGann, pp. 162–79.

Gautier, Léon. *Histoire de la poésie liturgique au moyen âge: Les tropes*. Paris, 1886.

Georgiades, Thrasybulos G., ed. *Musikalische Edition im Wandel des historischen Bewußtseins*. Musikwissenschaftliche Arbeiten Herausgegeben von der Gesellschaft für Musikforschung, 23. Kassel, Basel, Tours and London, 1971.

Glahn, Henrik, Søren Sørensen and Peter Ryom, eds. *International Musicological Society, Report of Eleventh Congress Copenhagen 1972*. 2 vols. Copenhagen, 1974.

Godt, Irving, and Benito Rivera, eds. and trans. "The Vatican Organum Treatise: A

Colour Reproduction, Transcription and Translation," in *Gordon Athol Anderson (1929–1981): In Memoriam*. 2 vols. Wissenschaftliche Abhandlungen, 39. Henryville, Ottawa and Binningen, 1984, II, 264–345.

Goehr, Lydia. *The Imaginary Museum of Musical Works: An Essay in the Philosophy of Music*. Oxford, 1992.

Goodman, Nelson. *Languages of Art: An Approach to a Theory of Symbols*. 2nd edn. Indianapolis, 1976.

Grasberger, Franz, ed. *Bruckner Symposion "Die Fassungen": Im Rahmen des Internationalen Brucknerfestes Linz 1980*. Linz, 1981.

Greg, W. W. *The Calculus of Variants: An Essay on Textual Criticism*. Oxford, 1927.

"The Rationale of Copy-Text." *Studies in Bibliography*, 3 (1950–51), 19–36.

Grier, James. "*Ecce sanctum quem deus elegit Marcialem apostolum*: Adémar de Chabannes and the Tropes for the Feast of Saint Martial," in *Beyond the Moon: Festschrift Luther Dittmer*, ed. Bryan Gillingham and Paul Merkley. Wissenschaftliche Abhandlungen, 53. Ottawa, 1990, pp. 28–74.

"Editing Adémar de Chabannes' Liturgy for the Feast of Saint Martial," in *Music Discourse from Classical to Early Modern Times: Editing and Translating Texts*, ed. Maria Rika Maniates. Conference on Editorial Problems, no. 26: 1990. New York, 1993, pp. 17–43.

"Lachmann, Bédier and the Bipartite Stemma: Towards a Responsible Application of the Common-Error Method." *Revue d'Histoire des Textes*, 18 (1988), 263–78.

"A New Voice in the Monastery: Tropes and *Versus* from Eleventh- and Twelfth-Century Aquitaine." *Speculum*, 69 (1994), 1023–69.

"Roger de Chabannes († 1025), Cantor of Saint Martial de Limoges." *Early Music History*, 14 (1995), 53–119.

"Scribal Practices in the Aquitanian Versaria of the Twelfth Century: Towards a Typology of Error and Variant." *Journal of the American Musicological Society*, 45 (1992), 373–427.

"Some Codicological Observations on the Aquitanian Versaria." *Musica Disciplina*, 44 (1990), 5–56.

"The Stemma of the Aquitanian Versaria." *Journal of the American Musicological Society*, 41 (1988), 250–88.

Gruber, Gerold W. "'Doppel'-Editionen für den interpretatorischen Freiraum." *Österreichische Musikzeitschrift*, 46 (1991), 710a–11b.

Guido of Arezzo. *Micrologus*, ed. Jos. Smits van Waesberghe. Corpus Scriptorum de Musica, 4. N.p., 1955.

Gülke, Peter. "Philologie und musikalische Praxis." *Österreichische Musikzeitschrift*, 46 (1991), 535–39.

Günther, Ursula. "La genèse de *Don Carlos*, opéra en cinq actes de Giuseppe Verdi, représenté pour la première fois à Paris le 11 mars 1867." *Revue de Musicologie*, 58 (1972), 16–64; *ibid.*, 60 (1974), 87–158.

Günther, Ursula, and Ludwig Finscher, eds. *Musik und Text in der Mehrstimmigkeit des 14. und 15. Jahrhunderts*. Göttinger Musikwissenschaftliche Arbeiten, 10. Kassel, Basel and London, 1984.

Hamm, Charles. "Interrelationships between Manuscript and Printed Sources of Polyphonic Music in the Early Sixteenth Century – An Overview," in *Quellenstudien zur Musik der Renaissance*, II, *Datierung und Filiation*, ed. Finscher, 1–13.

"Manuscript Structure in the Dufay Era." *Acta Musicologica*, 34 (1962), 166–84.

Harrán, Don. "In Pursuit of Origins: The Earliest Writing on Text Underlay (c. 1440)." *Acta Musicologica*, 50 (1978), 217–40.

"New Light on the Question of Text Underlay Prior to Zarlino." *Acta Musicologica*, 45 (1973), 24–56.

"On the Question of Word–Tone Relations in Early Music," in *Musik und Text*, ed. Günther and Finscher, pp. 269–89.

"Vicentino and His Rules of Text Underlay." *The Musical Quarterly*, 59 (1973), 620–32.

Hawkins, John. *A General History of the Science and Practice of Music*. 2 vols. London, 1853; repr. New York, 1963.

Henle, Günter. "Über die Herausgabe von Urtexten." *Musica*, 8 (1954), 377–80.

Herttrich, Ernst. "Autograph–Edition–Interpretation," in *Internationales Symposium Musikerautographe 5.–8. Juni 1989*, ed. Hilmar, pp. 165–84.

Hesbert, René-Jean. *Corpus antiphonalium officii*. 6 vols. Rerum Ecclesiasticarum Documenta, Series Maior, Fontes, 7–12. Rome, 1963–79.

Heussenstamm, George. *The Norton Manual of Music Notation*. New York and London, 1987.

Hilmar, Ernst, ed. *Internationales Symposium Musikerautographe 5.–8. Juni 1989*. Publikationen des Instituts für Österreichische Musikdokumentation, 16. Tutzing, 1990.

Hilzinger, Klaus Harro. "Über kritische Edition literarischer und musikalischer Texte." *Euphorion*, 68 (1974), 198–210.

Hindemith, Paul. *Unterweisung in Tonsatz: Theoretischer Teil*. Mainz, 1937. English translation: *The Craft of Musical Composition*, I, *Theoretical Part*, trans. Arthur Mendel. London, 1942.

Hitchcock, H. Wiley, ed. *The Phonograph and Our Musical Life: Proceedings of a Centennial Conference, 7–10 December 1977*. Institute for Studies in American Music, Monographs, 14. Brooklyn, 1980.

Hoboken, Anthony van. "Probleme der musikbibliographischen Terminologie." *Fontes Artis Musicae*, 5 (1958), 6–15.

Hoffmann-Erbrecht, Lothar. "Problems in the Interdependence of Josquin Sources," in *Josquin des Prez*, ed. Lowinsky and Blackburn, pp. 285–93.

Honigmann, E. A. J. *The Stability of Shakespeare's Text*. Lincoln, 1965.

Hooreman, Paul. "Saint-Martial de Limoges au temps de l'Abbé Odolric (1025–1040): Essai sur une pièce oubliée du répertoire limousin." *Revue Belge de Musicologie*, 3 (1949), 5–36.

Hoppin, Richard H. *Medieval Music*. The Norton Introduction to Music History. New York, 1978.

Howard-Hill, T. H. "Theory and Praxis in the Social Approach to Editing." *Text: Transactions of the Society for Textual Scholarship*, 5 (1991), 31–46.

"Variety in Editing and Reading: A Response to McGann and Shillingsburg," in *Devils and Angels*, ed. Cohen, pp. 44–56.

Huglo, Michel. "Codicologie et musicologie," in *Miscellanea codicologica F. Masai dicata MCMLXXIX*, 2 vols., ed. Pierre Cockshaw, Monique-Cécile Garand and Pierre Jodogne. Les Publications de Scriptorium, 8. Gand, 1979, I, 71–82.

"Les *Libelli* de tropes et les premiers tropaires-prosaires," in *Pax et sapientia: Studies* in *Text and Music of Liturgical Tropes and Sequences in Memory of Gordon Anderson*, ed. Ritva Jacobsson. Acta Universitatis Stockholmiensis, Studia Latina Stockholmiensia, 29. Stockholm, 1986, pp. 13–22.

Les livres de chant liturgique. Typologie des Sources du Moyen Âge Occidental, 52. Turnhout, 1988.

"On the Origins of the Troper-Proser." *Journal of the Plainsong & Mediaeval Music Society*, 2 (1979), 11–18. Translation of "Aux origines du Tropaire-Prosaire," in *Nordiskt kollokvium i latinsk liturgiforskning*, IV (Oslo, 1978), 53–65.

"Règlement du XIIIe siècle pour la transcription des livres notés," in *Festschrift Bruno Stäblein*, ed. Ruhnke, pp. 121–33.

Review of Finn Egeland Hansen, *The Grammar of Gregorian Tonality: An Investigation Based on the Repertory in Codex H 159, Montpellier*. *Journal of the American Musicological Society*, 37 (1984), 416–24 (trans. Paul Merkley).

Les tonaires: Inventaire, analyse, comparaison. Publications de la Société Française de Musicologie, ser. 3, 2. Paris, 1971.

Humbert of Romans. *Opera de uita regulari*, 2 vols., ed. Joachim Joseph Berthier. Rome, 1888–89.

Husmann, Heinrich. "The Enlargement of the *Magnus liber organi* and the Paris Churches of St. Germain l'Auxerrois and Ste. Geneviève-du-Mont." *Journal of the American Musicological Society*, 16 (1963), 176–203.

"The Origin and Destination of the *Magnus liber organi*." *The Musical Quarterly*, 59 (1963), 311–30.

Tropen- und Sequenzenhandschriften. Répertoire International des Sources Musicales, B/5, 1. Munich–Duisburg, 1964.

Ingarden, Roman. *The Work of Music and the Problem of Its Identity*, trans. Adam Czerniawski, ed. Jean G. Harell. Berkeley and Los Angeles, 1987. Translation of *Utwór muzyczny i sprawa jego tożsamości*. Warsaw, 1966.

Inventory of Western Manuscripts in the Biblioteca Ambrosiana. 2 vols. Publications in Medieval Studies, 22. Notre Dame, 1984.

Irigoin, Jean. "Accidents matériels et critique des textes." *Revue d'Histoire des Textes*, 16 (1986), 1–36.

Jeffery, Peter. "Music Manuscripts on Microfilm in the Hill Monastic Microfilm Library." *Notes: Journal of the Music Library Association*, 35 (1978–79), 7–30.

"The New Chantbooks from Solesmes." *Notes: Journal of the Music Library Association*, 47 (1990–91), 1039–63.

Jocqué, Luc, and Louis Milis, eds. *Liber ordinis sancti Victoris parisiensis*. Corpus Christianorum Continuatio Mediaeualis, 61. Turnhout, 1984.

Johnson, Douglas. "Beethoven Scholars and Beethoven's Sketches." *19th Century Music*, 2 (1978–79), 3–17.

Johnson, Douglas, Alan Tyson and Robert Winter. *The Beethoven Sketchbooks: History, Reconstruction, Inventory*, ed. Douglas Johnson. Oxford, 1985.

"Joseph Haydn. Werke. Herausgegeben vom Joseph Haydn-Institut, Köln. Richtlinien für die Mitarbeiter. Dritte Ausgabe (1966)," in *Editionsrichtlinien*, ed. Dadelsen, pp. 81–98.

Kallberg, Jeffrey. "Are Variants a Problem? 'Composer's Intentions' in Editing Chopin." *Chopin Studies*, 3 (1990), 257–67.

Kane, George, ed. *Piers Plowman: The Three Versions*. Rev. edn. 2 vols. London and Berkeley, 1988.

Karkoschka, Erhard. *Das Schriftbild der neuen Musik: Bestandsaufnahme neuer Notationssymbole, Anleitung zu deren Deutung, Realisation und Kritik*. Celle, 1966. English translation: *Notation in New Music: A Critical Guide to Interpretation and Realisation*, trans. Ruth Koenig. New York and Washington, 1972.

Karp, Theodore. *The Polyphony of Saint Martial and Santiago de Compostela*. 2 vols. Oxford, 1992.

Kenney, E. J. *The Classical Text: Aspects of Editing in the Age of the Printed Book*. Sather Classical Lectures, 44. Berkeley, Los Angeles and London, 1974.

Kerman, Joseph. *Musicology*. London, 1985. American edition: *Contemplating Music: Challenges to Musicology*. Cambridge, MA, 1985.

Kinsky, Georg and Hans Halm. *Das Werk Beethovens: Thematisch-bibliographisches Verzeichnis seiner sämtlichen vollendeten Kompositionen*. Munich–Duisburg, 1955.

Kirsch, Winfried. "Josquin's Motets in the German Tradition," in *Josquin des Prez*, ed. Lowinsky and Blackburn, pp. 261–78.

Kraft, Herbert. *Die Geschichtlichkeit literarischer Texte: Eine Theorie der Edition*. Bebenhausen, 1973.

Kramer, Lawrence. *Music as Cultural Practice, 1800–1900*. California Studies in 19th Century Music, 8. Berkeley, Los Angeles and Oxford, 1990.

Krohn, Ernst C. "Music in the Vatican Film Library at Saint Louis University." *Notes: Journal of the Music Library Association*, 14 (1956–57), 317–24.

Kropfinger, Klaus. "Von der Werkstatt zur Aufführung: Was bedeuten Beethovens Skizzen für die Werkinterpretation?" in *Festschrift Arno Forchert*, ed. Allrogen and Altenburg, pp. 169–74.

Krummel, D. W. "Citing the Score: Descriptive Bibliography and Printed Music." *The Library*, ser. 6, 9 (1987), 329–46.

The Literature of Music Bibliography: An Account of the Writings on the History of Music Printing & Publishing. Fallen Leaf Reference Books in Music, 21. Berkeley, CA, 1992.

———, compiler. *Guide for Dating Early Published Music: A Manual of Bibliographical Practices*. Hackensack, NJ, 1974.

Kurkela, Kari. *Note and Tone: A Semantic Analysis of Conventional Music Notation*. Acta Musicologica Fennica, 15. Helsinki, 1986.

Lachmann, Karl. "Rechenschaft über seine Ausgabe des Neuen Testaments." *Theologische Studien und Kritiken*, 3 (1830), 817–45. Reprinted in *Kleinere Schriften von Karl Lachmann*, II, *Kleinere Schriften zur Classischen Philologie von Karl Lachmann*, ed. J. Vahlen. Berlin, 1876, pp. 250–72.

———, ed. *In T. Lucretii Cari De rerum natura libros commentarius*. Berlin, 1850.

Lachmann, Karl, and Philip Buttmann, eds. *Nouum Testamentum Graece et Latine*. 2 vols. Berlin, 1842–50.

Lambert, J. Philip. "Communication." *Journal of the American Musicological Society*, 42 (1989), 204–9.

Landes, Richard. "The Making of a Medieval Historian: Ademar of Chabannes and Aquitaine at the Turn of the Millennium." Unpublished Ph.D. dissertation, Princeton, 1984.

Landon, H. C. Robbins. "The *Jena* Symphony." *Music Review*, 18 (1957), 109–13.

Lang, Paul Henry. *Music in Western Civilization.* New York, 1941.

LaRue, Jan. *Guidelines for Style Analysis.* New York and London, 1970.

Lefferts, Peter M., and Margaret Bent, compilers. "New Sources of English Thirteenth- and Fourteenth-Century Polyphony." *Early Music History*, 2 (1982), 273–362.

Leichtentritt, Hugo. *Music, History, and Ideas.* Cambridge, MA, 1938.

Leppert, Richard, and Susan McClary, eds. *Music and Society: The Politics of Composition, Performance and Reception.* Cambridge, 1987.

Lissa, Zofia. "Some Remarks on Ingardenian Theory of a Musical Work," trans. Ursula Niklas, in *Roman Ingarden and Contemporary Polish Aesthetics*, ed. Piotr Graff and Sław Krzemień-Ojak. Warsaw, 1975, pp. 129–44.

Lombardi, Daniele. *Scrittura e suono: La notazione nella musica contemporanea.* Rome, 1980.

Lowinsky, Edward E. "Early Scores in Manuscript." *Journal of the American Musicological Society*, 13 (1960), 126–73.

"On the Use of Scores by Sixteenth-Century Musicians." *Journal of the American Musicological Society*, 1 (1948), 17–23.

"A Treatise on Text Underlay by a German Disciple of Francisco de Salinas," in *Festschrift Heinrich Besseler zum sechzigsten Geburtstag.* Leipzig, 1961, pp. 231–51.

Lowinsky, Edward E., and Bonnie J. Blackburn, eds. *Josquin des Prez: Proceedings of the International Josquin Festival-Conference Held at the Juilliard School at Lincoln Center in New York City, 21–25 June 1971.* London, 1976.

Maas, Paul. *Textkritik.* 4th edn. Leipzig, 1960. English translation from the 3rd German edn (Leipzig, 1957): *Textual Criticism*, trans. Barbara Flower. Oxford, 1958.

Mann, Alfred. "Haydn as Student and Critic of Fux," in *Studies in Eighteenth-Century Music: A Tribute to Karl Geiringer on His Seventieth Birthday*, ed. H. C. Robbins Landon and Roger E. Chapman. London, 1970, pp. 323–32.

"Haydn's Elementarbuch: A Document of Classic Counterpoint Instruction." *The Music Forum*, 3 (1973), 197–237.

Marchetto of Padua. *Lucidarium*, ed. and trans. Jan W. Herlinger, *The Lucidarium of Marchetto of Padua: A Critical Edition, Translation, and Commentary.* Chicago and London, 1985.

Marco, Guy A. *The Earliest Music Printers of Continental Europe: A Checklist of Facsimiles Illustrating Their Work.* N.p., n.d.

Marston, Nicholas. "Approaching the Sketches for Beethoven's 'Hammerklavier' Sonata." *Journal of the American Musicological Society*, 44 (1991), 404–50.

Martens, Gunter, and Hans Zeller, eds. *Texte und Varianten: Probleme ihrer Edition und Interpretation.* Munich, 1971.

McGann, Jerome J. *The Beauty of Inflections: Literary Investigations in Historical Method and Theory.* Oxford, 1985.

A Critique of Modern Textual Criticism. Chicago and London, 1983.

"Literary Pragmatics and the Editorial Horizon," in *Devils and Angels*, ed. Cohen, pp. 1–21.

"A Response to T. H. Howard-Hill." *Text: Transactions of the Society for Textual Scholarship*, 5 (1991), 47–48.

The Romantic Ideology: A Critical Investigation. Chicago and London, 1983.

Social Values and Poetic Acts: The Historical Judgement of Literary Work. Cambridge, MA, and London, 1988.

"The Text, the Poem, and the Problem of Historical Method." *New Literary History*, 12 (1981), 269–88.

The Textual Condition. Princeton Studies in Culture/Power/History. Princeton, 1991.

Towards a Literature of Knowledge. Chicago, 1989.

———, ed. *Textual Criticism and Literary Interpretation*. Chicago and London, 1985.

McKenzie, D. F. *Bibliography and the Sociology of Texts*. The Panizzi Lectures: 1985. London, 1986.

McLeod, Randall, ed. *Crisis in Editing: Texts of the English Renaissance*. Conference on Editorial Problems, no. 24: 1988. New York, 1994.

Meister, Hubert. "Die Praxis der 'gelenkten Improvisation' und der 'Urtext': Ein editorisches Problem?" in *Musik–Edition–Interpretation*, ed. Bente, pp. 355–68.

Mendel, Arthur. "The Purposes and Desirable Characteristics of Text-Critical Editions," in *Modern Musical Scholarship*, ed. Edward Olleson. Oxford International Symposia. Stocksfield, 1980, pp. 14–27.

Mender, Mona. *Music Manuscript Preparation: A Concise Guide*. Metuchen, NJ, 1991.

Merkley, Paul. *Modal Assignments in Northern Tonaries*. Wissenschaftliche Abhandlungen, 56. Ottawa, 1992.

Merriam, Alan P. *The Anthropology of Music*. Evanston, IL, 1964.

Metzger, Bruce M. *The Text of the New Testament: Its Transmission, Corruption, and Restoration*. 3rd edn. New York and Oxford, 1992.

Meyer, Ann R. "Shakespeare's Art and the Texts of *King Lear*." *Studies in Bibliography*, 47 (1994), 128–46.

Meyer, Leonard B. *Emotion and Meaning in Music*. Chicago, 1956.

Style and Music: Theory, History, and Ideology. Studies in the Criticism and Theory of Music. Philadelphia, 1989.

Mies, Paul. *Textkritische Untersuchungen bei Beethoven*. Veröffentlichungen des Beethovenhauses in Bonn, new ser., part 4, Schriften zur Beethovenforschung, 2. Bonn, Munich and Duisburg, 1957.

Mitchell, Donald. *Gustav Mahler: The Wunderhorn Years, Chronicles and Commentaries*. Boulder, CO, 1976; 1st edn. London, 1975.

Nattiez, Jean-Jacques. *Music and Discourse: Toward a Semiology of Music*, trans. Carolyn Abbate. Princeton, 1990. Translation and revision of *Musicologie générale et sémiologie*. Collection Musique/Passé/Présent. N.p., 1987.

Neighbour, O. W. Review of Arnold Schönberg, *Sämtliche Werke*, Abteilung V, Reihe A, Bd. 19: *Chorwerke II*, ed. Josef Rufer and Christian Martin Schmidt; *Die Jakobsleiter*, piano score, arr. Winfried Zillig; and *Weihnachtsmusik*, ed. Leonard Stein. *Music and Letters*, 57 (1976), 443–46.

"Neue Mozart-Ausgabe," in *Musikalisches Erbe und Gegenwart*, ed. Bennwitz, *et al.*, pp. 61–69.

"Neue Schubert-Ausgabe," in *Musikalisches Erbe und Gegenwart*, ed. Bennwitz, *et. al.*, pp. 79–88.

Neumeyer, David. *The Music of Paul Hindemith*. Composers of the Twentieth Century. New Haven and London, 1986.

Newman, William S. "On the Problem of Determining Beethoven's Most

Authoritative Lifetime Editions," in *Beiträge zur Beethoven-Bibliographie*, ed. Dorfmüller, pp. 128–36.

Noblitt, Thomas. "Filiation vis-à-vis its Alternatives: Approaches to Textual Criticism," in *Quellenstudien zur Musik der Renaissance*, II, *Datierung und Filiation*, ed. Finscher, 111–27.

"Textual Criticism and Selected Works Published by Petrucci," in *Quellenstudien zur Musik der Renaissance*, I, *Formen und Probleme*, ed. Finscher, 201–44.

Nottebohm, Gustav. *Beethoveniana: Aufsätze und Mittheilungen*. Leipzig, 1872; repr. New York and London, 1970.

Zweite Beethoveniana: Nachgelassene Aufsätze, ed. E. Mandyczewski. Leipzig, 1887; repr. New York and London, 1970.

Osthoff, Wolfgang. "Neue Beobachtungen zu Quellen und Geschichte von Monteverdis 'Incoronazione di Poppea'." *Die Musikforschung*, 11 (1958), 129–38.

"Zu den Quellen von Monteverdis 'Ritorno di Ulisse in Patria'." *Studien zur Musikwissenschaft*, 23 (1956), 67–78.

Palmer, Humphrey. *The Logic of Gospel Criticism*. London, Melbourne, Toronto and New York, 1968.

"Proving Uniqueness in a Pedigree of Manuscripts," in *La pratique des ordinateurs dans la critique des textes: Paris 29–31 mars 1978*. Colloques Internationaux du Centre National de la Recherche Scientifique, 579. Paris, 1979, pp. 185–89.

Pascall, Robert. "Brahms and the Definitive Text," in *Brahms: Biographical, Documentary and Analytical Studies*, ed. Robert Pascall. Cambridge, 1983, pp. 59–75.

Pasquali, Giorgio. *Storia della tradizione e critica del testo*. 2nd edn. Florence, 1952.

Patterson, Lee. "The Logic of Textual Criticism and the Way of Genius: The Kane–Donaldson *Piers Plowman* in Historical Perspective," in *Textual Criticism and Literary Interpretation*, ed. McGann, pp. 55–91.

Pearsall, Derek. "Editing Medieval Texts: Some Developments and Some Problems," in *Textual Criticism and Literary Interpretation*, ed. McGann, pp. 92–106.

Penesco, Anne. *Les instruments à archet dans les musiques du XXe siècle*. Musique–Musicologie, 21–22. Paris, 1992.

Perkins, Leeman L. "Toward a Rational Approach to Text Placement in the Secular Music of Dufay's Time," in *Papers Read at the Dufay Quincentenary Conference, Brooklyn College December 6–7, 1974*, ed. Allan W. Atlas. Brooklyn, 1976, pp. 102–14.

Perz, Mirosław. "Zur Textunterlegungspraxis in der Mehrstimmigkeit des 14. und 15. Jahrhunderts und über einige in Polen neu- und wiedergefundene Quellen dieser Zeit," in *Musik und Text*, ed. Günther and Finscher, pp. 327–49.

Pesce, Dolores. *The Affinities and Medieval Transposition*. Music: Scholarship and Performance. Bloomington and Indianapolis, 1987.

Peyser, Joan. "Commentary: 'The Phonograph and Our Musical Life'." *The Musical Quarterly*, 64 (1978), 250–54.

Pfeiffer, Rudolf. *History of Classical Scholarship: From the Beginnings to the End of the Hellenistic Age*. Oxford, 1968.

History of Classical Scholarship: From 1300 to 1850. Oxford, 1976.

Planchart, Alejandro Enrique. *The Repertory of Tropes at Winchester*. 2 vols. Princeton, 1977.

"The Transmission of Medieval Chant," in *Music in Medieval and Early Modern Europe*, ed. Fenlon, pp. 347–63.

Porter, Andrew. Review of Giuseppe Verdi, *Don Carlos*, ed. Ursula Günther. *Journal of the American Musicological Society*, 35 (1982), 360b–70b.

"Problems in Editing the Music of Josquin des Prez: A Critique of the First Edition and Proposals for the Second Edition," in *Josquin des Prez*, ed. Lowinsky and Blackburn, pp. 723–54.

Quentin, Dom Henri. *Essais de critique textuelle (ecdotique)*. Paris, 1926.

Mémoire sur l'établissement du texte de la Vulgate. Collectanea Biblica Latina, 6. Rome and Paris, 1922.

Querbach, Michael. "Der konstruierte Ursprung: Zur Problematik musikalischer Urtext-Ausgaben." *Neue Zeitschrift für Musik*, 149 no. 1 (January 1988), 15a–21b.

Review of Georg Feder, *Musikphilologie: Eine Einführung in die musikalische Textkritik, Hermeneutik und Editionstechnik*. *Neue Zeitschrift für Musik*, 149 no. 7–8 (July/August 1988), 107a–8a.

Rastall, Richard. *The Notation of Western Music: An Introduction*. London, 1983.

Reaney, Gilbert. "Text Underlay in Early Fifteenth-Century Musical Manuscripts," in *Essays in Musicology in Honor of Dragan Plamenac on his 70th Birthday*, ed. Gustave Reese and Robert J. Snow. N.p., 1969, pp. 245–51.

Reeve, Michael D. "Archetypes." *Sileno*, 11 (1985), 193–201.

"*Eliminatio codicum descriptorum*: A Methodological Problem," in *Editing Greek and Latin Texts*, ed. John N. Grant. Conference on Editorial Problems, no. 23: 1987. New York, 1989, pp. 1–35.

"Stemmatic Method: 'Qualcosa che non funziona'?" in *The Role of the Book in Medieval Culture: Proceedings of the Oxford International Symposium 26 September–1 October 1982*, 2 vols., ed. Peter Ganz. Bibliologia: Elementa ad Librorum Studia Pertinentia, 3–4. Turnhout, 1986, I, 57–69.

Rehm, Wolfgang. "Notenschrift und Aufführung: Die Rolle der Musikverlage," in *Notenschrift und Aufführung: Symposium zur Jahrestagung der Gesellschaft für Musikforschung 1977 in München*, ed. Theodor Göllner. Münchner Veröffentlichungen zur Musikgeschichte, 30. Tutzing, 1980, pp. 99–120. Also published in *Fontes Artis Musicae*, 25 (1978), 135–41.

Reynolds, L. D., and N. G. Wilson. *Scribes and Scholars: A Guide to the Transmission of Greek and Latin Literature*. 3rd edn. Oxford, 1991.

Risatti, Howard. *New Music Vocabulary: A Guide to Notational Signs for Contemporary Music*. Urbana, Chicago and London, 1975.

Roemer, Clinton. *The Art of Music Copying: The Preparation of Music for Performance*. 2nd edn. Sherman Oaks, CA, 1985.

Roesner, Edward H. "The Origins of W_1." *Journal of the American Musicological Society*, 29 (1976), 337–80.

Roesner, Linda Correll. "The Autograph of Schumann's Piano Sonata in F Minor, Opus 14." *The Musical Quarterly*, 61 (1975), 98–130.

Rönnau, Klaus. "Bemerkungen zum 'Urtext' der Violinsoli J. S. Bachs," in *Musik–Edition–Interpretation*, ed. Bente, pp. 417–22.

"Regnum tuum solidum," in *Festschrift Bruno Stäblein*, ed. Ruhnke, pp. 195–205.

Die Tropen zum Gloria in excelsis Deo: Unter besonderer Berücksichtigung des Repertoires der St. Martial-Handschriften. Wiesbaden, 1967.

Rosand, Ellen. "The Bow of Ulysses." *Journal of Musicology*, 12 (1994), 376–95.

Rosen, Charles. *The Classical Style: Haydn, Mozart, Beethoven.* New York, 1972.

Rosen, David. "Le quattro stesure del duetto Filippo-Posa," in *Atti del IIo Congresso Internazionale di Studi Verdiani* (Parma, 1971), pp. 368–88.

Rousseau, Norbert. *L'école grégorienne de Solesmes 1833–1910.* Rome and Tournai, 1910.

Ruhnke, Martin, ed. *Festschrift Bruno Stäblein zum 70. Geburtstag.* Kassel, 1967.

Salzedo, Carlos. *Modern Study of the Harp.* 2nd edn. New York, 1948.

Salzman, Eric. "On Reading Cosima Wagner's *Diaries.*" *The Musical Quarterly*, 68 (1982), 337–52.

Saussure, Ferdinand de. *Cours de linguistique générale*, ed. Charles Bally and Albert Sechehaye. Paris, 1972. English translation: *Course in General Linguistics*, trans. Roy Harris. London, 1983.

Schmidt, Hans. "Verzeichnis der Skizzen Beethovens." *Beethoven-Jahrbuch*, ser. 2, 6 (1965–68), 7–128.

Schmidt, P. L. "Lachmann's Method: On the History of a Misunderstanding," in *The Uses of Greek and Latin: Historical Essays*, ed. A. C. Dionisotti, Anthony Grafton and Jill Kraye. Warburg Institute Surveys and Texts, 16. London, 1988, pp. 227–36.

Schmieder, Wolfgang. "Nochmals: Originalhandschrift oder Erstdruck?" *Allgemeine Musikzeitung*, 67 (1940), 258b–59a.

Schnapp, Friedrich. "Neue Mozart-Funde in Donaueschingen." *Neues Mozart-Jahrbuch*, 2 (1942), 211–23.

Schulze, Hans-Joachim. *Studien zur Bach-Überlieferung im 18. Jahrhundert.* Musikwissenschaftliche Studienbibliothek Peters. Leipzig and Dresden, 1984.

Schwandt, Erich. "Questions Concerning the Edition of the 'Goldberg Variations' in the *Neue Bach Ausgabe.*" *Performance Practice Review*, 3 (1990), 58–69.

Schwarz, Boris. "Joseph Joachim and the Genesis of Brahms's Violin Concerto." *The Musical Quarterly*, 69 (1983), 503–26.

Seeger, Charles. "Prescriptive and Descriptive Music-Writing." *The Musical Quarterly*, 44 (1958), 184–95.

Shepherd, John. *Music as Social Text.* Cambridge, 1991.

Sherwood, Gayle. "Questions and Veracities: Reassessing the Chronology of Ives's Choral Works." *The Musical Quarterly*, 78 (1994), 403–21.

Shillingsburg, Peter L. "The Autonomous Author, the Sociology of Texts, and the Polemics of Textual Criticism," in *Devils and Angels*, ed. Cohen, pp. 22–43.

"An Inquiry into the Social Status of Texts and Modes of Textual Criticism." *Studies in Bibliography*, 42 (1989), 55–79.

Slim, H. Colin. "Dosso Dossi's Allegory at Florence about Music." *Journal of the American Musicological Society*, 43 (1990), 43–98.

Solie, Ruth A., ed. *Musicology and Difference: Gender and Sexuality in Music Scholarship.* Berkeley, Los Angeles and London, 1993.

Solomon, Maynard. "Charles Ives: Some Questions of Veracity." *Journal of the American Musicological Society*, 40 (1987), 443–70.

"Communication." *Journal of the American Musicological Society*, 42 (1989), 209–18.

Squire, William Barclay. "Publishers' Numbers." *Sammelbände der Internationalen Musikgesellschaft*, 15 (1914), 420–27.

Staehelin, Martin. "Bemerkungen zum Verhältnis von Werkcharakter und Filiation in der Musik der Renaissance," in *Quellenstudien zur Musik der Renaissance*, II, *Datierung und Filiation*, ed. Finscher, 199–215.

Stinson, Russell. *The Bach Manuscripts of Johann Peter Kellner and His Circle: A Case Study in Reception History*. Sources of Music and Their Interpretation: Duke Studies in Music. Durham, NC, and London, 1989.

Stockmann, Doris. "Die Transkription in der Musikethnologie: Geschichte, Probleme, Methoden." *Acta Musicologica*, 51 (1979), 204–45.

Stone, Kurt. *Music Notation in the Twentieth Century: A Practical Guidebook*. New York and London, 1980.

Strohm, Reinhard. "Quellenkritische Untersuchungen an der Missa 'Caput'," in *Quellenstudien zur Musik der Renaissance*, II, *Datierung und Filiation*, ed. Finscher, 153–76.

Subotnik, Rose Rosengard. *Developing Variations: Style and Ideology in Western Music*. Minneapolis, 1991.

Tanselle, G. Thomas. "Editing without a Copy-Text." *Studies in Bibliography*, 47 (1994), 1–22.

"The Editorial Problem of Final Authorial Intention." *Studies in Bibliography*, 29 (1976), 167–211.

"Greg's Theory of Copy-Text and the Editing of American Literature." *Studies in Bibliography*, 28 (1975), 167–229.

"Historicism and Critical Editing." *Studies in Bibliography*, 39 (1986), 1–46.

"Literary Editing," in *Literary & Historical Editing*, ed. George L. Vogt and John Bush Jones. Lawrence, 1981, pp. 35–56. Reprinted as "Texts of Documents and Texts of Works," in Tanselle. *Textual Criticism and Scholarly Editing*, pp. 3–23.

"Problems and Accomplishments in the Editing of the Novel," in Tanselle, *Textual Criticism and Scholarly Editing*, pp. 179–217. Corrected version of the article of the same title in *Studies in the Novel*, 7 (1975), 323–60.

A Rationale of Textual Criticism. Philadelphia, 1989.

"Recent Editorial Discussion and the Central Questions of Editing." *Studies in Bibliography*, 34 (1981), 23–65.

"Reproductions and Scholarship." *Studies in Bibliography*, 42 (1989), 25–54.

"Some Principles for Editorial Apparatus." *Studies in Bibliography*, 25 (1972), 41–88.

Textual Criticism and Scholarly Editing. Charlottesville and London, 1990.

Taylor, Gary. "Revising Shakespeare." *Text: Transactions of the Society for Textual Scholarship*, 3 (1987), 285–304.

Taylor, Gary, and Michael J. Warren, eds. *The Division of the Kingdoms: Shakespeare's Two Versions of King Lear*. Oxford Shakespeare Studies. Oxford, 1983.

Thorpe, James. *Principles of Textual Criticism*. San Marino, CA, 1972.

Timpanaro, Sebastiano. *La genesi del metodo del Lachmann*. 2nd edn., corr. Biblioteca di Cultura, Saggi, 5. Padua, 1985.

"*Recentiores* e *deteriores*, *codices descripti* e *codices inutiles*." *Filologia e Critica*, 10 (1985), 164–92.

Tomlinson, Gary. "The Web of Culture: A Context for Musicology." *19th-Century Music*, 7 (1983–84), 350–62.

Treitler, Leo. "The Early History of Music Writing in the West." *Journal of the American Musicological Society*, 35 (1982), 237–79.

"History and the Ontology of the Musical Work." *Journal of Aesthetics and Art Criticism*, 51 (1993), 483–97.

"Methods, Style, Analysis," in *International Musicological Society, Report of Eleventh Congress*, ed. Glahn, *et al.*, I, 61–70.

"Observations on the Transmission of some Aquitanian Tropes," in *Forum Musicologicum: Basler Beiträge zur Musikgeschichte*, III, *Aktuelle Fragen der musikbezogenen Mittelalterforschung: Texte zu einem Basler Kolloquium des Jahres 1975*, ed. Hans Oesch and Wulf Arlt. Winterthur, 1982, pp. 11–60.

"Oral, Written, and Literate Process in the Transmission of Medieval Music." *Speculum*, 56 (1981), 471–91.

"Paleography and Semiotics," in *Musicologie médiévale: Notations et séquences*, ed. Michel Huglo. Paris, 1987, pp. 17–27.

"Reading and Singing: On the Genesis of Occidental Music-Writing." *Early Music History*, 4 (1984), 135–208.

"Transmission and the Study of Music History," in *International Musicological Society: Report of the Twelfth Congress Berkeley 1977*, ed. Daniel Heartz and Bonnie Wade. Kassel, Basel and London, 1981, pp. 202–11.

"The 'Unwritten' and 'Written Transmission' of Medieval Chant and the Start-Up of Musical Notation." *Journal of Musicology*, 10 (1992), 131–91.

Tyson, Alan. *The Authentic English Editions of Beethoven*. All Souls Studies, 1. London, 1963.

Unverricht, Hubert. *Die Eigenschriften und die Originalausgaben von Werken Beethovens in ihrer Bedeutung für die moderne Textkritik*. Musikwissenschaftliche Arbeiten Herausgegeben von der Gesellschaft für Musikforschung, 17. Kassel, Basel, London and New York, 1960.

van der Werf, Hendrik. *The Oldest Extant Part Music and the Origin of Western Polyphony*. 2 vols. Rochester, 1993.

van Dijk, S. J. P., O. F. M. *Sources of the Modern Roman Liturgy*. 2 vols. Studia et Documenta Franciscana, 1–2. Leiden, 1963.

Vicentino, Nicola. *L'antica musica ridotta alla moderna prattica*. Rome, 1555; repr. Kassel and New York, 1959.

Vötterle, Karl. "Die Stunde der Gesamtausgabe," in *Haus unterm Stern: Über Entstehen, Zerstörung und Wiederaufbau des Bärenreiter-Werke*. 3rd edn. Kassel, Basel, Paris, London and New York, 1963, pp. 287–95. Revised version of the article of the same title published in *Musica*, 10 (1956), 33–36.

Wagner, Peter. *Die Gesänge der Jakobsliturgie zu Santiago de Compostela*. Collectanea Friburgensia, Veröffentlichungen der Universität Freiburg, Neue Folge, 20. Freiburg, 1931.

Wallnig, Josef. "'Produkt im Kopf' contra 'Produkt im Ohr'." *Österreichische Musikzeitschrift*, 46 (1991), 539–42.

Warfield, Gerald. *Writings on Contemporary Music Notation: An Annotated Bibliography*. Ann Arbor, MI, 1976.

Wathey, Andrew. *Manuscripts of Polyphonic Music: The British Isles, 1100–1400*. Répertoire International des Sources Musicales, B/4, 1–2, Suppl. 1. Munich, 1993.

Weinhold, Liesbeth. "Die Erst- und Frühdrucke von Beethovens Werken in den Musiksammlungen der Bundesrepublik Deutschland und West-Berlins:

Verzeichnis und Kommentar. 2. Zur Definition der Ausgabe-Typen. 3. Die Gestalt des Titelblatters und ihre Veränderung," in *Beiträge zur Beethoven-Bibliographie*, ed. Dorfmüller, pp. 245–68.

Wells, Stanley. "Revision in Shakespeare's Plays," in *Editing and Editors: A Retrospect*, ed. Richard Landon. Conference on Editorial Problems, no. 21: 1985. New York, 1988, pp. 67–97.

West, Martin L. *Textual Criticism and Editorial Technique Applicable to Greek and Latin Texts*. Stuttgart, 1973.

Westcott, Brooke Foss, and Fenton John Anthony Hort, eds. *The New Testament in the Original Greek*. 2 vols. New York, 1882; 1st edn., Cambridge and London, 1881.

Westergaard, Peter. "On the Notion of Style," in *International Musicological Society, Report of Eleventh Congress*, ed. Glahn, *et al.*, I, 71–74.

Willis, James. *Latin Textual Criticism*. Illinois Studies in Language and Literature, 61. Urbana, Chicago and London, 1972.

Wolf, Eugene K., and Jean K. Wolf. "A Newly Identified Complex of Manuscripts from Mannheim." *Journal of the American Musicological Society*, 27 (1974), 379–437.

"Rastrology and Its Use in Eighteenth-Century Manuscript Studies," in *Studies in Musical Sources and Style: Essays in Honor of Jan LaRue*, ed. Eugene K. Wolf and Edward H. Roesner. Madison, 1990, pp. 237–91.

Wolff, Christoph. "Bach's *Handexemplar* of the Goldberg Variations: A New Source." *Journal of the American Musicological Society*, 29 (1976), 224–41.

"Towards a Methodology of Dialectic Style Consideration: Preliminary Terminological and Historical Considerations," in *International Musicological Society, Report of Eleventh Congress*, ed. Glahn, *et al.*, I, 74–80.

"Wolfgang Amadeus Mozart. Neue Ausgabe sämtlicher Werke. In Verbindung mit den Mozartstädten Augsburg, Salzburg und Wien herausgegeben von der Internationalen Stiftung Mozarteum Salzburg. Editionsrichtlinien 3. Fassung (1962)," in *Editionsrichtlinien*, ed. Dadelsen, pp. 99–129.

Wright, Craig. *Music and Ceremony at Notre Dame of Paris 500–1550*. Cambridge Studies in Music. Cambridge, 1989.

Yudkin, Jeremy. "The Anonymous of St. Emmeram and Anonymous IV on the *Copula*." *The Musical Quarterly*, 70 (1984), 1–22.

"The *Copula* According to Johannes de Garlandia." *Musica Disciplina*, 34 (1980), 67–84.

Zarlino, Gioseffo. *Le istitutioni harmoniche*. Venice, 1558.

Index

Index

Index